DEER HUNTING

DEER HUNTING

2nd Edition

Richard P. Smith

STACKPOLE
BOOKS

Published by
STACKPOLE BOOKS
Cameron and Kelker Streets
P.O. Box 1831
Harrisburg, PA 17105

All photos by the author unless otherwise credited
Cover photo by Richard P. Smith
Cover design by Caroline Miller

Printed in the United States of America

Second Edition

10 9 8 7 6 5 4

Library of Congress Cataloging-in-Publication Data

Smith, Richard P., 1949–
    Deer hunting / Richard P. Smith. — 2nd ed.
        p.   cm.
    Includes bibliographical references and index.
    ISBN 0-8117-3036-0
    1. Deer hunting—North America.   I. Title.
SK301.S567   1991
799.2'77357—dc20   90-27250
                                                                          CIP

To my father,
who taught me to be
a sportsman

Contents

Acknowledgments

I would like to take this opportunity to thank all of my friends and relatives who have let me be a part of their deer hunts. Every experience made me a better and richer hunter.

My dad deserves recognition, of course, for cultivating my interest in hunting. George Smith, an uncle, deserves special appreciation for making many of my deer hunts possible. Leonard Yelle, another uncle, took me on my first successful deer hunt. My brother Bruce has shared many deer hunts with me. Rudy Rudibaugh taught me about mule deer and how to hunt them.

I want to thank Bill Jordan for his part in making hunts to Georgia possible; Jimmy Dean for allowing me to hunt with him in Montana; Andy Kaul and the gang at Trout Run for excellent Pennsylvania hunts; Mike Aftanas and John Bardahl for Saskatchewan adventures; Dick Rintamaki for valuable assistance in Wyoming; Al Hofacker for sharing his Wisconsin camp; and Hayward Simmons and Rob Keck for making trips to South Carolina possible. The Markesbery Brothers, Tony Knight, Greg Bambenek, and Herb Boldt have made hunts in various locations possible and so have Bob Eastman, George Gardner, and Lennie Rezmer.

A number of people have also been helpful in terms of photographing deer. They include Mark Eby, Bill Mattson, the Harrison Brothers, George and Ellen Planck, and Justin Blain. Deer researcher John Ozoga has helped with photography as well as passing along some of his vast knowledge about whitetails.

Beryl Jensen, Ed Lindstrom, Mike Hogan, Fred and Tom DeRocher, Jim Haveman, Dave Raikko, Bob DeLongchamp, Bill Robinson, Phil Doepke, Kirwin Werner, Keith Chapel, Craig Smith, and many more can be added to the list.

This book wouldn't have been possible without the help of Ken Lowe, who gave me the encouragement necessary to start writing, and Dave Richey, who has assisted in countless ways. My friends and relatives have all been a source of encouragement in this endeavor, especially my wife, Lucy.

Last, but not least, the state and provincial departments of fish and game and natural resources deserve thanks for providing information that went into this book. I would like to give special thanks to Anne Cascadden at the Canadian Consulate in Detroit for help in gathering information about deer hunting across Canada.

Preface

I was all set to write a lengthy introduction, but remembering the speaker at the podium who didn't want to bore his audience, I won't. This book is about deer and deer hunting; it's as simple as that. The table of contents tells you exactly what is included. If you have any interest in whitetails or mule deer there is something in this book for you.

Researching and writing this book has made me a more knowledgeable deer hunter. If you learn as much from reading these words as I have from writing them, both efforts will have been worthwhile.

Preface to the Second Edition

Much of the first edition of *Deer Hunting* still applies, but there have been changes in techniques, equipment, and clothing since I wrote it. The book has been expanded to include this new information. The most important changes, though, involve an almost universal increase in deer populations and deer hunting opportunities across North America. Hunting seasons are longer than ever before and bag limits are barely keeping pace with growing herds in many cases.

Since I wrote the first edition of this book I've shot approximately 100 deer in various states and provinces with centerfire firearms, muzzle-loaders, and archery equipment and photographed many times that number. The added experience has made me a better hunter and now that experience, as well as the knowledge gleaned by interviewing some of the most successful deer hunters in North America, can make you a better hunter, too.

You will learn how best to take advantage of those expanded opportunities in this revised and updated version of *Deer Hunting*. Good luck!

1

About the Quarry

There are two native species of deer in North America: the whitetail and the mule deer. Within each species a number of subspecies exist that exhibit variations that set them apart from each other. Some of the variations are minor, others are more noticeable.

Thirty subspecies of whitetails have been identified in North America. Seventeen of these are found in the United States and Canada (forty-eight contiguous states and eight provinces). Another thirteen exist south of the border. Where subspecies overlap, they frequently interbreed. Some states have more than one race of whitetails.

The northern whitetail is the largest and most widespread of the subspecies. Two 402-pound (dressed weight) members of this variety are the heaviest known specimens. They were shot in Minnesota. Northern whitetails are found in seventeen states and five Canadian provinces. They include Michigan, Minnesota, Wisconsin, New York, New Jersey, Massachusetts, New Hampshire, Maryland, Pennsylvania, Ohio, Delaware, Indiana, Illinois, Connecticut, Rhode Island, Maine, Vermont, Ontario, Quebec, Manitoba, New Brunswick, and Nova Scotia.

Virginia whitetails are found in Virginia, the Carolinas, Kentucky, Georgia, Mississippi, Tennessee, and Alabama.

Dakota whitetails inhabit the Dakotas, Kansas, Wyoming, Nebraska, Montana, Manitoba, Saskatchewan, and Alberta.

The northwest variety calls the states of Oregon, Idaho, Montana, Washington, Nevada, California, and Utah home. They also reside in British Columbia and Alberta in Canada.

A Coues whitetail buck in Arizona.

In contrast to most other whitetails, the Columbian subspecies is endangered. It is only found in Oregon and Washington.

Coues, or fantail, whitetails inhabit desert regions of California, Arizona, New Mexico, and Mexico.

The Texas whitetail is also found in parts of New Mexico and Mexico as well as in Texas, Kansas, Colorado, and Oklahoma.

A Kansas strain lives in its home state plus Oklahoma, Nebraska, Arkansas, eastern Texas, Missouri, Iowa, and Louisiana.

Florida coastal whitetails are distributed in Florida's panhandle, southern Alabama, and Mississippi.

Eight subspecies of whitetails in the U.S. have very limited distribution as indicated by their names: Carmen Mountains (Texas); Avery Island (Texas and Louisiana); Bull's Island, Hunting Island, and Hilton Head Island (all in South Carolina); Blackbeard Island (Georgia); Florida (Georgia and Florida); and the Florida Keys whitetail, the smallest of the species. Keys deer, like the Columbian type, are protected.

Some species of whitetails have been introduced into areas where they wouldn't otherwise be found, which may account for some variations in the distributions listed above.

There are eleven subspecies of mule deer, but they are commonly lumped into four categories. The Rocky Mountain variety is the most widely distributed. Desert mule deer, Columbian blacktails, and sitka blacktails are the other three types.

Mule deer are primarily western animals. They are found from the southeastern portion of Alaska to northern Mexico. Their extreme eastern range includes western portions of Iowa, Minnesota, Kansas, Oklahoma, and Texas. They inhabit the entire Pacific Coast, including the Baja Peninsula. In Canada representatives of the species are established in the southern limits of the Yukon and Northwest Territories. They are common in British Columbia, Alberta, Saskatchewan, and the southwest corner of Manitoba.

As with some of the subspecies of whitetails, mule deer are not hunted in every state or province where they are found. Low densities in the extreme limits of their range are not huntable populations.

Columbian blacktails call Washington, Oregon, California, and British Columbia home. Sitkas occupy the northern portion of the mule deer range in Alaska, the Yukon, and British Columbia. Desert and Rocky Mountain mulies occupy the rest of this deer's range.

The variety of subspecies of white-tailed and mule deer is basically reflected in size variations, coat color, tail markings, and other habitat adaptations. Most whitetails look alike. To the untrained observer, it can be difficult to tell many of the subspecies from the others. The differences among the blacktail subspecies and mule deer are more apparent.

Mulies have narrow, ropelike tails. The undersides of mule deer tails are hairless. When running, this deer holds its tail clamped against its distinctive white rump. Blacktail tails are wider than those of mule deer.

Mule deer have small, black-tipped tails and white rumps. The tines fork on bucks, as shown by this fine specimen. *Lee Kline*

Whitetails have longer, wider tails than all types of mule deer. Their tails are brown or black and brown on the back with white trim. The species gets its name from the white underside, which is visible when the deer waves its tail from side to side in an elevated position while it runs.

There is also an obvious difference between the antler structure of adult whitetails and that of mature mule deer bucks. Typical whitetail racks exhibit unbranched tines arising from main beams. Points beyond the brow tine on mule deer antlers typically fork. Blacktail antlers are generally smaller than those of their mule deer relatives.

Another feature that usually varies between mulies and white-tailed deer is ear size. Mulies typically have larger ears than whitetails. Coues whitetails have larger ears than normal for the species, which is thought to be an adaptation to their desert environment.

A less obvious external difference between whitetail and mule deer is the size of their metatarsal glands. Metatarsals are located on the outside of the lower hind legs of deer. A patch of white hair marks the location of each metatarsal. Metatarsals are about an inch long on whitetails, more than two inches on blacktails, and about five inches on other mule deer.

Whitetails and mulies have three additional external glands. Tarsal glands are on the inside of the hind legs at the knee joint. Interdigital glands are found between the toes on each foot. Preorbitals are directly in the corner of the eyes; these release tears to cleanse the eyes.

When running, the two species can be differentiated by their gait. Mule deer employ a stiff-legged bounce. Whitetails run in typical headlong fashion, but also make lengthy leaps or bounds. Deer may cover as much as thirty feet in a forward leap or bound. Whitetails have been known to scale barriers eight and one-half feet high.

Top speed for mule deer has been clocked at from twenty-five to thirty miles an hour. Whitetails are capable of speeds from thirty-five to forty miles per hour, but are probably moving at closer to twenty or twenty-five miles per hour in hunting conditions.

Most deer hunters overestimate the size, both in height and weight, of deer. Mule deer typically measure from thirty-six to forty-two inches high at the shoulder. The smaller blacktails stand a maximum of thirty-eight inches at the shoulder. Big whitetail bucks will measure thirty-six inches at the shoulder. The smallest whitetails (Keys deer) stand only twenty-four to twenty-six inches high at the shoulder.

The estimated live weight of the biggest mule deer is 512.5 pounds. A buck bagged in Colorado by Laurence Rowe in 1938 had an actual dressed weight of 410 pounds. Average field-dressed weights for adult bucks fall in a range from 150 to 200 pounds. Northern whitetails are about the same.

The two record-weight whitetails from Minnesota had estimated live weights of 502.5 pounds. Carl Lenander, Jr., shot one of the monster

Most hunters overestimate the height of deer. This whitetail being used for a browse selection study isn't even waist-high on researcher Bill Bauer. It would take a big buck to measure thirty-six inches at the shoulder.

bucks in 1926. George Himango got the second one in 1981 on the Fond du Lac Indian Reservation. Dressed weights of blacktails and southern whitetails range from 80 to 150 pounds.

Generally, deer will lose one-fifth of their weight during field dressing. A rough determination of a whitetail's or mule deer's live weight can be made by dividing the dressed weight by four, then adding the resulting number to the dressed weight. The weights listed below (dressed weight first, followed by live weight) should be accurate in most cases: 80, 105; 90, 115; 100, 130; 110, 140; 120, 155; 130, 165; 140, 180; 150, 190; 160, 205; 170, 215; 180, 230; 190, 240; 200, 255.

Bucks may lose as much as 20 percent of their weight during the breeding season (rut), which occurs in the fall.

Deer are colorblind. They see shades of black and white. Movement attracts their attention. Hunters who remain motionless are often a source of curiosity rather than alarm. White-tailed and mule deer's sight is better to the sides than straight ahead because of the position of their eyes. Animals that live in open country tend to depend on their vision more than those in heavily wooded terrain.

It isn't unusual to have deer cautiously approach an immobile person they can't smell. They recognize the object as an addition to the landscape, but are unsure of what it is, so are curious. Sometimes they nervously stamp a front foot if they suspect danger. I have frequently seen deer do this while I was bowhunting or trying to photograph them. Occasionally, a wise doe will whirl as if to run off, but then will stop quickly and look back in an apparent attempt to catch me in the act of moving.

The sense of hearing is well-developed in deer. Only sounds that are not normal in their environment, such as human voices, metallic sounds, fabric rubbing against brush, or noisy human feet, unduly alarm them.

Deer rely heavily on their sense of smell. It is probably their strongest defense against hunters. If the wind is right, deer often smell hunters before they are within sight of their quarry. Animals that "wind" hunters sometimes make a noise by blowing through their nostrils. This sound is often referred to as a snort. Both bucks and does make this sound. It serves as a warning signal to other deer in the area. The noise they make sounds like a train whistle or someone blowing on an empty rifle cartridge.

Whitetails and mulies make more sounds with their mouths than most hunters realize, and a variety of calls that duplicate these sounds are available on the market. The most common vocalizations are between does and fawns when the offspring are young, between bucks and does during the rut, and from deer that are distressed. These sounds are seldom heard by hunters, though. On a number of occasions while hunting I have heard bucks following does during the rut make noises. They were very distinctive, throaty, rasping grunts. I have heard penned bucks make similar noises. While deer are being handled by biologists during live-trapping and marking operations, they sometimes bleat or baa.

Both whitetails and the blacktail variety of mule deer inhabit thick, brushy terrain. Blacktail habitat rivals whitetail country for denseness and short sight distances in many cases. The larger varieties of mule deer are usually found in more open terrain than either black- or whitetails, but they can be found in stands of timber, too.

Mule deer are generally considered a migratory species; whitetails usually spend their entire lives in a limited home range of two square miles, and in many cases, less. The truth of the matter is that both species exhibit these traits.

Most mule deer have distinct summer and winter ranges. Summers are often spent at higher elevations than winters. There is a downhill migration in the fall to escape heavy snows. As the snow melts in the

spring or early summer the deer move uphill. Whitetails that live in mountainous or hilly terrain do the same. In South Dakota's Black Hills, for
example, whitetails migrate between their low winter range and high summer range twice a year. Distance of travel is as great as twenty miles.

Some white-tailed deer in northern climates migrate to wintering
areas called yards, which are primarily lowland swampy areas. Deer yards
vary in size from a few square miles to hundreds of square miles. To reach
yarding areas, many deer move south, toward an area where snow depths
are less. Most of the time there is little or no elevation change between
yards and summer range.

Deer that make seasonal movements, regardless of species, often
use the same routes year after year, unless habitat change requires an
adjustment.

Most white-tailed deer spend their lives in a limited home range.
Some blacktails and mule deer have adapted similarly where the climate
permits. Whitetails mark territory during the breeding season. Mule deer
are generally not territorial, roaming at will during the summer and fall.
Mulies spooked by hunters may travel miles to a new area. Whitetails
seldom roam far. If pushed out of their territory, they usually return.

In the wild, most bucks don't live past three or four years, but older
ones occur in remote or lightly hunted areas. Does tend to live longer than
bucks because they aren't as sought after by hunters. The oldest whitetails
and mule deer occur in captivity where ages of nineteen and twenty-two
years have been recorded. Ten-year-old deer are not common in the wild,
but they do occur. A pair of whitetail does taken by hunters in Alabama
were over twenty years old. One was twenty-one and the other was twenty-
three. A doe that was 14½ years old was bagged in Michigan during the
fall of 1987. Bucks estimated to be 12½ and 10½ years old were taken in
Michigan during 1988 and 1989, respectively. The ages of the old Michigan
deer were verified by counting rings (annuli) in cross sections of the animals' teeth.

The most common method of determining the age of deer is by
examining their cheek teeth. Fawns generally have four cheek teeth on
each of the upper and lower jaws. Three are premolars and one is a molar.
Yearlings typically have two more molars, although one is usually not
showing completely. By age 2½ all molars are completely visible and the
three premolars, which were temporary, have been replaced by permanent
premolars. After that point the amount of tooth wear is a primary age
indicator. Criteria for determining age by tooth wear vary slightly between
species of deer and even among members of the same species found in
different regions.

A buck's age is seldom reflected by the number of tines on his antlers.
Antler beam circumference is more closely related to age. In Nebraska, for

instance, if the beam circumference one inch above the burr is greater than 3⁵/₁₆ inches on whitetails, the buck is usually 2½ years or older. Mule deer of the same age will have a circumference greater than 3¹/₁₆ inches.

Bucks are polygamous. When mature they service a number of does. Bucks are capable of impregnating about twenty does, but this is seldom necessary in the wild unless there is an extremely lopsided sex ratio. The rut usually takes place from October to December, but may be as late as February and March in some parts of the south.

Under optimum conditions a percentage of young-of-the-year does will produce fawns. In poor habitat does may not be productive until they are 2½ years old. Does must breed within a twenty-four-hour period when in heat. If they don't, they will come into breeding condition again at twenty-eight-day intervals. Most adult does give birth to one or two fawns, but triplets are possible. The gestation period for deer is seven months.

At birth fawns usually weigh from five to eight pounds, but some males have weighed over ten pounds. The percentage of bucks born is usually slightly higher than does. Young deer rely on their spotted coats to camouflage them against predators. If fawns are scentless at birth, the condition lasts for a short time. When one to three weeks old, deer are able to run well. Milk is the primary source of nourishment for deer during their first two or three months of life, but they begin foraging on grass when they are between two and three weeks old. When a month old, fawns often eat solid foods. They are usually weaned by three months of age, but may continue nursing longer.

Fawns lose their spotted coats when they are between three and four months old. Adults go through two coat changes a year. A reddish-colored summer coat replaces the winter pelage in late spring or early summer. The heavier, darker winter dress takes its place in the fall.

Abnormalities in coat color are exhibited by some deer. Partial albinos (piebald deer) are most common. These mutants exhibit varying amounts of white, but don't have the pink eyes of true albinos. Melanistic deer (black-colored) are not as common as albinos; in fact, they are very rare. Despite their rarity, Dick Giles from Milford, Michigan, bagged two melanistic bucks from the same location in the state. He got an eight-pointer in 1977 and a spike in 1981. Genetics of the local deer obviously favored that coat-color mutation.

I have been fortunate enough to have photographed a number of true albino whitetails. The first one was a doe. She was a strange sight. Her eyes, ears, and nose were pink; and she was all white except for the tarsal glands on her back legs. There were plenty of normal deer in the area that

Left: Fawns weigh five to eight pounds at birth and lose their spotted coats at three or four months of age. The mottled color serves to camouflage young deer. *Right:* The piebald (partially white) deer represents the most common coat-color mutation.

Dick Giles of Milford, Michigan, bagged these melanistic bucks.

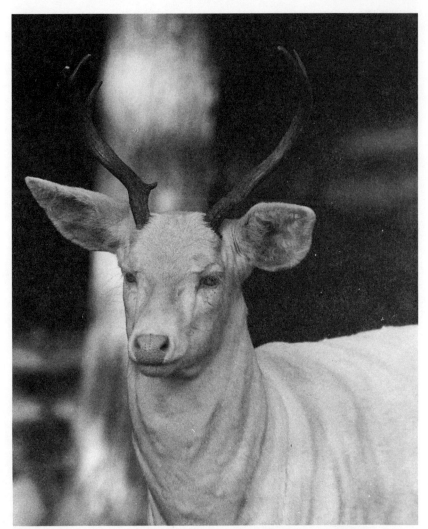

True albinos, like this buck with pink eyes, nose, and inside of the ears, are rare.

seemed to accept her presence. She was spookier than the other animals though.

Additional abnormalities occur with varying frequency in deer herds. Does with antlers are not uncommon. Some have antlers in velvet. Antler growth among does is caused by abnormal amounts of male hormones. Nonetheless, these does breed normally. I photographed one antlered doe that had velvet-covered buttons on her head throughout her life. She pro-

This "antlered" doe produced fawns every year.

duced fawns every year. Does with polished antlers are usually hermaphroditic; that is, they have both male and female sex organs and are often sterile.

Occasionally, bucks will grow three antlers. There is a record of a Canadian buck that sprouted a third antler on its nose. A Montana buck developed an extra antler below its right eye. Castrated bucks or those with a hormonal imbalance may grow oddball antlers, fail to shed their velvet, or not develop antlers at all.

Undershot jaws are seen on some deer. This mutation doesn't affect a deer's ability to feed. My brother shot a short-jawed doe that was eight or ten years old and in good health. Jim Strelec bagged a yearling buck in Georgia that had a short lower jaw, too.

Warts or tumors called papillomas or fibromas are also found on deer. In bad cases they give the animals an unappealing appearance. These tumors are usually not malignant nor do they affect the edibility of venison from a whitetail or mule deer that has them. Warts are commonly on the head, but they may occur elsewhere on the body. Jim Shope from Rapid River, Michigan, encountered a doe one fall that had so many growths on her head that she was blinded.

A buck with no testicles. Note the odd growths on his head in place of antlers.

Jim Strelec bagged this short-jawed three-pointer in Georgia.

A doe with bad case of fibromas that blinded her. *Jim Shope*

With few exceptions, disease doesn't affect deer to a significant extent. A viral disease thought to be transmitted by an insect—Epizootic Hemorrhagic Disease (EHD)—accounts for significant losses in various parts of the United States. Ninety percent of the deer exposed to the virus usually die.

Diseased animals develop a fever, lose their appetite, and have difficulty breathing. The fever seems to induce excessive thirst, so deer that succumb to EHD are often found near water. Before death, deer go into a state of shock. The disease causes destruction of blood vessel walls, causing hemorrhaging. EHD outbreaks occur in the summer. Incidence of the disease ceases after a frost.

There was a recorded outbreak of hoof-and-mouth disease among mule deer in California during 1924. Since that time, its occurrence has been minimal.

Additional disease-related losses stem from parasite infestations. Significant mortality has occurred among Alabama's herd, for one, as a result of lungworm. Other internal parasites that sometimes cause problems are brainworm, liver flukes, and nasal botfly larvae. External parasites include lice and ticks.

Parasites, both internal and external, are common among deer, but their incidence is low in healthy whitetail and mule deer herds. Problems from parasites usually arise in populations on poor range or when herds overpopulate an area.

Extremes in weather such as prolonged cold winters, floods, and hurricanes take further tolls on deer. Here again, healthy deer herds are least susceptible to these conditions. Thousands of whitetails and mulies also die on highways yearly as a result of being struck by automobiles. Less significant accidents account for more deer deaths, including getting stuck in fences and trees, and falls.

During a recent winter I photographed three whitetails that died in upper Michigan after getting stuck in trees. Amazingly, two of them were mature bucks that had already shed their antlers and died together when a front leg of each animal lodged in the crotch between two maple trees. They had been facing each other when they became stuck and the left front leg of the larger buck was on top of the right front leg of the smaller animal. The only way they could have become stuck in this fashion is to

Left: **A pair of mature bucks that died with their front legs stuck in tree crotch.** *Right:* **An adult doe found dead at a cutting in Delta County with her head stuck in a tree cavity.**

have been striking at each other with front feet while standing on hind legs, and when their front quarters dropped toward the ground the bigger buck pushed the smaller one's front foot into the tree crotch with enough force to wedge them there.

The third deer was an adult doe that had her head in a tree cavity where it became stuck. All three deer died of exposure.

Predation is probably the most common mortality factor among deer herds. Mountain lions, wolves, bobcats, and coyotes all take their toll, but humans are the most important deer predator today. Planned predation through hunting is the best means of maintaining healthy deer popula-

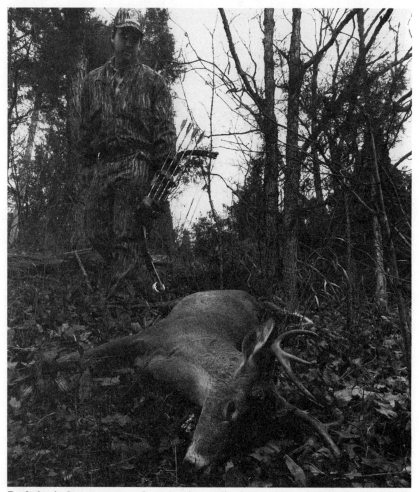

Predation is the most commonly accepted mortality factor of deer, and man is the most important predator.

tions. The reproductive capacity of whitetails and mule deer is geared toward annual production of surplus animals in response to the many mortality factors they are subject to. If the surplus isn't removed through predation, population compensation will occur through disease, extremes in weather, road kills, and other factors.

Losses to disease, weather, and accidents are less desirable than predation as a means of controlling deer populations. Adequate annual harvest through hunting will keep deer mortality from other causes at a minimum. For more information on deer management, refer to chapter 17.

Fawns normally stay with their mothers through the winter and into the next spring. Does chase their offspring from the previous year away before giving birth. Disowned yearlings sometimes travel long distances before settling into a home range of their own. Most, however, probably disperse less than five miles from the area where they were raised.

Nebraska and South Dakota have some interesting findings on dispersal of young whitetails and mule deer. In South Dakota ten male mule deer tagged as fawns moved an average of 36.7 miles from that time to when they were killed as yearlings or adults. Some whitetails also disperse over long distances. Twenty-three members of this species moved an average of 38 miles in Nebraska. A pair of whitetails traveled 125 and 137 miles from points where they were tagged to points of recovery in that state.

Bucks frequently seek the company of other male deer before the rut starts. From my experiences, mule deer males seem to be more gregarious

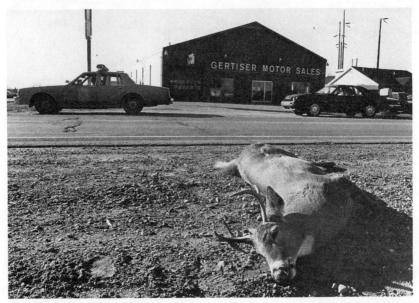

Countless deer are hit by cars every year.

An ear-tagged deer is released by volunteers of U.P. Whitetails, Inc. Collars can also be used to mark deer.

than whitetail bucks. Once breeding begins, the same group of bucks may fight among themselves competing for does. In these contests the stronger of the two deer usually wins without any injury to either contestant. Occasionally, however, the animals' antlers become hopelessly locked. Both deer usually die of exposure, unless they're found by hunters.

On October 20 one fall Gary Yancey of Lincoln Park, Michigan, and partner Dave Papas of Howell, Michigan, were bird hunting when they encountered a pair of bucks with locked antlers. Bow deer season was open and they both had unfilled tags, so they exchanged shotguns for bows and arrows as quickly as they could. Yancey filled his tag with the bigger of the two bucks, which had an eight-point rack, and Papas arrowed the six-pointer.

Brothers Eric and Dave Norden of Rock, Michigan, bagged with firearms a pair of trophy bucks that got their antlers locked in late November. Eric encountered the bucks first and returned to the scene with his

In the summer, groups of bucks assemble and are congenial, but once the rut starts they sometimes fight.

brother and father. The buck Eric shot had a twelve-point rack and Dave's trophy sported eleven points.

A buck will sometimes kill a rival during the course of a fight over breeding rights. Death is usually caused by stab wounds from sharp antler tines. One buck killed in a fight was stabbed in the heart.

Broken antlers and superficial injuries sometimes result from fights between bucks, too. One fall, a local taxidermist found a broken tine imbedded in the skull of a buck's head he was skinning. Apparently, the piece of antler was lost by another buck in a fight.

Whitetails and mule deer are good swimmers. Reports of them swimming for miles are common. When chased by dogs or predators, deer sometimes head for water to escape. Animals may also go in water to escape biting insects during the summer. Some deer feed on aquatic vegetation in the summer, too.

Basically, whitetail and mule deer are browsers, but they also graze on grasses and weeds when they are available. Additionally, deer are fond of a variety of agricultural crops. Leaves from trees and plants make up a large part of their diet in the summer and a lesser part in the fall. They do most of their browsing in late fall and winter. Woody material such as the buds and the tender tips of saplings and shrubs from sagebrush, mountain mahogany, dogwood, willow, maple, and oak are preferred. Evergreen leaves from yew, cedar, juniper, hemlock, and some pines are also favored. Acorns, beechnuts, and apples are prime fall and winter deer foods, when available. It is not uncommon for deer to stand on their hind legs to reach morsels of food on trees, especially in the winter when rations are sometimes in short supply.

Deer break or pull woody material that they ingest. Since only the lower jaw has front teeth, a deer can't bite through stems. For this reason, the ends of limbs or stems that deer feed on will be ragged. Farther back in the mouth, deer have teeth on both the top and bottom jaws, which are used for chewing.

Ingested food is chewed when taken in, but is later chewed again. Deer have four cavities in their stomachs: the rumen, reticulum, omasum, and abomasum. When first swallowed, food goes in the rumen. Bacteria mix with the material here to help break it down. The strain of bacteria in the rumen depends on what type of food is being consumed; so bacteria may vary during different seasons of the year. Cuds of food are regurgi-

Deer are primarily browsers. This one is munching the tops of felled trees.

tated from the rumen and then rechewed. The digestion process is completed in the other three cavities of the stomach.

Whitetails and mule deer require a daily average of five to ten pounds of food per 100 pounds of weight. Food requirements are greatest during periods of cold weather.

A fairly recent biological discovery about deer in areas where winters are typically severe is that they go into a physiological state similar to hibernation during the height of the cold season. The animals don't go to sleep, but their metabolism slows down. It seems to be an adaptation for conserving energy reserves necessary to carry them through the critical period.

2

Where to Hunt

One of the first steps on the way to a satisfying deer hunt is to choose wisely where to hunt. To do so often takes time and effort, but every consideration this phase of the hunt gets can prove to be well worth it. The process of picking the best location possible increases anticipation of the upcoming season and adds an important touch of confidence to a trip, which can make the difference between success and failure.

Planning where to go on a deer hunt should be done as far in advance of the season as possible. Most of the work involved can be done from home. This stage of deer hunting fills the gap between one season and the next. It is homework deer hunters shouldn't mind doing.

Preseason selection of an area for deer season is important on any deer hunt, but it is vital in some states. These states require hunters to specify a region or management unit in which they wish to hunt. That area is marked on their licenses and restricts them to hunting within that area. This requirement will probably become more prevalent in the future.

Planning where to go is just as important for deer hunters who hunt in their home region or state as it is for those who travel to another state. Typically, deer hunters who confine their hunting to home territory know little about deer densities a county or two away, and so miss out on what might be better deer hunting. These hunters hunt the same locations year after year and often accept the hunting available in their spots as representative of what is available throughout the region or state. In many cases this is far from the truth.

My home region, the Upper Peninsula of Michigan, will serve as a perfect illustration of how deer densities can vary regionally. Some of the best and some of the worst deer hunting in the state can be found in this fifteen-county area. Northern counties that border Lake Superior have mature forests and long, cold winters. Farming is common in southern counties of the region, younger forests are also found there, and winters aren't as severe as farther north. Some of the best deer hunting in the state is found in southern counties. A drive of 50 to 100 miles south in upper Michigan can take hunters from poor to excellent deer hunting.

Deer density is one of the most important considerations in deciding where to hunt, but other factors must be considered, too. These include hunter densities, availability of public land to hunt, and antler growth. Many times where there are the most deer, there will also be the most hunters. I, for one, do not like to hunt deer where the odds favor seeing more hunters than whitetails or mule deer. If little or no public land is available in an area of high deer density, permission to hunt private property must be obtained. When that isn't possible, an alternate location must be found. Deer hunters interested in trophy heads won't often find them in areas of high deer concentrations, unless the spot is lightly hunted.

When interested in hunting out of state, a number of additional factors should be considered. They include season dates, bag limits, availability of licenses, license fees, and hunter success ratios. Sometimes season dates and differing hunter success are considerations from area to area in one state, too.

Most of the necessary information on deer densities, harvest figures, hunter success, seasons, licenses, antler growth, and availability of public land can be obtained from state fish and game agencies or departments of natural resources. All states publish an annual hunting digest that contains pertinent information on licenses and seasons. Outdoor magazines are sources of information on seasons and license fees, too. *Outdoor Life,* for example, publishes state-by-state and province-by-province listings every fall. The National Rifle Association also publishes a hunting annual that is packed with helpful facts.

Most game departments also compile data on deer harvests, populations, or other indices that reflect the general abundance of deer by county, management unit, districts, or regions. The largest harvests normally occur where deer numbers are greatest. Hunt digests and harvest figures will often be available upon written request to the state agency's main office. Their addresses are given in chapter 3. A regional or district office would be a better source of information if you are interested in only a portion of a state or province.

Wildlife biologists are usually the best contacts for queries on deer densities, antler growth, and hunter success. A phone call or personal visit is generally the best way to reach biologists for information. Try to write questions down on paper before calling or stopping in, to prevent forgetting what you want to ask.

Maps that show public and private lands should also be available from state or provincial offices. Sometimes there is a charge for these. If maps aren't available from state offices, try other sources. In Michigan, for instance, the Michigan United Conservation Clubs publishes a booklet of county maps for the entire state. Plat books can be obtained from individual counties, and U.S. Forest Service offices usually have maps of any areas in their jurisdiction.

Maps are not only good references for determining land ownership, but they can also be used to determine where roadless tracts of land are located. Areas without roads that are at least a square mile in size are prime locations for getting away from large numbers of deer hunters. Few hunters penetrate far into tracts that aren't easily accessible.

The Boone and Crockett and Pope and Young record books are great references for learning where most of the big-antlered bucks are taken in individual states. If you are looking for a record or trophy head, these books will give you an idea of what parts of a state or which states big racks come from. Additional large-racked bucks are likely to be found in regions where others were bagged. Characteristics of the habitat in these parts of the country plus the genetics of the herd are often conducive to producing outstanding antlers on bucks.

Virginia, Pennsylvania, New York, Maine, Michigan, Wisconsin, Ohio, and some other states have big buck clubs. Their records show where trophy deer are likely to be found within their state.

When planning a deer hunt, try to dig up as much information as possible that will be helpful in determining which state and which region within it is most likely to provide the deer hunt you want.

To illustrate how to go about choosing a place to hunt deer, let's look at a couple of examples. For convenience we will assume that hunters want to hunt somewhere in the Upper Peninsula of Michigan. The first group of hunters want to see deer. They will be satisfied with any legal whitetail — other hunters in the area won't bother them.

Michigan's Department of Natural Resources (DNR) compiles a yearly list of the number of deer seen by its field personnel for each county. The number of hours involved in the sightings is also noted. This information is used to determine the average number of deer seen for every 100 hours DNR employees are in the field. The figures for each county represent an index of the general abundance of deer there. It is easy to determine which county has the highest density of deer by comparing the number of animals seen per 100 hours in each one.

Menominee County stands out as the number-one choice for this group of hunters. For July through August one year, an average of 165 deer were seen for every 100 hours in deer country. The next highest count was 52.5, which was for Dickinson County.

A check of the deer harvest for that year by counties would show there were an average of more than two bucks per square mile taken by hunters in Menominee County. Further checking would show there were from seven to twelve hunters per square mile in Menominee County during gun season, which is about medium pressure. Part of the reason for the lower-than-expected hunting pressure is private ownership of much of the county's land.

A look at a county map would show that since there is enough public land to choose from, there wouldn't be any problem finding a place to hunt if permission couldn't be obtained to hunt on private property. Heavy hunting pressure isn't always the rule in areas with limited public hunting land and lots of deer. I have hunted for days at a time in locations in both Menominee and Dickinson counties (hunter density is supposed to be as high as twenty per square mile in Dickinson) without seeing any hunters who didn't belong to our group. Few hunters make the effort to reach out-of-the-way locations. One area we frequent is surrounded by a marshy bog. We wear chest waders to get across the marsh, then put boots on when we reach dry ground.

Horses provide a convenient means of transportation to get away from crowds of hunters when hunting mule deer in western states.

To avoid other hunters when hunting in areas with a lot of deer, look for places that are difficult to reach.

Hunters interested in trying for trophy bucks in upper Michigan would find that thirty bucks from upper Michigan qualified for Boone and Crockett listing by looking at the current edition of *Michigan Big Game Records*. Seven of them were taken in Iron and Alger counties and eight in Baraga County. *Michigan Big Game Records* is published by Commemorative Bucks of Michigan (CBM), the state's record-keeping organization. Copies of this book can be obtained by writing to CBM at 3215 Old Farm Lane, Walled Lake, MI 48088.

For those who want to compete with as few hunters as possible, Alger or Baraga counties would be the best selection. Hunting pressure data show there were 7 to 12 hunters per square mile in Iron County. Alger had 4.6 to 7 hunters per square mile, and Baraga had fewer than 4.5.

Knowledge of deer densities in these counties would make the choice among them fairly easy. An average of 22.3 deer were seen per 100 hours in Alger, but only 3.6 in Baraga. An average of 31.4 deer were seen for every 100 hours spent in Iron County.

Public hunting land wouldn't be a problem in any of those three big-buck counties.

The same sort of information used in these examples can be used to help determine where best to hunt in any region, state, or province, if it is available. When hunting out of state, such factors as the number of licenses available to nonresidents must also be considered. Some states sell their quotas, at least those for preferred areas, well in advance of season openings.

After general hunting locations have been determined, hunters should concern themselves with isolating the best huntable-size chunks of terrain available. We have already seen that deer densities are not the same throughout a state. By the same token their distribution is not equal throughout a square mile of cover. There can be ten whitetails or mulies utilizing an area a fraction of that size and only a few throughout the rest of it. Some portions of deer habitat are simply more attractive to the animals than others.

Sources of large quantities of high-quality food are great for attracting concentrations of deer. Agricultural crops are favored by whitetails and mule deer. A good crop of acorns will attract a lot of local deer, too. Other favored deer haunts are areas that have been burned or logged in recent years. Young vegetation that mulies and whitetails thrive on grows profusely in either type of opening.

When in hilly or mountainous terrain the biggest bucks are usually found at the highest elevations. Islands in lakes or large rivers also can be hotspots for deer hunting. Whitetails and mulies that reside on some islands aren't often hunted. The same is true of any piece of deer habitat that is exceptionally thick or difficult to reach.

Hunting from horse or mule is a good way to get away from crowds of deer hunters.

Some of these locations can be pinpointed on maps. Talking with wildlife biologists, conservation officers or game wardens, sport shop owners, and other deer hunters in the area you plan to hunt is a good idea, too. From that point on, the final decision of where to hunt should be made after spending time in the field scouting the area.

There is one more consideration that can play a decisive role for some hunters in determining where to hunt deer. That factor is familiarity. Hunters who have spent a season or two or maybe a dozen in one area are bound to become familiar with the terrain, its deer, and the deer's behavior. The more familiar a hunter is with an area and its deer, the better his chances of scoring there. For this reason, some hunters may prefer to hunt locations with low densities of deer over those that have more animals, especially if they don't have time to check out distant spots. Many deer hunters simply don't have as much time to devote to deer hunting as they would like.

Tradition has a lot to do with return trips to familiar deer hunting grounds, too. Over the years the list of fond memories associated with a location grows. Each season then becomes an opportunity to recall past experiences, as much as it is an opportunity to have new ones.

3

Hunting Regulations

It is surprising how much hunting regulations vary from state to state. What may be legal in one could be illegal in another. Some states prohibit hunting on Sunday, for instance; many others allow it. Variations are also evident on minimum age requirements, hunter safety courses, legal weapons, clothing requirements, plus others.

While there are differences in hunting regulations across the country, there are also many that are universal. It is illegal to shoot deer while they are in water or to hunt them with rimfire firearms throughout North America. Legal hunting hours in most areas are a half-hour before sunrise until a half-hour after sunset. Motorized vehicles, including boats and aircraft, are not permitted to aid in collecting deer. Guns carried in vehicles must be unloaded and cased in most states, too.

Additional regulations relating to weapons that are commonly accepted are as follows: semiautomatic firearms must be restricted to a five-shell capacity; .410 and 28-gauge shotguns are inadequate for deer hunting; nonexpanding bullets are prohibited; and broadheads must be at least seven-eighths of an inch wide for deer hunting.

To avoid inadvertently breaking laws relating to deer hunting, hunters should read the guides published by states and provinces they intend to hunt. In Canada handguns are prohibited for deer hunting throughout. Fifty rounds of ammunition can be brought into Canada duty free. Additionally, hunters going into Canada should leave descriptions and serial numbers of their guns with customs officials when entering the country to avoid problems when reentering the U.S. If you can't prove they weren't purchased in Canada, a duty will have to be paid on them.

The following listings will give deer hunters a general idea of some of the regulations and requirements in various states and provinces. This information does not represent a total picture of all regulations in any given area, just some of the more pertinent ones that may be useful when planning a hunting trip. Some of those listed may change at any time. Certain counties or management units may have more restrictive regulations than a state or province as a whole. Keep these things in mind when referring to the following listings.

Deer herd estimates, harvests, hunting success percentiles, and addresses of main state or provincial natural resources or fish and game offices and their phone numbers will be listed in addition to hunting regulations. These are intended to help in planning or preparing for deer hunts. Figures on herd sizes, harvests, and success percentiles are the latest available. They are intended to give hunters a general idea of the hunting situations in each state and province. These figures may vary markedly from year to year.

United States

Alabama: There are an estimated 1.5 million whitetails in Alabama, according to state Deer Studies Project Leader David K. Nelson. He said approximately 300,000 deer are bagged annually, 75 percent of which are antlered bucks. There are about 200,000 deer hunters in Alabama, 50,000 of which hunt with bow and arrow.

One deer a day may be legally taken by hunters in Alabama. Archers can shoot a deer of either sex. Gun hunters are limited to antlered bucks, with bare antlers visible above the natural hairline, except during hunters'-choice seasons when one antlered and one unantlered deer can be taken per day.

The 1990–91 statewide archery season was October 15 to January 31. Gun seasons varied by county and on public and private lands, so consult a current hunting seasons booklet for accurate information. Separate hunts are usually held for chasing deer with dogs and stalk-hunting. Buckshot can be used when hunting with dogs, but not during seasons set aside for stalk-hunting.

Gun hunters are required to wear a solid orange hat or cap or an outer garment above the waist. Bows must have a minimum draw weight of thirty-five pounds for deer hunting. Muzzleloaders must be a minimum of .40 caliber. The toll-free phone number to report game law violations is 800-272-4263.

Game and Fish Division, Wildlife Section, 64 North Union St., Montgomery, AL 36130 (205-261-3469).

Alaska: Black-tailed deer "numbers are currently at very high levels throughout the state," according to Acting Planning Chief Bruce Dinneford. He said there are an estimated 350,000 present. Hunters bagged an estimated 16,310 blacktails during 1988 compared to 19,000 in 1987, but they still enjoyed a 69 percent success rate.

Deer hunts began on August 1 in 1989 and closing dates varied by management unit, ranging from October 31 through January 31. Annual bag limits ranged from one to six, depending on management unit.

Although it is illegal to hunt most big game species in Alaska the same day you've flown in an airplane, that restriction does not apply to deer. To report game violations, call 800-478-3377.

Department of Fish and Game, Box 3-2000, Juneau, AK 99802-2000 (907-465-4190).

Arizona: There are an estimated 160,000 mule deer in Arizona, according to Game Program Supervisor Tice Supplee. She said 110,000 are the Rocky Mountain subspecies and 50,000 are desert mule deer. The state is also home to about 55,000 Coues whitetails, according to Supplee.

She said the state's 1989 deer harvest by firearm was 15,645 mulies and 2,735 whitetails. Approximately 3,600 of the mulies were the desert variety. Supplee said archers bag about 1,000 deer a year in the state, most of which are mule deer.

Participation in Arizona gun hunts is limited by permit allocation through drawings. The number of bowhunting licenses, however, is unlimited. Supplee said archers will be restricted to taking antlered bucks only starting in 1990. Archery seasons for 1990 included the months of August, September, December, and January. The lengths and dates of gun hunts vary by management unit and range from four to seventeen days. To report poachers, call 800-352-0700.

Game & Fish Department, 2222 West Greenway Rd., Phoenix, AZ 85023 (602-942-3000).

Arkansas: An estimated 700,000 to 800,000 whitetails inhabit Arkansas, according to Forest Wildlife Research Coordinator Michael Cartwright, and the population is increasing. Record harvests have been achieved in each of the last four years. There were 113,079 deer registered by hunters in this state during 1989 compared to 110,207 in 1988 and 106,392 in 1987. All deer taken by hunters must be taken to check stations.

There were 223,053 licensed deer hunters in Arkansas during 1988.

Archery season generally begins October 1 and continues through February across most of the state. During 1990, bow deer season closed at the end of December in zone 4, though. Crossbows can be used during the archery season. Crossbows must have a minimum draw weight of 125 pounds and the minimum for conventional bows is 40 pounds.

Two black-powder deer hunts were held during October and December in 1990. Centerfire gun seasons began November 10 during 1990 and extended through December 2 or 9, depending upon zone.

Deer hunting with dogs is legal in designated zones during specified gun seasons (November 19–25 during 1990). As many as three whitetails can be bagged per year in Arkansas, but no more than two of them can be antlered bucks. Legal bucks must have antlers at least two inches long.

All gun hunters must wear a minimum of 400 square inches of blaze-orange above the waist in addition to an orange hat or cap. Completion of a Hunter Education Course is mandatory for anyone born after January 1, 1969, who wishes to hunt. This state's toll-free game violations number is 800-482-9262.

Game & Fish Commission, 2 Natural Resources Dr., Little Rock, AR 72205 (501-223-6300).

California: There are an estimated 850,000 mule deer in California. Six subspecies of mulies inhabit the state, according to Big Game Biologist Doug Updike. A little more than half of the deer population—approximately 435,175—is composed of coastal blacktails. The reported deer harvest for 1989 was 28,600, but Updike said the actual harvest was around 70,000, based on results of a mail survey of hunters.

Bow and gun deer seasons vary widely based on zones, so refer to a current state hunting regulation booklet for accurate season dates. Archery seasons start as early as July in some zones. The annual bag limit is two bucks with forked antlers in some zones and one buck in others.

Updike said one of the changes for 1990 was lowering the antler size for legal bucks in northeast zones X1, X2, and X3a and b to conform to the rest of the state. Bucks in those zones now only have to have a forked antler to be legal game. Previously, bucks had to have an antler with three points or more before they were legal.

Another change will allow hunters trying their luck in D zones to buy a second tag, if any are left after first-round applications are processed. Updike said the number of tags available for D zones has usually exceeded the number of people applying.

Crossbows can be used for deer hunting in California, but only during gun seasons, not archery seasons. Muzzleloaders must be at least .40 caliber and equipped with iron sights only. In areas where the discharge of centerfire rifles is prohibited, shotgun hunters may use sizes 0 or 00 buckshot. In all other areas, shotgun hunters are restricted to the use of slugs. The toll-free phone number to report poachers is 800-952-5400.

Department of Fish and Game, 1416 Ninth St., Box 944209, Sacramento, CA 94244-2090 (916-445-3531).

Colorado: Colorado's deer population was estimated at 674,410 animals before 1990 deer seasons opened. Most of those are mule deer. Division of Wildlife spokesman Harlan Riffel said there are some 900 to 1,000 whitetails harvested by hunters in the state annually. He added that most whitetails occupy the plains east of Interstate 25. A few show up on the Wyoming border.

There were 79,749 deer harvested in Colorado during 1989 seasons, according to Riffel. Archers accounted for 5,251, and another 2,237 were taken during muzzleloader hunts.

Dates for the 1990 archery season were August 23 to September 25. Gun seasons were held October 13–17, October 20–31, and November 3–11. A limited number of permits are available for muzzleloader and high-country hunts in September and for the plains deer hunt during October. The bag limit is one deer per year. To report poaching call 800-332-4155.

Division of Wildlife, 6060 Broadway, Denver, CO 80216 (303-297-1192).

Connecticut: This state's deer herd is increasing and so is its deer harvest, according to Wildlife Bureau spokesman Jim Spignesi. He said the state's whitetail herd contained 40,000 to 45,000 animals prior to the opening of 1990's hunting seasons. He said there were 8,763 whitetails harvested by hunters in the state during 1989, 926 of which were tagged by archers.

This compares with harvests of 7,642 in 1988 and 6,472 during 1987. Spignesi said better hunter access to private land was as much a factor in the increased kill as the availability of more deer. This state has liberal bag limits. Hunters who take advantage of all opportunities can shoot as many as eleven whitetails per year, according to Spignesi.

Shotgun deer hunts are controlled by permit on state land. Hunters who drew A permits during 1990 could hunt from November 19–28. The B hunt was held November 29 to December 8. The shotgun/rifle season on private land was November 19–December 8. A muzzleloader season on both public and private lands ran from December 10–22. Bow hunt dates were October 1 to November 17 and December 24–31.

Gun deer hunters are required to wear at least 200 square inches of orange visible from all sides. Bagged deer must be brought to check stations. Sunday hunting is not allowed.

Muzzleloaders used for deer hunting have to be at least .45 caliber and they may not be mounted with scopes. Shotguns are limited to 20 gauge and larger, shooting rifled slugs only. Centerfire rifles .243 caliber and larger may only be used on private property encompassing ten acres or more. Report poachers by dialing 800-842-HELP.

Department of Environmental Protection, 165 Capitol Ave., Hartford, CT 06106 (203-566-4683/5599).

Delaware: An estimated 15,000 whitetails occupy Delaware, according to Wildlife Division spokesman Ken Reynolds. He said the population has been increasing along with the annual kill since the late 1970s. Hunters bagged 4,504 deer in the state during 1989 seasons, according to Reynolds. Those using shotguns claimed 3,889, black-powder enthusiasts got 403, and archers tagged 212.

The bag limit has been two whitetails of either sex per year, but Reynolds said a bonus antlerless deer may be added to that limit for 1991. Muzzleloaders must be at least .42 caliber with iron sights only. Shotguns smaller than 20 gauge are prohibited for deer hunting. Gun hunters must wear at least 400 square inches of orange above the waist. The toll-free phone number to report poachers is 800-292-3030.

Department of Natural Resources & Environmental Control, Division of Fish & Wildlife, 89 Kings Hwy., P.O. Box 1401, Dover, DE 19903 (302-736-5297).

Florida: Florida's population of whitetails has been increasing, but Frank Smith, chief of the state's Bureau of Wildlife Management, expects numbers to level off soon due to the loss of habitat to development. He said there are approximately 800,000 to 900,000 deer in the state and he expects the population to level off at 110,000 to 115,000.

Harvest figures from 1989 seasons weren't available, but Smith said hunters took an estimated 107,240 whitetails during 1988, 105,917 in 1987, and 89,212 during 1986 seasons.

Florida is divided into three zones and deer seasons are set by zone. In the Northwest Zone, archery season was October 13 through November 11, 1990; the muzzleloader season took place November 16–18; gun season for antlered bucks was November 22–25, and December 8 to February 13; antlerless deer were legal game December 15 and 16.

In the Central Zone, bow season was September 22 to October 21; the muzzleloader hunt was October 26–28; antlered bucks were legal for gun hunters November 10 to January 20; and antlerless days were November 17 and 18. In the South Zone, archers could try their luck September 8 to October 7; muskets were legal October 12–24; antlered buck season was October 27 to January 6; and antlerless days were November 3 and 4.

Smith said special post-season archery and muzzleloader hunts were held in the Northwest Zone only. Dates for that season were February 14–24, 1991.

The daily bag limit for antlered bucks in Florida is two. The possession limit is four. There is no season limit. Legal bucks must have one antler protruding an inch above the hairline. Only one antlerless deer a year can be taken, except by special permit.

Gun hunters must wear a minimum of 500 square inches of orange above the waist. Hunting deer with dogs is legal. To report game law violations in the Northwestern Region dial 800-342-1676; Northeastern Region, 800-342-8105; Central Region, 800-342-9620; South Region, 800-282-8002; Everglades Region, 800-432-2046.

Game and Fresh Water Fish Commission, Farris Bryant Bldg., Tallahassee, FL 32399-1600 (904-488-1960).

Georgia: There are an estimated 1.15 million whitetails in Georgia, according to state Game Management spokesperson Kate Schumacher. She added that hunters bagged 320,000 deer during the course of recent gun and bow seasons. Dates for the 1990 bow season in Georgia were September 15 to October 19. Gun season opens the day after the archery season ends. In the southern zone, gun season remained open through January 6, 1991. In the northern zone, gun hunting ended December 2, then reopened December 25 through January 1.

Five whitetails per year can be legally taken per hunter in this state, but only three can be shot with firearms and no more than two can be antlered bucks. Shotguns used for deer hunting must be at least 20 gauge. Buckshot is not allowed on wildlife management areas. Muzzleloaders that are .44 caliber or larger are required for deer hunting.

At least 500 square inches of orange must be worn above the waist during gun hunts. Deer hunting with dogs is legal in designated counties at specified times. The toll-free phone number to report poachers is 800-241-4113.

Department of Natural Resources, Game and Fish Division, 205 Butler St., S.E., Suite 1362, Atlanta, GA 30334 (404-656-3523).

Idaho: Both mule deer and whitetails reside in Idaho. There are an estimated 290,000 mulies and 70,000 whitetails, according to Fish and Game spokesman Lonn Kuck. He said there has been a substantial increase in mule deer numbers during recent years due to several mild winters, and whitetails are also doing fine.

Kuck said hunters bagged an estimated 90,300 deer in the state during 1989 hunting seasons. Another 3,200 were claimed during muzzleloader season, and archers accounted for 1,700 deer. Seventy-six percent of the total harvest of 95,200 were mulies, Kuck said.

Archery seasons are usually from September through December; gun hunts are primarily during October and November, and the muzzleloader season takes place during November and early December. Poachers can be reported by dialing 800-632-5999.

Department of Fish & Game, 600 South Walnut St., P.O. Box 25, Boise, ID 83707 (208-334-3700).

Illinois: "Currently, Illinois does not attempt to provide a deer population estimate. . . ," Forest Wildlife Program Manager John Kube said. "Harvest records indicate deer densities are increasing and [the] health of the herd is excellent."

Whitetail harvests during gun seasons have steadily increased since 1970. There were 56,143 deer bagged during the 1989 firearm hunt compared with 47,786 in 1988 and 42,932 during 1987. An estimated 10,000 whitetails were tagged by bowhunters in the state during 1989 compared to 7,820 in 1988 and 6,646 during 1987.

Deer hunting permits are issued in a by-county drawing in Illinois. Once the drawing is held, any remaining permits are issued on a first come, first served basis. Hunters who were unsuccessful in the drawing get first crack at leftover tags. If enough permits are available, some hunters can obtain a second one.

Archery season dates for 1990 were October 1 to December 31 in counties without a firearm hunt. In counties having a firearm hunt, bowhunting is prohibited during gun seasons. Dates for gun hunts in 1990, during which only shotguns and muzzleloaders are legal, were November 16–18 and December 14–16.

Starting in 1990, archers are required to bring deer they bag to check stations. Gun deer hunters are required to wear at least 400 square inches of orange above the waist. Shotguns must be at least 20 gauge. Minimum caliber for muzzleloaders is .45. Legal bucks must have antlers at least three inches long. All white deer are protected in Illinois. Report poaching by dialing 800-252-0163.

Department of Conservation, Lincoln Tower Plaza, 524 South Second St., Springfield, IL 62701-1787 (217-782-6384).

Indiana: Indiana is home to an estimated 400,000 whitetails and the herd is increasing. A record 79,318 deer were bagged by hunters in the state during 1989 seasons. The tally was 56,521 for the gun hunt, 16,192 during bow seasons, and 6,605 with muzzleloaders.

In an effort to control the deer population, bonus licenses will be increased to 79,000 for 1990 from 20,000 the year before. Archery seasons were October 6 to November 9 and the month of December during 1990. A muzzleloader hunt was held December 1–9. Firearms season was November 10–25.

There's a two-deer bag limit with bow and arrow. One antlered buck is legal during firearms season and a deer of either sex is legal during the black-powder hunt. Hunters are required to wear orange during gun seasons. Shotguns must be at least 20 gauge and slugs are required. Muzzleloaders of .44 caliber and larger are legal. Deer must be checked at check stations.

Turn in poachers by dialing 800-TIP-IDNR.

Department of Natural Resources, Fish & Wildlife Division, 607 State Office Bldg., Indianapolis, IN 46204 (317-232-4080).

Iowa: An estimated 200,000 whitetails were in Iowa before the fawn crop of 1990, according to Wildlife Research Biologist Willie Suchy. The state's deer population has been increasing. Suchy said the total harvest for 1989 was 99,712. Bowhunters tallied 11,857 of those, black-powder hunters got 6,334, and shotgunners tagged 81,521.

As many as three deer can be taken per year, one per each type of license. Deer that are predominantly white are protected. Wearing orange is required during gun seasons. Anyone born after January 1, 1967, must complete a hunter safety course.

Dates for 1990 bow seasons were October 1 to November 30 and December 17 to January 10. Shotgun hunts were held December 1–15 and December 9–16. Muzzleloader seasons were October 13–21 and December 17 to January 10, 1991.

Shotguns must be at least 20 gauge and rifled slugs are the only projectiles legal for all gauges. Muzzleloaders must be at least .44 caliber. Poachers can be reported by dialing 800-532-2020.

Department of Natural Resources, Wallace State Office Bldg., Des Moines, IA 50319-0034 (515-281-5145).

Kansas: Approximately 300,000 deer live in Kansas, according to deer biologist Keith Sexson. He said about 50,000 of those are mulies and the rest are whitetails. Firearms hunters harvested an estimated 31,000 deer during 1989, archers got another 5,500, and black-powder hunters tallied 3,000 deer. Sexson said about 25 percent were mule deer.

Deer hunting in Kansas is limited to residents only. The bag limit is one deer per permit, and in some cases hunters can obtain two permits. The 1990 archery seasons were October 1 to November 27 and December 9–31. Gun season was November 28 to December 9, and the muzzleloader hunt was September 22–30. Call 800-228-4263 to report poaching.

Department of Wildlife & Parks, Route 2, Box 54A, Pratt, KS 67124-9599 (316-672-5911).

Kentucky: As many as 450,000 whitetails inhabited Kentucky prior to the opening of 1989 hunting seasons, according to state Deer Program Coordinator John Phillips. He said there were 64,000 deer harvested by hunters during 1988, 6,700 of which were claimed by archers, compared to a kill of 39,000 whitetails in 1986. Phillips added that he expects the herd and harvest to continue increasing. He anticipates a peak population of 650,000 deer in ten years with an annual harvest of 120,000 animals.

Bowhunting was legal from October 1 to December 31, 1990, in Kentucky. Gun season dates were November 10–19. Black-powder hunts were held October 20–21 and December 8–14.

Crossbows can be used for deer hunting during all gun seasons and on designated days late in the bow season. Shotguns must be at least 20 gauge and slugs are the only loads legal for deer hunting. Muzzleloaders must be at least .40 caliber.

The annual bag limit is two deer and animals must be brought to check stations. Legal bucks must have antlers four inches or more in length. A minimum of 500 square inches of orange must be worn above the waist during gun hunts. To report poachers, call 800-25ALERT.

Department of Fish and Wildlife Resources, Division of Public Relations, #1 Game Farm Rd., Frankfort, KY 40601 (502-564-4336).

Louisiana: Approximately 650,000 whitetails were present in Louisiana prior to the 1990 hunting seasons, according to Deer Study Leader Jerry Farrar. He said hunters harvested 165,000 deer during 1989–90 seasons, about 10,000 of which were taken by bowhunters. He added that hunters enjoyed an 82 percent success rate during 1989.

The daily bag limit is one whitetail, but hunters are allowed to tag six deer per year. A deer with a visible antler above the hairline is considered a legal buck.

Bowhunting is legal from October 1 to January 20 during 1990–91. Gun hunts are divided into three segments between November and mid-January, with actual dates varying by area, but totaling no more than sixty days. A seven-day muzzleloader hunt is also held.

Deer hunting with dogs is legal in certain areas at designated times. Report game thieves by dialing 800-442-2511.

Department of Wildlife and Fisheries, P.O. Box 15570, Baton Rouge, LA 70806 (504-765-2806).

Maine: Maine's deer population is increasing. The state had an estimated post-hunt herd of 160,000 animals prior to 1983 and 250,000 in 1988.

There's been a corresponding increase in hunter harvests. Maine's deer kill was 23,729 in 1987, 28,056 during 1988, and 30,260 by 1989.

The 1989 harvest comprised 17,009 antlered bucks and 13,251 antlerless deer. Only 416 whitetails were registered by archers, and 134 were taken by black-powder hunters, so the bulk of the kill took place during gun season. Firearms deer season was from October 29 to November 24 during 1990, with October 27 set aside for residents only. Archery season was October 1–26 and the muzzleloader hunt took place November 26 to December 1.

There's a bag limit of one deer a year in Maine and Sunday hunting is prohibited. Legal bucks must have antlers at least three inches long. Wearing an article of solid orange clothing is mandatory during gun seasons. All deer must be registered. The toll-free phone number to report game law violations is 800-253-7887.

Department of Inland Fisheries & Wildlife, 284 State St., State House Station 41, Augusta, ME 04333 (800-322-3606 or 207-289-2175).

Maryland: Maryland is the only state with a huntable population of sika deer. There are an estimated 4,000 to 5,000 of these deer in the state, with most of them found in Dorchester County and on Assateague Island in Worchester County. A few turn up in Wicomico and Somerset counties, too. There were 1,283 sikas taken by hunters in Maryland during 1989.

Whitetails are the primary species of deer found in the state and there are an estimated 150,000 of them. Hunters bagged 45,010 whitetails in Maryland during 1989 seasons compared to 33,597 the previous year. There were 34,518 tagged during the gun hunt, 7,988 were taken by archers, and 3,787 fell to front-loading rifles.

Archery seasons during 1990 were September 15 to November 23, December 4–21 and January 7–31, 1991. The bag limit was two deer of either sex. Black-powder season was December 22 to January 5 with a one-deer bag limit in most of the state, but two could be taken in some counties. The same limits apply to the eight-day firearms hunt held during late November and early December.

Registration of deer is mandatory. Deer hunting is prohibited on Sundays. Wearing orange is required during gun hunts. Shotguns must be at least 20 gauge and loads are limited to slugs, except in Dorchester County, where buckshot can be used. Scopes are prohibited on muzzleloaders. Report poachers by dialing 800-635-6124.

Department of Natural Resources, Forest, Park and Wildlife Service, Tawes State Office Bldg., Annapolis, MD 21401 (301-974-3776).

Massachusetts: An estimated 50,000 whitetails inhabited this state prior to 1990 hunting seasons, according to Assistant Wildlife Director Steven

Williams. He said a record harvest of 6,720 deer was logged in 1989, which is 20 percent greater than the previous record harvest.

Archery season during 1990 was November 5–24. Shotgun seasons were November 26 to December 5 in zones 1 through 11, and November 26 to December 1 in zones 12 through 14. A muzzleloader hunt was held December 17–19. Front-loading rifles must be .44 caliber or larger. Scopes are prohibited during this hunt and rifles must be loaded with round balls only.

The annual bag limit is two deer. Legal bucks must have antlers at least three inches long. Bagged deer must be brought to check stations. At least 500 square inches of orange must be worn during gun hunts. There's no hunting on Sundays. Poachers can be reported by calling 800-632-8075.

Division of Fisheries and Wildlife, Leverett Saltonstall Bldg., Government Center, 100 Cambridge St., Boston, MA 02202 (617-727-3151).

Michigan: Michigan's whitetail population has steadily increased during recent years and the annual deer harvest has kept pace with that trend. An estimated two million deer inhabited the state prior to 1989 hunting seasons and the population was considered close to that level again during the fall of 1990.

Record deer harvests have been achieved from 1986 through 1989, and that trend was expected to continue through 1990. Hunters bagged an estimated 244,000 whitetails in 1986, 315,000 for 1987, 379,390 by 1988, and 445,240 during 1989. Regulations and bag limits have been liberalized in order to try to control the herd's rapid growth.

The combined bow and gun season bag limits allow four deer, and a variety of bonus licenses are available for antlerless animals. Traditional season dates for archers are October 1 to November 14 and December 1 to January 1. The regular gun season is from November 15–30 and a ten-day muzzleloader hunt is held during December. The black-powder season is usually earlier in the Upper Peninsula than in the rest of the state.

Starting in 1990, all white deer are protected in the state, but partially white, or piebald, whitetails are legal to hunters. Front-loading rifles must be a minimum of .44 caliber. At least one item of orange is required for outer-wear during all gun hunts. Firearms hunters may not hunt from elevated stands, but archers may.

The minimum age for deer hunting with bow and arrow is twelve, and fourteen for firearms. Hunter safety training is mandatory for first-time hunters. To report game law violations dial 800-292-7800.

Department of Natural Resources, Wildlife Division, Box 30028, Lansing, MI 48909 (517-373-1263).

Minnesota: Minnesota had an estimated 900,000 whitetails within its borders prior to the opening of 1990 seasons, according to Forest Wildlife Program Leader Dave Schad. He said the herd has stabilized at that level for several years. The total deer harvest for the state was 139,480 for 1989 compared to 148,394 in 1988, 143,073 for 1987, and 137,923 in 1986.

While the gun season harvest dipped to 129,551 during 1989 compared to 138,946 the previous year, archers did better in 1989 (9,307) than in 1988 (8,262) and 1987 (7,535). Only one whitetail a year is legal in Minnesota, so there may be an increase in two-season hunters. Those who connect with bow and arrow may not hunt during gun season.

The 1990 archery season opened September 15 and ended at different times according to zones. The muzzleloader season was November 24 to December 9. Gun season opened November 3. It is mandatory to register all deer bagged in the state. Legal bucks must have one antler at least three inches long.

Only iron sights are legal on black-powder guns during muzzleloader season. Bows must be at least 40-pound pull. Gun hunters must wear a hat and outer garment that is either bright red or orange above the waist. To report violations dial 800-652-9093.

Division of Fish & Wildlife, Department of Natural Resources, 500 Lafayette Rd., St. Paul, MN 55155-4007 (612-296-6157).

Mississippi: Deer Biologist Bill Lundceford said there are between 1.5 million and 1.75 million whitetails in Mississippi. He also said that hunters harvest from 250,000 to 275,000 deer per year.

Deer seasons usually begin the first week of October with the archery hunt and continue through most of December. Gun hunts begin during the second half of November. Hunting with dogs is allowed during some segments of the season. A primitive-weapons hunt is held during the first half of December.

As many as five bucks can be taken per season, but no more than one per day. The daily bag limit on antlerless deer is also one, with a season limit of three. A deer with antlers visible above the hairline is a legal buck. Spotted fawns are protected.

Hunters are required to wear a minimum of 500 square inches of solid orange above the waist during gun seasons. Telescopic sights are prohibited on muzzleloaders. Persons born on or after January 1, 1972, must complete a hunter education course before purchasing a license. Game violations can be reported by dialing 800-237-6278.

Department of Wildlife, Fisheries and Parks, P.O. Box 451, Jackson, MS 39205-0451 (601-961-5300).

Missouri: Between 600,000 and 1 million whitetails live in Missouri. The total kill during 1989 was 168,476. Firearms hunters accounted for 157,506 animals, and archers tagged 10,970. During 1988 there were 151,367 whitetails bagged by hunters in Missouri, 10,183 of which were taken during bow season.

Archery seasons for 1990 were October 1 to November 9 and November 19 to December 31, with a bag limit of two deer, but only one whitetail could be taken by November 9. Dates for the regular firearm season were November 10–18. A muzzleloading hunt was held December 1–9.

Scopes may not be mounted on firearms used by muzzleloading permit holders. Shotguns used for deer hunting must be a minimum of 20 gauge. Gun hunters must wear a hat or cap and shirt, vest, or coat that is solid orange in color. Hunters born on or after January 1, 1967, are required to have an approved hunter safety card to obtain a hunting license. It is mandatory to have bagged deer examined at check stations. Legal bucks must have one antler at least three inches long. The toll-free phone number to report poaching is 800-392-1111.

Department of Conservation, P.O. Box 180, Jefferson City, MO 65102-0180 (314-751-4115).

Montana: Both whitetails and mule deer inhabit Montana. No statewide deer-population estimates are available, but deer herds are healthy. Special Projects Coordinator Heidi Youmans said hunters harvested 122,324 deer during 1989 seasons. Mule deer contributed 78,063 to the kill and 44,261 were whitetails.

Proposed dates for 1991 archery deer seasons in Montana are September 7 to October 20. A back-country deer hunt is planned for September 15–December 1, and the general gun deer season should be October 27 to December 1, 1991.

Muzzleloaders used for deer hunting in Montana must be at least .45 caliber. Shotgun hunters are limited to the use of slugs, and 0 and 00 buckshot. Hunters must wear a minimum of 400 square inches of orange above the waist during gun hunts. Persons between the ages of twelve and seventeen must complete a hunter education program. The toll-free phone number to report violations is 800-847-6668.

Department of Fish, Wildlife & Parks, 1420 E. 6th Ave., Helena, MT 59620 (406-444-2535).

Nebraska: This state is home to an estimated 160,000 whitetails and 40,000 mule deer. An estimated 24,334 whitetails and 9,659 mulies were taken by hunters in Nebraska during the 1989 gun season.

Gun season dates for 1990 were November 10–18 and January 5–13. Archery season was September 15 to November 9. A muzzleloader hunt was from December 8–23.

All deer hunting in this state is by permit and are issued in drawings. Hunters may obtain two permits per year. Deer must be brought to check stations. The minimum age for deer hunting is fourteen. Gun deer hunters are required to wear at least 400 square inches of orange on their heads, backs, and chests.

Crossbows with a minimum draw weight of 125 pounds are legal for deer hunting in Nebraska. Other bows must have a draw weight of at least 40 pounds. Muzzleloaders must be at least .40 caliber. Only shotguns 20 gauge or larger, firing slugs, can be used on deer. Dial 800-742-SNAP to report violations.

Game and Parks Commission, P.O. Box 30370, Lincoln, NE 68503 (402-471-0641).

Nevada: State Big Game Biologist Mike Hess estimates there are 200,000 mule deer in Nevada. He said the total number of deer bagged during 1989 seasons was 17,782. Only 349 of those were taken by archers, and 271 by black-powder hunters.

All deer hunting in the state is controlled by permit quotas, according to Hess. He said the application deadline for bow and black-powder hunts is usually mid-June, and late June for gun seasons. If enough permits are available, a hunter could get two: one for a buck and another for an antlerless animal. Hunt dates vary by management unit.

Muzzleloaders must be at least .44 caliber with iron sights only. Shotguns used for deer hunting must be at least 20 gauge and rifled slugs are the only legal shotgun loads. A hunter safety course must be completed by persons born after January 1, 1960. Deer kills must be reported. It is illegal to camp within 100 yards of any water hole in such a manner that wildlife and livestock are denied access to water. Report poachers by dialing 800-992-3030.

Department of Wildlife, 1100 Valley Rd., P.O. Box 30040, Reno, NV 89520-3040 (702-789-0500).

New Hampshire: Whitetails number approximately 40,000 in New Hampshire, according to Deer Project Leader Scot Williamson. He said the herd is increasing in most of the state's management units, but at varying rates.

A total of 7,238 whitetails were taken by hunters in the state during 1989 seasons, according to Williamson. There were 5,410 bagged during gun season, 1,339 during the muzzleloader hunt, and 489 in bow season.

Dates for the 1990 archery season were September 15 to December 16.

Black-powder hunting was held October 24 to November 6, and the general firearms hunt was November 7 to December 2. Report poachers by calling 800-344-4262.

Fish and Game Department, 2 Hazen Dr., Concord, NH 03301 (603-271-3421).

New Jersey: An estimated 160,000 whitetails live in New Jersey. State hunters harvested 48,462 deer during 1989–90 seasons compared to 45,900 in 1988–89. Bowhunters accounted for 13,714 of those, and muzzleloader hunters tagged 5,899.

Bag limits are liberal in this state for hunters who participate in a variety of seasons and are willing to travel to different areas. By buying a number of permits, hunters can collect as many as a dozen deer per year. For 1990, archery hunts have been modified in zones 1 and 4 to allow only the taking of antlered bucks during the first three weeks, with deer of either sex legal during the second half of the season.

New Jersey has three separate bow seasons. The fall hunt was September 29 to November 9, 1990. A permit hunt was held November 10 to December 1. The winter hunt took place January 2–25, 1991.

The 1990 shotgun season was held December 3–8 and permit shotgun hunts were held on designated days during December and January by zone. A permit muzzleloader hunt took place on fifteen specified days in December.

Gun hunters must wear at least 200 square inches of solid orange above the waist. Deer hunting on Sundays is prohibited. Shotguns used for deer hunting must be at least 20 gauge and those loaded with buckshot must be at least 12 gauge. Muzzleloaders must be a minimum of .44 caliber and only iron sights are permitted. A minimum draw weight of thirty-five pounds is required for bows. To report violations, call 800-222-0456.

Department of Environmental Protection, Division of Fish, Game & Wildlife, CN400, Trenton, NJ 08625 (609-292-2965).

New Mexico: Mulies are the major deer species in New Mexico, with an estimated 350,000 present, according to Assistant Chief of Research Wally Haussamen. He said some whitetails live in the state, but they number fewer than 35,000. The whitetails are the small southwestern subspecies referred to as Coues deer.

Haussamen said state hunters bagged just over 19,000 deer of both species during 1989, with at least 95 percent of them being mulies. Rifle hunters accounted for 16,900 of the total kill, muzzleloader hunters 1,620, and archers claimed about 500 animals.

Deer seasons vary by area for centerfire firearms, muzzleloaders, and archery equipment. Participation in some hunts is limited by permit. The bag limit is one antlered deer per year. Legal bucks must have one antler at least two inches long.

Shotguns used for deer hunting must be at least 28 gauge and buckshot loads are prohibited. Muzzleloaders must be a minimum of .40 caliber and are limited to iron sights. People under eighteen must complete a hunter education course. Without permission, it is illegal to park a vehicle or camp within 300 yards of a man-made water hole, well, or tank used by wildlife. To report violations dial 800-432-4263.

Department of Game & Fish, Villagra Bldg., State Capitol, Santa Fe, NM 87503 (505-827-7911).

New York: An estimated 700,000 whitetails live in New York. Hunters harvested 181,879 in the state during 1989 compared to 193,464 in 1988. The major reason for the lower kill during 1989 was a reduction in the number of does. There were actually more bucks shot during 1989 (99,589) than 1988 (92,987).

Archers claimed 12,770 deer during 1988, accounting for 6.6 percent of the total harvest. Bowhunters who bag a whitetail can get a permit for a second whitetail. Only one deer can be taken during other seasons, except by the member of a group having a deer management permit.

In the state's northern zone, archery season was September 27 to October 19, 1990. The black-powder hunt was October 13–19, and regular gun season was October 20 to December 2. In the southern zone, bow seasons were October 15 to November 18, December 12–16, and November 1 to December 31 (in Westchester County). Gun season was November 19 to December 11 in the southern zone, and musket hunters could be in the field December 12–18.

Scopes are prohibited on muzzleloaders, which must be loaded with patched round balls only. The minimum caliber for muskets is .44. Shotguns must be at least 20 gauge for deer hunting and buckshot is prohibited. Hunter education courses are required for first-time hunters. The minimum age for deer hunting with bow and arrow is fourteen, sixteen with firearms. Sunday hunting is prohibited in some parts of the state. To report poachers call 800-847-7332.

Department of Environmental Conservation, 50 Wolf Rd., Albany, NY 12233 (518-457-5400).

North Carolina: North Carolina's whitetail population is estimated at 600,000, according to Deer Project Leader J. Scott Osborne. There were 89,690 animals harvested by hunters in the state during 1989–90 seasons.

Archers accounted for 4,660 of that total.

Bow season started September 10, 1990, statewide, but ended during October or November, depending upon region. Dates for the gun hunt in the eastern region were October 15 to January 1, November 12 to January 1 in the central region, November 19 to December 1 in the northwestern region, and November 19 to December 8 in the western region. Muzzleloader seasons were October 8–13 in the eastern and western regions, November 5–10 in the central region, and November 12–17 in the northwestern region.

Bows must have a minimum draw weight of forty-five pounds. Broadheads that mechanically open upon impact are prohibited. Gun hunters must wear an orange hat or cap or other outer garment. Dogs may be used for deer hunting during regular gun seasons. Whitetails with visible antlers are considered legal bucks. The daily bag limit is two deer, with a season limit of four animals. Bagged deer must be reported. The toll-free phone number to report game law violations is 800-662-7137.

Wildlife Resources Commission, 512 N. Salisbury St., Raleigh, NC 27611 (919-733-3391).

North Dakota: Both mule deer and whitetails are present in North Dakota, with about 25,000 of the former and 145,000 of the latter. Game and Fish Department spokesman Arlen Harmoning said herds are down from record levels, but are generally stable to slightly increasing.

Firearms hunters bagged 46,700 whitetails and 5,400 mulies during the 1989 season, according to Harmoning. Archers claimed 2,900 whitetails and 350 mule deer. Black-powder shooters got 300 whitetails.

All gun licenses are available on a permit basis and no more than one percent of them are allocated for nonresidents. There's an unlimited number of archery licenses. All deer hunts begin at noon. To report poaching call 800-472-2121.

Dates for 1990 bow seasons were August 31 to November 8 and November 13 to December 31. Gun season was from November 9–25. Muzzleloader hunts were held November 30 to December 3 and December 7–10. The bag limit was one deer per person.

Lighted and light-gathering sight pins are prohibited for bowhunting in North Dakota. Wearing an orange hat and vest is required during firearms hunts.

Game and Fish Department, 100 North Bismarck Expressway, Bismarck, ND 58501-5095 (701-221-6300).

Ohio: There are in excess of 250,000 whitetails in Ohio, according to state Wildlife Education Officer Chip Gross. Hunters harvested 91,236 deer in

Ohio during 1989 compared to 100,674 in 1988. Archers using both cross-bows and conventional bows claimed 10,038 of the total kill in 1988 and 9,437 during 1989.

Dates for Ohio's 1989 archery season were October 7 to January 31. Gun season opens on the first Monday after Thanksgiving (November 26, 1990) and runs for six days. A special primitive-weapons hunt is usually held on three public hunting areas in late October. The statewide primitive-weapons hunt has been open during early January.

Conventional bows must have minimum draw weights of 40 pounds, while crossbows are restricted to a maximum draw weight of 200 pounds. Muzzleloaders of .38 caliber and larger can be used for deer hunting. Shotguns of at least 20 gauge, with slugs only, can also be used. Bagged deer must be taken to a check station.

All first-time hunters are required to complete a hunter training course. To report game law violations dial 800-POACHER.

Department of Natural Resources, Division of Wildlife, Fountain Square, Bldg. G, Columbus, OH 43224-1329 (614-265-6330).

Oklahoma: Deer populations are increasing in Oklahoma, with an estimated 250,000 whitetails and 2,500 mule deer, according to Deer Project Biologist Michael Shaw. A record deer harvest of 38,850 was achieved during 1988, which only included 232 mulies. He said the 1989 harvest was slightly lower, at 38,341, due to difficult hunting conditions during the primitive-weapons season.

Archers contributed 4,414 deer to the 1988 harvest and 4,589 during 1989. Muzzleloader hunters bagged 5,034 deer in 1988 and 4,406 in 1989. A total of 29,402 animals were tagged during the regular gun season in 1988 and 29,346 during 1989. The bag limit was two deer during bow season, one of which had to be a buck with at least three-inch antlers. The bag limit was the same during gun season in designated areas. Primitive-weapons hunters were limited to shooting one antlered buck.

The 1990 archery season was from October 1 to November 11 and December 1-31. Gun season was November 17-25 and the muzzleloader hunt was October 20-28. All deer must be taken to check stations.

Persons born on or after January 1, 1972, must have a hunter safety certificate to purchase a hunting license. Wearing 500 square inches of orange above the waist is required during gun season. Muzzleloaders used during primitive season can only be equipped with iron sights. Shotguns used for deer hunting must be at least 20 gauge. Dial 800-522-8039 to report game law violations.

Department of Wildlife Conservation, 1801 N. Lincoln, P.O. Box 53465, Oklahoma City, OK 73105 (405-521-3851).

Oregon: There are an estimated 480,000 blacktails and 256,000 mule deer in Oregon, according to Big Game Staff Biologist Chris Wheaton. He said gun hunters harvested 43,150 blacktails and 26,809 mulies during 1989 seasons. Archers claimed 2,163 blacktails and 1,079 mulies.

Wheaton said the state is also home to two small populations of whitetails. A hunted herd resides in eastern Oregon and about 100 of them are harvested annually. Columbian whitetails live in western Oregon and they are classified as a threatened species, so are protected.

Hunting seasons vary by management unit. Limited permits are available for some special deer hunts and applications must be in by April. Bows used for deer hunting in Oregon must be at least forty-pound pull. Front-loaders are required to be a minimum of .40 caliber. Dial 800-452-7888 to turn in poachers.

Department of Fish and Wildlife, P.O. Box 59, Portland, OR 97207 (503-229-5403).

Pennsylvania: More than a million whitetails roam Pennsylvania, according to Game Commission spokesman Ted Godshall. He said the total deer harvest in the state during 1989 was 388,601. Archers bagged 11,008 of those and another 6,553 were taken during the state's flintlock season.

Archery seasons for 1990 were September 29 to October 26 and December 26 to January 12. Buck hunting with firearms took place November 26 to December 8 and antlerless deer were legal December 10–12. Dates for the black-powder season were the same as the late archery hunt.

Only flintlock muzzleloaders .44 caliber and larger can be used during the state's black-powder season and loads are limited to patched round balls. Shotguns must be at least 20 gauge and buckshot loads are prohibited for deer hunting. Semiautomatic rifles and shotguns are illegal for deer hunting, too, except in designated areas. Wearing orange is mandatory during gun seasons.

Game Commission, 2001 Elmerton Ave., Harrisburg, PA 17110-9797 (717-787-4250).

Rhode Island: In excess of 3,000 whitetails live in this small state, according to Wildlife Technician Sharon Bugbee, and the population is increasing. She said the 1989 deer harvest included 161 during archery season, 186 collected by black-powder users, and 280 by shotgun hunters for a total of 627. This compares with a kill of 456 during 1988.

Bowhunting for deer is legal from October through January. Dates for the shotgun season were December 2–10, 1989. A special shotgun hunt for paraplegics is held during October. Black-powder hunts were held November 18 to December 1 and December 11–24. Only iron sights are legal on front-loaders during these hunts.

Archers and muzzleloader hunters who bag deer must register the animals with conservation officers or at check stations and then they can get a free tag for a second deer. Deer shot during shotgun seasons must also be checked, but the bag limit is one whitetail. The wearing of at least 500 square inches of orange is required during shotgun hunts; 200 square inches during muzzleloader seasons. First-time hunters must complete a hunter safety course.

Game law violations can be reported twenty-four hours a day by dialing 401-277-3070 in Providence.

Department of Environmental Management, Division of Fish & Wildlife, Washington County Government Center, Tower Hill Rd., Wakefield, RI 02879 (401-789-3094 or 277-3075).

South Carolina: Deer Project Supervisor Derrel Shipes estimates South Carolina's whitetail population at 750,000 animals. There was a minimum harvest of 107,081 deer in the state during 1989–90 seasons, of which 63,866 were bucks and 40,422 were does.

Dates for deer seasons vary by zone in this state. Gun hunts begin as early as August 15 in some zones, September 15 in others, but not until October in additional zones. There is no bag limit on bucks in some zones, but it varies from three to seven in others. The antlerless harvest is controlled by permit quotas. Legal bucks must have an antler at least two inches in length in most zones.

Mandatory checking of bagged deer is required in some portions of the state. Deer hunting with dogs is allowed in designated areas. Hunters must wear an orange hat, cap, vest, or coat during gun seasons. The toll-free phone number to report violations is 800-922-5431.

Wildlife and Marine Resources Department, P.O. Box 167, Columbia, SC 29202 (803-734-3886).

South Dakota: South Dakota has an estimated 225,000 whitetails and 75,000 mule deer, according to state Game Specialist Ron Fowler. The projected deer harvest for 1989 included 42,828 whitetails and 9,682 mulies for an average hunter success rate of 67 percent.

An unlimited number of bow deer licenses are available. The same is true for gun licenses in the Black Hills. Special applications are required for firearms hunts in other areas of the state.

Archery season generally runs from October 1 to December 31 in South Dakota. The Black Hills gun hunt usually encompasses the month of November. Season dates vary in other locations. Some special deer hunts on wildlife refuges are limited to the use of muzzleloaders.

An exterior garment of orange must be worn during gun hunts. Shooting at deer from the right-of-way of any road is illegal. Black-powder guns have to be at least .44 caliber. Buckshot may not be used for deer hunting. Lighted sight pins and telescopic sights are prohibited on bows. The toll-free phone number to report violations is 800-592-5522.

Department of Game, Fish and Parks, Sigurd Anderson Bldg., 445 East Capitol, Pierre, SD 57501-3185 (605-773-3381).

Tennessee: There were an estimated 600,000 to 700,000 whitetails in Tennessee during the spring of 1990, according to Deer Project Coordinator Greg Wathen. Hunters bagged a record 100,687 deer during 1989–90 seasons compared to 84,561 in 1988 and 90,580 during 1987. Archers claimed 11,660 deer during 1989 and muzzleloader hunters bagged 16,186.

Hunting seasons vary among the state's four deer units. Hunts are provided for archers, black-powder shooters, and centerfire firearms users. As many as four whitetails can be taken during some seasons in designated units. Legal bucks must have antlers at least three inches long. Taking bagged deer to check stations is mandatory.

Persons born on or after January 1, 1969, must complete a hunter education course. Wearing at least 500 square inches of orange above the waist is required during gun hunts. Buckshot is prohibited for deer hunting. Crossbows can only be used for deer hunting during bow seasons by hunters who are severely handicapped. Dial 800-255-TWRA to report violations.

Wildlife Resources Agency, Ellington Agricultural Center, P.O. Box 40747, Nashville, TN 37204 (800-624-7406 or 615-781-6622).

Texas: This large state has a correspondingly large population of whitetails, numbering 3,537,560 during 1989, according to assistant Deer Program Leader Mike Reagan. Deer numbers have gradually declined over the past four years, having reached a peak population of 4,177,672 in 1986. There's still no shortage of whitetails in Texas, however.

Reagan said there are an estimated 207,000 mule deer in the state. There were 6,839 mulies harvested by 20,492 hunters during the 1989–90 season. A total of 477,491 whitetails were claimed by 564,120 hunters.

Bow season dates for both whitetails and mulies were October 1–31 during 1990. Gun seasons for whitetails were from November 3 to January 6 in north Texas and November 10 to January 13 in south Texas. Mule deer gun hunts were from November 17 to December 2 in the Panhandle and November 24 to December 9 for the Trans-Pecos Region.

Hunters may legally take as many as four whitetails a year, with no more than two of those being bucks. There's a two-deer limit on mulies, but only one can be a buck. A legal buck is a deer with a hardened antler protruding through the skin.

Bows must have a minimum draw weight of forty pounds. Hunters handicapped in such a way that they can not shoot a conventional bow may use a crossbow during archery seasons. Crossbows must have a minimum draw weight of 125 pounds.

Hunters born on or after September 2, 1971, must complete a hunter education course. The toll-free phone number to report game violations is 800-792-GAME.

Parks & Wildlife Department, 4200 Smith School Rd., Austin, TX 78744. Call 800-792-1112 in Texas for information. From out of state, dial 512-389-4505.

Utah: No attempt is made to estimate the number of mule deer in Utah, according to Big Game Program Coordinator Wes Shields. He said hunters bagged a total of 78,372 mulies in the state during 1989 seasons. That includes 3,078 taken by archers and 2,370 brought down with muzzleloaders.

The bag limit is one buck per year, but Shields said some additional antlerless permits are issued. Something new for 1990 is that no antler restrictions will be in effect. Any antlered buck will be legal. A minimum three-point antler limit was in effect in some units previously.

Archery season was August 18 to September 3, 1990. The rifle hunt took place October 20–30 and muzzleloaders were legal November 3–11. All hunters born after December 31, 1965, must show proof of completing a certified hunter education course to buy a license.

Shotguns must be at least 20 gauge and only rifled slugs can be used for deer hunting. Front-loaders must be at least .40 caliber with iron sights only. Saboted bullets are prohibited for black-powder deer hunting. Bows must have a minimum draw weight of forty pounds. Wearing orange is required for gun hunts. Turn in poachers by dialing 800-662-DEER.

Department of Natural Resources, Division of Wildlife Resources, 1596 West North Temple, Salt Lake City, UT 84116-3195 (801-538-4700).

Vermont: An estimated 90,000 to 100,000 whitetails are expected to be in Vermont when the 1990 hunting seasons open, according to state Deer Project Leader Ronald Regan. Hunters harvested 9,227 deer in the state during 1989 compared to 7,078 in 1988. There were 7,913 whitetails taken during the regular gun season in 1989, 1,206 during bow season, and 108 on the muzzleloader hunt. Harvests for the same seasons during 1988 were 6,429, 627, and 22.

Archery seasons were October 6–28 and December 1–9 during 1990. One deer of either sex was legal during the early hunt. Only antlered bucks with at least three-inch antlers could be taken on the late hunt. Crossbows are legal for handicapped hunters unable to use a standard bow.

Dates for the regular gun season were November 10–25, 1990. The muzzleloader deer season was December 1-9. The bag limit during those hunts is one antlered buck. No more than two whitetails can be taken per year. All deer shot by hunters must be reported. The toll-free phone number to report game violations is 800-75ALERT.

Agency of Natural Resources, Fish and Wildlife Department, 103 South Main St., Waterbury, VT 05676 (802-244-7331).

Virginia: An estimated 650,000 to 700,000 whitetails inhabit Virginia, according to Jerry Sims, assistant chief of the state's Wildlife Division. Hunters registered 134,646 deer in the state during 1989 seasons compared to 114,562 in 1988.

Virginia's bow deer season for 1990 took place from October 13 to November 10. West of Blue Ridge, bowhunting was also legal from December 3 to January 5. The general gun season began November 19 and ended December 1 or January 5, depending upon location. A number of counties in the southeast corner of Virginia held gun hunts starting October 1 that lasted for two months. A muzzleloader hunt was held in designated western counties from December 17 to January 5.

As many as three deer a year could be legally taken in Virginia during 1989, with no more than one per day allowed. No more than two bucks can be taken. A legal buck is classified as a deer with antlers visible above the hairline.

Gun deer hunters are required to wear a solid orange hat or upper body covering. Completion of a hunter education program is required of youngsters between the ages of twelve and fifteen, as well as older individuals who have not hunted previously. The state's toll-free phone number to report poachers is 800-237-5712.

Department of Game and Inland Fisheries, 4010 West Broad St., Richmond, VA 23230 (800-252-7717 or 804-367-1000).

Washington: An estimated 400,000 deer roam Washington, according to state Wildlife Biologist Rolf Johnson, and that figure includes blacktails, mulies, and whitetails. He said the population is composed of 200,000 blacktails, 133,000 mule deer, and 67,000 whitetail.

Deer licenses are valid for any one of the three, so the kill isn't indexed according to species. Johnson said hunters bagged a total of 48,071 deer during 1989. Gun hunters accounted for 42,636 of those, bowhunters tagged 3,654, and black-powder enthusiasts were credited with 1,791 deer.

Early and late deer seasons for centerfire firearms, muzzleloaders, and archery equipment are held in the state. Season openers for 1990 were September 15 and October 13 for centerfire firearms, September 15 and November 21 for bow and arrow, and September 29 and November 21 for muzzleloaders. Closing dates of seasons vary by management units. Only one deer a year may be taken by each hunter in the state.

One major change in regulations for 1990 in the Blue Mountains of southeast Washington is that mule deer bucks must have antlers with at least three points to be legally taken. Previously, any antlered buck was legal. That rule is still in effect for whitetails from that area.

Shotguns used for deer hunting must be at least 20 gauge. Muzzleloading rifles carried during designated hunts must have iron sights only and black-powder substitutes are prohibited. Albino deer are protected. To report violations, dial 800-562-5626.

Department of Wildlife, 600 North Capitol Way, Olympia, WA 98504-0091 (206-753-5700).

West Virginia: This state's whitetail population numbers between 700,000 and 800,000 animals, according to Deer Manager Dick Hall. He said the herd is stable to increasing.

Hunters harvested 145,567 deer during 1989 seasons. Of that total, 123,436 were tagged during the firearms hunt, 16,217 were collected by archers, and muzzleloader users took 5,914. Hall said as many as six whitetails a year can be claimed by hunters taking part in all of the state's seasons.

Bowhunting started October 13 during 1990 and extended through most of December. Bucks were legal to gun hunters November 19 to December 1 and antlerless deer could be taken December 6–8. The muzzleloading season was December 17–22.

Sunday hunting is prohibited in this state. At least 400 square inches of orange is required for gun hunts. All deer taken by hunters must be checked. Legal bucks must have an antler at least three inches long. Buckshot is illegal for deer hunting. No scopes are allowed on muzzleloaders and the minimum caliber for deer hunting is .44. Report poachers by dialing 800-638-4263.

Wildlife Resources Division, 1800 Washington St., East, Charleston, WV 25305 (304-348-2771).

Wisconsin: In excess of 1.3 million whitetails inhabit Wisconsin. Hunters harvested 356,586 deer in the state during 1989 seasons. The gun season harvest was 310,192 and archers bagged 46,394.

The bag limit is one whitetail with a gun and one with bow and arrow. Albinos are protected. All deer must be registered at check stations. Wearing orange is required during gun seasons. Deer hunting in three state parks was limited to muzzleloaders during 1990.

Bowhunting was legal from September 15 to November 11, 1990, and the entire month of December. Gun season was held November 17–25.

Poachers can be reported by calling 800-847-9367.

Department of Natural Resources, Box 7921, Madison, WI 53707 (608-266-2193).

Wyoming: Both mule deer and whitetails roam Wyoming. Game and Fish Department Information Manager Al Langston said there were an estimated 450,000 mulies and 60,000 whitetails in the state at the end of 1989 seasons. He added that 89,097 deer hunters bagged 69,415 deer during 1989, enjoying a 78 percent rate of success. Of that harvest, 60,330 were mule deer and 9,085 were whitetails, according to Langston.

Nonresident deer hunters interested in trying their luck in Wyoming should apply for a license during January or February. Eleven new deer regions were established for 1990. The minimum age for deer hunting in this state is fourteen. Persons born after January 1, 1966, must have a hunter safety certificate. Gun hunters are required to wear at least one orange outer garment. The toll-free phone number to report poaching is 800-442-4331.

Seasons vary by hunt areas. Obtain current regulations by writing Game and Fish Department, 5400 Bishop Blvd., Cheyenne, WY 82006 (307-777-7735).

Canada

One of the most important things to remember about hunting in Canada is that it is illegal to possess a handgun. Severe penalties are possible for hunters breaking this law. Luggage is routinely inspected at border crossings and airport terminals.

If you fly into Canada, all luggage will be unloaded at the first airport reached in the country. You must then take it through customs. All guns and bows must be reported. It helps if you carry with you proof that they were purchased in the United States. Allow plenty of time to go through customs when planning connecting flights.

Proof of U.S. citizenship can also be helpful. Birth certificates and voter-registration cards are acceptable. A passport is fine, too, but not required. Under normal circumstances it only takes a few minutes to go through customs when entering and leaving the country.

Mail is slow between the United States and Canada. Allow at least a month for receipt of requested material.

Alberta: Alberta has approximately 144,000 whitetails and 88,000 mule deer. Harvest figures for 1988 included 27,393 whitetails and 13,967 mule deer, according to provincial spokesperson Sylvia Schurman. She said the bow harvest included 313 whitetails and 316 mulies.

Harvest figures for 1989 weren't final yet, but Schurman said preliminary figures indicated that close to 29,000 whitetails were bagged and about 14,000 mule deer. Hunters can take one deer of each species in the province per year. Nonresidents must hunt with a guide or outfitter. Sunday hunting is allowed in the north, but not in the south.

Season dates vary by area. Dates for bowhunting during 1990 in several areas were August 27 to September 23 and September 4 to November 3. Gun hunts for whitetails open as early as September and extend through November. Firearms seasons for mulies are during November. To report poaching, call 800-642-3800.

Fish and Wildlife Division, Main Floor, North Tower, Petroleum Plaza, 9945 108 St., Edmonton, Alberta T5L 2G6 (403-427-8580).

British Columbia: Blacktails, mule deer, and whitetails are found in British Columbia in that order of abundance. Blacktails are estimated at 200,000, mule deer at 140,000, and whitetails number 45,000.

The 1989 harvest included approximately 30,000 mule deer, according to Wildlife Biologist John Thornton. He said about 8,000 of those were blacktails. The whitetail harvest was about 7,000. Thornton said the total archery deer harvest probably doesn't exceed 100 annually.

Bag limits and season lengths vary by zone, so refer to a current hunting synopsis for accurate information. Nonresidents must hunt with a guide or outfitter. To report poaching dial 800-663-9453.

Wildlife Branch, Ministry of Environment and Parks, Parliament Bldgs., Victoria, British Columbia V8V 1X5 (604-387-9422).

Manitoba: Big Game Biologist Ron Larche said Manitoba had a prefawning whitetail population numbering 100,000 during 1990. The province's mule deer herd is small. Only a small harvest of mulies is taken by hunters every year, according to Larche. He said the 1989 harvest included 24,158 deer taken during gun season, 1,129 on the bow hunt, and 1,852 during muzzleloader season.

As many as five deer can be taken per year, two of which must be antlerless. The 1990 bow season was August 27 to December 1. Blackpowder season was between two and three weeks in duration and started October 22. Rifle season was the same length and started November 12.

Licensed guides must accompany nonresidents. Gun hunters are required to wear a blaze-orange hat in addition to 400 square inches of orange above the waist. Muzzleloaders must be a minimum of .44 caliber and buckshot is prohibited. Dial 800-782-0076 to report violations.

Department of Natural Resources, 1495 St. James St., Box 24, Winnipeg, Manitoba R3H 0W9 (204-945-6784).

New Brunswick: There's no attempt to estimate this province's whitetail numbers, according to Big Game Biologist Gerry Redmond. He said the population has been declining, though, due to a series of bad winters.

The deer harvest was 19,692 during 1989, according to Redmond. Archers accounted for 102 of those. Registering deer is required and there's a one-animal bag limit. Most hunting is bucks-only, but antlerless permits are issued for some management units. Bow season was October 1–20, 1990, and gun season was October 22 to November 17.

All hunters, including bowhunters, must wear at least 400 square inches of orange from September 15 to November 30. Guides are required for nonresidents. To report poaching, call 800-222-8477.

Department of Natural Resources, Fish & Wildlife Branch, P.O. Box 6000, Fredericton, New Brunswick E3B 5H1 (506-453-2440).

Nova Scotia: An estimated 150,000 whitetails roam Nova Scotia. Hunters harvested 27,228 deer in the province during 1989, according to wildlife technician Morton Stewart. He said 140 of those were claimed by archers.

The 1990 bow season was October 1–13. Archers could hunt the Chignecto Sanctuary October 26 to December 1. Dates for the provincial gun season were also October 26 to December 1. The province's first black-powder hunt was held October 22–27 on the Tobeatic Sanctuary.

The bag limit is one deer of either sex and deer must be registered. Gun hunters are required to wear a hat and/or garment of solid orange. First-time hunters must complete a hunter education course. Guides are required for nonresidents.

Department of Lands & Forests, P.O. Box 698, Halifax, Nova Scotia B3J 2T9 (902-424-8925).

Ontario: Whitetails number approximately 300,000 in Ontario. A total of 144,579 hunters harvested 44,736 deer in the province during 1989 seasons for a 30.94 rate of success.

The bag limit is one deer a year and seasons vary by management unit. Bow seasons usually open during September and gun hunts generally take place in November. Dogs are legal for deer hunting in some areas.

Ministry of Natural Resources, Public Information Center, Parliament Bldg., Toronto, Ontario M7A 1W3 (416-965-4251).

Quebec: An estimated 250,000 whitetails live in Quebec, according to provincial spokesman Francois Potvin. He said about 130,000 of those are on the mainland and 120,000 are on Anticosti Island. There were an estimated 20,538 deer taken in the province during 1989 seasons, according to Potvin, 7,823 of which came from Anticosti. Archers accounted for 1,139 deer out of the total harvest.

Deer season usually runs from August through November on Anticosti, but most hunting doesn't get under way until September. Hunts vary by unit on the mainland. Bow seasons usually begin during late September, while gun seasons normally get under way by early November. The bag limit is one deer per year except on Anticosti, where two can be taken.

An orange vest must be worn during gun deer seasons. Shotguns used for deer hunting must be at least 20 gauge. The minimum caliber for muzzleloaders is .45. Crossbows can be used for deer hunting and must have a minimum draw weight of 120 pounds, while a 40-pound-pull minimum is required for conventional bows. Poachers can be reported by dialing 800-463-2191.

Department of Loisir, Chasse et Peche, 150 St. Cyrille E., Quebec City, Quebec G1R 4Y1 (418-643-2464).

Saskatchewan: Big Game Manager Dave Brewster said there are between 200,000 and 250,000 whitetails and 40,000 mule deer in the province. He said hunters tallied 39,998 whitetails and 15,047 mulies during 1989 seasons. All mule deer hunting is controlled by permit quotas. Nonresidents must hunt with guides and are limited to hunting northern forested zones.

The bag limit is one deer per license. Second whitetail licenses are available in northern forested areas. There's no Sunday hunting. Gun hunters must wear a solid red or orange hat and a full outer suit of solid red, orange, or white.

Archery seasons for 1990 were September 3 to October 13. A muzzleloader hunt took place October 1–13. Firearms season for whitetails in the north was November 5 to December 1 and November 17 to December 1 in the south. Rifle season for mule deer bucks was November 5–10 and antlerless deer were legal November 12–17. Call 800-667-7561 to report poaching.

Tourism Saskatchewan, 2103 11th Ave., Regina, Saskatchewan S4P 3V7 (800-667-7191). Parks and Renewable Resources, Wildlife Branch, 3211 Albert St., Regina, Saskatchewan S4S 5W6 (306-787-2314).

4

Preseason Scouting

Preseason scouting is one of the most important parts of any deer hunt, whether hunting an area frequented for years or a location being tried for the first time. Granted, preseason checks of familiar hunting grounds need not take as much time as is required to look over new territory. Nonetheless, doing it or not doing it can play a significant role in determining the number of whitetails or mulies that end up on the game pole by the end of the season.

It is not unusual for centers of deer activity to shift from year to year for a variety of reasons. Hunters who fail to detect a change in movement or use patterns before the season opens can lose the most valuable day of hunting of the season: opening day.

Two years ago an uncle of mine found what proved to be a hot spot for bucks on state land. The first day of the season he missed a whitetail with a six- or eight-point rack. A spikehorn he saw the next day wasn't as lucky.

Last season he was all set to go back to the same spot but routinely went to check it out before the season began. It was a good thing he did. A road had been opened in the area and a large field created right where his stand had been. Since there were a few days until opening day he had a chance to locate an alternate position.

This isn't likely to happen on private land, but changes in other factors from year to year such as weather, food availability, or maturing of the habitat can cause shifts in deer abundance and activity in certain locations.

Something I try to do when scouting territory hunted year after year is to get into cover I haven't been in before or am not familiar with. This often results in the discovery of new deer hiding places. I often don't get into some of these deer hangouts because they are out-of-the-way or extremely thick. Deer easily find safety in such spots.

Some hunters who hunt the same territory every fall get in the habit of using the same stands, making the same drives, or still-hunting the same course all the time. There is nothing wrong with this, but it often leads to overlooking areas that are worth trying. In addition, deer that live in the vicinity are quick to catch on to the routine and may avoid spots where they have encountered hunters. A change of pace may be the ticket to some easy venison.

When visiting deer country that will be hunted for the first time, hunters should try to scout as much terrain as possible. At the same time they are familiarizing themselves with the deer situation, they are guarding against getting lost. This is a second advantage of preseason scouting in an unfamiliar area.

Along the same lines, features of the terrain such as boulders or stumps that might be mistaken for deer can be checked out while scouting. Then hunting time won't be wasted looking at these deerlike objects. This also makes out-of-place shapes that may be deer more noticeable.

Still a third benefit of visiting hunt locations ahead of deer season is the possibility of combining scouting missions with small-game hunting. Such small game as squirrels, rabbits, grouse, and other game birds provide action in many states right up to the time some deer seasons begin. Some states may prohibit carrying a gun in the field the week before deer season, however; so be sure it is legal before planning on hunting small game when scouting for deer.

My brother and an uncle collected three Canada geese and a pair of ruffed grouse during a preseason check for deer sign one fall. They bagged more game that day than they often do when intentionally hunting small game or waterfowl. Our luck isn't always that good on scouting trips, but the results of that day are indicative of what can be one of the peripheral benefits of preseason reconnaissance. In many states, bow deer season is open until gun season begins. Under these circumstances, you can be scouting for the gun hunt while afield with archery equipment.

The week before deer season opens is usually the best time to scout an area. Starting sooner is a good idea if the location isn't far from where you live and you will be hunting it for the first time. When hunting out of state, scouting must often be restricted to the two or three days before the season, but anything is better than starting cold at the crack of dawn on opening day.

Bowhunting for deer can be combined with scouting for upcoming gun hunts.

What do you look for when scouting an area for deer hunting? Feeding and bedding grounds, regularly used trails, signs of buck activity, and deer themselves are the primary things to watch for. Water holes should be considered in terrain where water is in short supply. I spend most of my time checking remote locations or those near heavy cover when visiting a new area. This type of terrain invariably get the heaviest use by good bucks throughout the year, but especially once the shooting starts.

While scouting the territory I also try to anticipate where other hunters might be. I prefer not to hunt too near other people, but sometimes it is unavoidable. If I find someone's blind, I go elsewhere in search of a place to hunt.

Left: **This hunter combined small-game hunting with scouting for deer. He examines an antler rub while holding a ruffed grouse he bagged.** *Right:* **This photo shows a rubbed sapling and a scrape made by a rutting buck. Hunters should look for these signs while scouting.**

In open country it is often possible to look over a lot of territory from observation points with the aid of binoculars or spotting scopes. Under these circumstances deer movements can usually be observed. Animals that aren't disturbed will generally be found in the same areas once deer season opens.

One fall Dave Raikko and I were hunting mule deer from a drop camp in the Colorado Rockies. We got to our camp a couple of days ahead of the season to look the area over and adjust to the altitude. The first morning out we located a group of bucks using a patch of willows above timber line. They were still there opening day. We both dropped our deer there on the first day of our hunt.

Centers of deer activity in wooded terrain can be determined by reading the signs. Trails or runways used regularly will usually be well worn. The course of a runway through grass or weeds is marked by a narrow lane of trampled vegetation. Trails through heavily wooded areas will be marked by a line of leaves that have been scuffed by whitetail or mule deer hooves. Good runways will sometimes be worn right down to

A well-used deer trail. Look for these while scouting.

the soil in certain spots and tracks can be seen there. Trails are most obvious in sandy areas or when snow is on the ground.

Most regularly traveled trails used by deer are routes they take from bedding to feeding areas and back again. Sometimes animals use different runways going each way. Where water is scarce, trails leading to watering areas are also common. Many times the same network of trails will be used as escape routes. Once a good trail is discovered, feeding and bedding areas can be located by following it both ways. Or, if a feeding area is located, runways leading from it will go to bedding grounds and vice versa if a bedding area is found.

Deer feeding grounds are often openings. For the most part they are agricultural or woodland fields, burned or logged-over areas, or orchards. Whitetails and mule deer also feed in locations where there is a lot of low brush and in groves of nut-bearing trees. Groups of deer droppings are common in feeding areas that get regular use.

Deer often bed down in heavy cover or where they have a good view, such as on the sides or tops of hills. Beds are oval-shaped areas where vegetation has been flattened under the weight of the animals. In sand or snow, beds will appear as shallow depressions. Beds can be found next to

Acorns are favored fall food for deer. Feeding areas can also be located by scouting.

tree trunks, among rocks, under evergreen boughs, under brush piles or
windfalls, or in open bogs and in other locations. A number of beds of
varying ages will be present in locations used regularly.

Whitetails and mulies generally move from higher to lower elevation
or from heavy cover toward openings when feeding and vice versa when
retiring. Since deer adapt to their habitats, which vary from state to state,
this isn't always true. I have encountered situations hunting both species of
deer when bedding and feeding locations were the same.

Some animals also feed uphill and others travel different trails on a
day-to-day basis.

Countless times I've watched mulie bucks feed and then lie down in
the same patch of cover. It doesn't take brush that is very high to conceal
deer. Animals frequently feed for a period of time then lie down out of
sight for a couple of hours, then get up and eat some more. They may do
this all day and cover very little ground while browsing.

Some of the bigger bucks are the least predictable. They often travel
routes only used by them and many times don't move during daylight
hours when they are vulnerable to hunters. Their normal cautiousness is
usually lost during the rut. During this time they frequent areas where
does are and travel with them.

Mature whitetail bucks leave telltale signs along the runways they use during the rut. They paw patches of ground that attract does. I believe these scrapes also serve as territorial markers for the benefit of other bucks. Scrapes are often checked at regular intervals by the bucks that made them. Bucks also rub their antlers on trees along trails they use during the rut.

I have seen rubs and scrapes in mulie country, too. Since mule deer are not territorial, however, there is no evidence that they return to check scrapes as do whitetail bucks.

Once trails or areas that are being used regularly by deer are located, hunters should try to spend a day or two determining when deer are using them. Deer use some runways only at night. Hunting these during the day is a waste of time. Watching promising locations from a distance during the hours you will be hunting is the best way to determine if deer will be there and their sex. Try not to alert or alarm deer during this time; it could upset their routine.

Several trails can be checked for use the same day by putting pieces of thread across them at daybreak and checking them a couple of times during the day. Trails where the thread is broken by noon are being used in the morning. Another survey of the trails by dark will show which avenues get use in the afternoon or evening.

Timers that are available on the market make it a lot easier to determine which trails are used when. The simplest models employ thread attached to a digital timer and are called Trail Timers. The clock stops at the time a deer breaks the thread. Additional information can be obtained from the manufacturer by writing or calling P.O. Box 19722, St. Paul, MN 55119 (612-738-0925).

More sophisticated timing devices called Trail Monitors record every passage of deer on runways, not just the first animal's. Trail use is monitored with an invisible infrared beam. Trail Monitors are manufactured by Gryphon Engineering, P.O. Box 050407, Roseville, MI 48066 (313-296-1177).

Timers can provide valuable information without the hunter's actually having to be there, which reduces human scent and disturbance of potential stand sites.

Preseason scouting increases the chances of hunters' collecting their deer the first couple of days of the season, if done properly; but it is no guarantee. Time and time again when I think I know exactly where to intercept a buck or doe something happens and I draw a blank. Whitetails and mulies simply are not always predictable. With this in mind, try not to forget about scouting once the season opens and even after it closes.

If I have failed to score after several days of sitting at a promising stand, I often combine still-hunting or tracking with a reconnaissance of

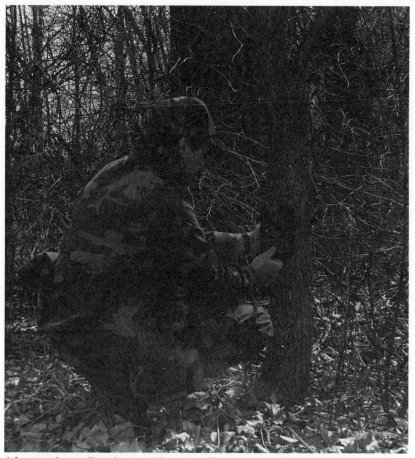

A hunter takes readings from a trail monitor. Timers can help hunters "scout."

my surroundings. Sometimes I roam around a little during the middle of each day. This practice has paid off more than once when hunting both whitetails and mule deer. In cases where I have scored and others in my party haven't, scouting during the season has been beneficial in locating more promising territory for them to try.

Tracking deer when snow is on the ground is a surprisingly good way to find animals. Pursued deer often lead trackers to areas where other mulies or whitetails are or have been.

One fall when I scored early in the season and a light covering of snow fell I started tracking deer in an effort to keep them moving, which would increase the chances of my partners getting shooting. The freshest tracks I located one morning were of a doe and her youngster. I tailed them for several hours and they led me to a patch of high ground surrounded by thick lowland swamp. There was a lot of buck sign there.

We didn't get a chance to hunt there that year, but we did in following seasons. Between my brother and me we have taken four bucks and missed a couple of others on that isolated patch of high ground. One of them was a trophy whitetail.

Another cold, snowy day I took a walk to a partner's stand at noon to warm up. I hadn't seen a thing. My partner saw one deer at a distance and was unable to tell if it was a buck or doe. I tracked the animal for a while and it led me through an area with a heavily used runway.

Three of us posted in that vicinity the next morning. An eight-point buck walked by me shortly after daylight. I missed it, but he made the mistake of running past my brother. Bruce downed him.

Post-season scouting can be valuable for hunting in the same area the next year. During the course of a hunting season deer frequently change their travel patterns as well as their bedding and feeding grounds. Whitetails and mule deer generally react to hunting pressure the same way each season. Learning which trails animals in your area use most once the shooting starts can help determine how to connect quickly the next fall.

It is difficult to do too much scouting for deer. Something new about whitetail or mulie behavior is often learned each trip. The more hunters know about deer in the area they hunt, the better their chances are of collecting one there consistently. That is what scouting is all about.

5

Stand Hunting

Patience is one of the most difficult and important attributes for a deer hunter to develop. It can make the difference between success and failure in most whitetail or mule deer hunting methods.

Patience is especially rewarding for the stand hunter. Hours or days may pass before a buck is sighted. But determined vigilance on a stand often pays off; in fact, stand hunting probably accounts for more downed deer in the fall than any other method.

The reasons for this success are easy to understand. Two of the more commonly used techniques available to solitary hunters, still-hunting and tracking, match pursuer and pursued on a one-to-one basis. The average deer hunter's senses and stealth in the field are simply no match for those of the quarry.

Hunting from a properly chosen stand places all the advantages in the hunter's favor. In a stationary position the sitter's strongest senses, sight and hearing, can be utilized to the fullest. At the same time, the effectiveness of a deer's faculties in detecting a hunter will be impaired.

By being downwind of where animals are expected to appear, the hunter's scent will often go undetected. The use of natural cover or a properly constructed blind to conceal yourself, combined with minimal movements, will reduce your visibility to a deer. With little or no movement, unnatural sounds are avoided and a deer is not likely to hear you.

Hunting from a stand can be productive most hours of the day and under most weather conditions. This is another factor in the technique's favor. The circumstance in which a stand hunter would be least likely to

A bagged buck in foreground with successful tree-stand hunter in background — the results of a well-placed stand and a patient hunter.

see game is during stormy weather, when both deer and hunter activity are at a minimum.

On most days during the fall, animals will travel to and from feeding areas or their reproductive drive will keep them on the move. Where hunting pressure is heavy, the vulnerability of deer to stand hunters is increased. Plenty of hunters in the woods are bound to keep the deer stirred up and increase the likelihood of trail-watchers seeing game.

Basically, stand hunting can be broken down into a sequence of four steps: selecting sites, preparing them for the hunt, hunter preparation, and procedure once in position.

Preseason work and scouting are important for successful stand hunting. Three of the four points mentioned above should be looked after before opening day. Far too many hunters waste opening day by not having any idea where they want to be once shooting time begins, or they spend the first few critical hours fixing up a stand selected the night before. The bulk of the nation's deer harvest occurs the first few days of the season, especially in heavily hunted whitetail country. A hunter who doesn't take advantage of every minute of the first few days is drastically reducing his or her chances of success.

Ideally, scouting activity should be concentrated one to two weeks before deer season begins. That way a hunter will get a handle on current conditions. Deer concentrations and movements can vary greatly from one month to the next. A shift in habits will often acaompany a weather change. As an example, deer will use different travel routes when snow is on the ground than when it is bare.

Without snow covering the landscape, whitetails and mulies blend into their surroundings fairly well, even in relatively open terrain. With a white backdrop of snow in open to semi-open country, deer stand out in stark contrast to their surroundings. They seem to sense their increased visibility to hunters under these circumstances and move into timber, swamps, or brush.

There is a swampy swale in Michigan that either my brother or I have taken a whitetail buck from the first couple days of the season for several years. Tag alders grow thick in the swale along with tall marsh grass, which provides plenty of concealment for whitetails. There was never snow on the ground when we met with success in that spot.

One year we had an early snowfall, and the ground was snow-covered the first week of the season. My brother sat in that swale for two days without seeing a single deer. Because of the snow, visibility was about three times greater than normal. The alders didn't look as dense as they did without snow, and the marsh grass was matted down.

Whitetails that normally traveled through that swale were probably using an alternate route through evergreens where they would be less conspicuous.

Sometimes the available cover itself will undergo a change, which will cause deer to adjust their travel patterns. A prime example is leaf fall from deciduous trees such as maple, beech, birch, oak, and aspen.

One fall when I was hunting mule deer in Colorado a heavy rain combined with strong wind practically defoliated all of the quaking aspens in my area overnight. Before that time my party had been seeing mulies in the quakies on a regular basis. After the leaves fell most of the deer moved into the surrounding timber.

If the time isn't available to visit the hunt area a week or two ahead, it is advisable to set up camp at least two days before the season opener. An early arrival has other advantages in addition to allowing time for scouting; you can also set up camp or arrange motel accommodations at a leisurely pace. Last-minute arrivals and the corresponding hassles that often arise can overtax your system and reduce productivity during the hunt.

If preseason scouting isn't possible, secure a guide who will do it for you. One who knows the habits of the deer in the area can be a distinct advantage. Guides will be discussed in greater detail in chapter 14.

The most important procedure in successful stand hunting is selecting a spot to wait for deer to show. Not only must the hunter consider the animals' normal movement patterns, but he or she must also try to anticipate how the deer will react to hunting pressure, unless he or she is in one of those rare locations where few other deer hunters tread. Otherwise, the number of competing hunters and access points are prime concerns.

Step number one in selecting a stand site is to become familiar with the locality that will be hunted by learning the lay of the land. County and topographic maps come in handy for deciding on an area that might be suitable for hunting. Try to isolate one chunk of terrain at a time. One square mile, or less, of country is plenty to work with. In many cases a forty-acre plot is enough. Territory completely surrounded by roads is easily defined. In many cases, however, a fence, river or creek, lake, ridge, or transition zone from one type of cover to another will have to be chosen as a boundary.

Once a feeling for the lay of the land is obtained from maps, get out there on foot with a compass. Walk as much of it as possible to familiarize yourself with the various cover types present and the basic features of the terrain. By becoming familiar with the tract, you will also be guarding against getting lost.

While familiarizing yourself with the terrain, keep an eye out for deer. Any sign of them, such as feeding and bedding areas or trails, are worthy of note.

Check trails after a rain to be sure they are receiving regular use. Or tie a piece of thread across the trail, one to two feet off the ground, early in the morning. If the thread is broken by nightfall, the trails were traveled during the day. A timer will record what time deer passed. Another way is to spend a day before the season in your stand (without a weapon, of course).

If, after scouting an area, you aren't satisfied with what you found— not many deer signs, too many roads, or some other displeasing factor— pick out another locality. Keep it up until finding circumstances you will be happy with. This is the advantage of beginning preparations well in advance of the season opening. If you don't allot enough time for scouting, you might end up hunting in a location with which you aren't completely satisfied.

Incidentally, a high density of deer isn't necessary in an area to be able to score from a stand. It's just a matter of being able to intercept one animal. Proper scouting is the key to accomplishing this.

In the northern counties of the Upper Peninsula of Michigan, which border Lake Superior, winters are long and severe and winter deer range is poor. As you would expect, deer densities are low. Nonetheless, my brother, my uncle, and I managed to collect at least one whitetail buck a year (one season we got two) among us from a spot within sight of the big lake for a number of consecutive years.

The location we hunted was a series of rugged hills that dropped off to lowland swamps on two sides. On preseason scouting trips the first year we hunted there we learned what runways whitetails used to get into the hills from the lowlands. When other hunters moved the deer out of the swamps on opening day at least one of us would drop a buck.

Once the lay of the land and areas of heaviest deer use have been pinpointed, choosing specific stands should be a simple matter. As a general rule, it is better to situate yourself closer to bedding areas than to feeding grounds. (There are exceptions to this that I will get to shortly.) The odds of seeing animals in these localities are best during daylight hours. Whitetail and mule deer often reach resting areas after daylight and leave before dark.

In addition, bedding grounds are usually in heavy cover or higher in elevation than feeding areas. Deer disturbed during any hour of the day by moving hunters commonly seek thick cover or gain altitude to escape; so they are apt to move your way.

During firearms seasons, deer often use the same escape routes year after year, trails that lead to exceptionally heavy cover or relatively in-accessible country. If you know where such a trail is from experience in your territory, posting along it could be productive.

Early in the fall, primarily during bow seasons, choosing a stand near feeding areas may be better than locating close to bedding grounds, at least for hunting during evenings. Deer often start feeding before it gets dark then. Where it is legal, some hunters bait deer with foods such as apples, corn, and potatoes.

If you are looking for a buck with a nice rack or if there is expected to be a high density of hunters in your area, it may be advisable to head for the remotest parcel of your scouted acreage. The harder a location is to reach, the better the chances mature bucks will be in residence. A large influx of hunters will usually push additional deer into remote sections, as well.

Big bucks are easier to locate once the rut has started. Moss-horned mulies will leave elevated haunts and go to lower areas in search of does. Both species of bucks are also more active during daylight hours when they are looking for does.

Antlered whitetails mark their territory with scrapes, or pawings. These are patches of ground from one foot to four feet across that have been pawed clear of leaves and other debris. Antler rubbings are small

Stand hunters will have their best chance at big bucks once the rut starts. They are more active during daylight hours than otherwise. This buck's swollen neck is a sign that he is in the rut. *Lee Kline*

Deer hunters who find a tree this large that has been rubbed by a buck will be in the territory of a trophy animal.

trees that have been rubbed free of bark on one side by bucks polishing their antlers.

Buck sign is usually noted while scouting. Bucks periodically check their network of pawings, and being located along a trail marked with scrapes can put you on the way to success. Here again, pick a spot in or near heavy cover. There is more of a chance a buck will cruise that stretch during daylight hours. Scrapes in open areas will, most likely, be saved for after dark.

Search out migration trails for a late-season stand. Once snow flies, mule deer head from mountains to valleys; whitetails, in some locations, move toward yarding areas, which are often expansive lowland swamps. The animals generally follow the same trails to winter quarters every year.

Consider prevailing wind currents when selecting specific sites for stands. You want to be downwind of where deer will appear. When in hilly country, remember that air currents rise in the morning and flow downhill in the evening. It may be advisable to watch a runway from up the slope early in the day and move to a vantage point below the trail later in the day.

Wind direction varies from day to day, and it is a good practice to have alternate stands to cover a hot trail. Going one step farther, a wise hunter will select one or two backup spots for stands before the season, separated by a quarter-mile or more, in the event his first choice doesn't pan out. This way there is no great loss of valuable time in relocating.

Another consideration in stand location is never to situate yourself where you can keep an eye on everything. Being able to see one well-used travel route or the junction of two runways is plenty. Also, stay within a reasonable shooting distance off to the side of the trails. This distance will vary, depending upon the terrain hunted. In brush country it may be only thirty yards, while in open areas it may be from 100 to 150 yards.

Once you've decided on one or several spots for stands, some cover will be necessary to break your outline while on stand. There are three options available: using natural cover, building a blind, or using an elevated platform, where legal. Natural cover is preferable whenever available.

Clumps of brush, fallen trees, large rocks, and low-hanging boughs of evergreen trees usually do the job. However, don't restrict freedom of movement and your visibility for concealment. It will do little good to be so well hidden from a buck that a good shot is impossible. Many times hunters are so screened they can't see the deer until it is too late.

When you are building blinds, try to use materials available nearby, such as dead limbs and pine boughs. If other materials are unavailable, camouflage netting or burlap can be used to fashion a blind.

One way to use netting is to wrap it around two or three trees that are close together. Sticks, stakes, brush, or bushes can also serve as a framework to attach the material to around the chosen stand site. Here again, never construct a covering that obscures sight, sound, or maneuverability.

A blind should be erected at least a week before the season so local animals will grow accustomed to it. A blind erected the day before the season may make deer wary of your position.

Whether using natural cover or building a blind, a backrest and comfortable seat will make the vigil more bearable, which is necessary to be able to stay in place for any length of time. Stumps or tree trunks serve well as backrests and can be used in conjunction with a log, boat cushion, or collapsible stool. A folding lawn chair is best of all if carrying it in isn't a problem. Placing it in position before the season can be an advantage.

A variation of the ground blind that isn't used by many deer hunters, but is effective, involves digging a pit, either circular or rectangular. The best position for a pit blind is on the slope or crest of a hill. When on level ground, brush and small mounds easily obstruct a hunter's view. A hatchet and shovel will be necessary to dig a satisfactory hole because roots are often encountered during the excavation.

A lawn chair provides perfect back support for this ground-based hunter.

Circular pit blinds resemble a Thermos bottle cap, stopper down, from the side. The upper portion of the hole should be about six feet across and three feet deep. It should be deep enough for all but a hunter's head to be out of sight when he or she is sitting. Another, smaller hole about three feet wide is then dug in the center of the first one to make a space for legs. With this design a hunter can sit facing any direction.

Squared-off pit blinds are also constructed with two levels so that it is possible to sit comfortably in them. Sides of the pit serve as a backrest. This type can be constructed to allow sitting at one or both ends of the pit. These can be six feet long and half as wide.

Dirt removed from holes can be distributed around the outside edge and should be covered with leaves or brush after the job is completed. Pine boughs can be used to cover a portion of the pit, leaving just enough room to sit. This protects foxhole hunters from cold. The side of the pit hunters will be leaning against can be covered with plastic to keep their backs dry. A boat cushion makes a comfortable seat.

Check to make sure this practice is permissible whether you are hunting on private or public land.

Elevated stands (where legal) are popular for deer hunting in wooded locations. With their use, hunters can get above their quarry's normal line of sight and escape detection. Whitetails and mulies do not expect danger from above and seldom look up, unless alerted by an out-of-place noise. Additionally, deer are less likely to wind a hunter in an elevated position.

While trying for a mule deer one fall in Wyoming with bow and arrow, I began the day from a ground stand. Wind currents were finicky that day. For a time it would be blowing one direction; then it would shift for fifteen minutes before changing again. Since it was morning, the general flow of air was uphill; so I chose a position on the uphill side of where I expected deer to show.

Several groups of does passed by at a distance; then a buck began working toward me. He was feeding uphill and the wind was in my favor. When that mulie buck was twenty yards away and I was about to draw, the wind shifted. He scented me and wasted little time getting out of there.

After that episode I found a tree with sturdy limbs to stand on about fifteen feet off the ground and continued my vigil. Within a half-hour another buck showed and came within twenty-five yards, where I arrowed him. Switching wind notwithstanding, that buck didn't know I was there.

In areas where permanent tree stands are permitted, those constructed of fresh lumber should be painted with green, brown, or black to reduce the boards' visibility. Injuring trees by installing stands with nails is prohibited in many states. In these locations portable stands are the best choice.

Tim Horner poses with a mulie buck he bagged from a well-placed tree stand in North Dakota.

When nails are used to install a tree stand, they should be removed when the platform is removed. Nails left in a tree can ruin a saw if the tree is ever cut.

Few tree-stand hunters take the time to consider a tree's market value as lumber or pulp, but they should. If possible, only use portable or permanent elevated stands in trees with low market value. If you don't know the difference between high-quality and low-quality trees, a visit with a local forester can be worthwhile.

Commercially manufactured, portable tree stands are becoming increasingly popular because of their versatility. Some come complete with a climbing tool, and others have ladders. Tree slings are also available. Changing stand sites with portable tree stands can be accomplished in a matter of minutes.

Shiny metallic surfaces on portable tree stands should be dulled by covering them with paint. Green, black, brown, or a combination of these colors work well.

Steve Wunderlee waits in an Amacker tree stand, one of the portables on the market.

Left: A hunter prepares for a shot from a ladder stand. *Right:* Jimmy Dean uses a tree sling for hunting. The straps are light and take up less room for carrying than portable platforms.

Lacking a platform, some hunters simply utilize a convenient crotch in a tree with ample space to get comfortable. I seldom climb higher than fifteen feet above the ground, but some hunters get as high as twenty to thirty feet.

Additionally, a tree stand should be located on the side of a tree opposite a deer trail. In this position there is less likelihood a deer will see the hunter. This is an especially useful tip for bowhunters. The movement an archer makes when drawing his or her bow sometimes attracts a deer's attention. When on the opposite side of a tree trunk, there is less chance of this happening.

All tree-stand hunters should be safety conscious when climbing into position. There is always a possibility of injuring yourself or damaging equipment in the event of a fall. The best practice is to raise and lower a weapon from a tree with a rope. Archers should have all broadheads in a covered quiver. Rifles and shotguns should be empty when raised or lowered from a tree.

It is also advisable to use a safety harness while hunting from a tree stand. The belt or rope guards against your falling from your perch if you get drowsy or lose your balance.

The next step in readying a stand is to clear away all forest litter within five feet of where you will be positioned if you are on the ground. A nervous foot crunching dead leaves won't do much for keeping your presence a secret. This is also a precaution in case you have to stand up to stretch cramped muscles or try to get a better look at a deer.

Similarly, branches and twigs that may restrict your view or bump your weapon when raising or swinging it should be removed where you will be sitting or standing. Check all quadrants — front, sides, and back — by shouldering or drawing and swinging your weapon.

Limbs that are trimmed should be cut flush with tree trunks rather than leaving stubs that are several inches long. Stubs of limbs will eventually die and fall off, which reduces the quality of the tree for lumber. When the stubs fall off they will leave holes in the wood.

A hunting companion of mine didn't get a shot at what he guessed was a ten-point whitetail buck one year because he failed to remove twigs on all sides that might be in his way. He was sitting with his back against a stump when he heard something walking behind him. It was making so much noise he thought it had to be another hunter. When my partner peeked around the stump he saw the big buck. He slowly brought his rifle around and up to take a shot. When the gun was halfway to his shoulder, the barrel hit a twig and the twig snapped off. That buck was gone in less time than it takes to tell about it.

Once interfering brush and limbs are removed, a bowhunter should consider pacing the distance from the stand to various points where shots at deer can be expected. Archers who don't know how long a step they take should measure it in order to gauge yardages accurately. It is important that bowhunters know how far a deer is when they shoot. Unlike bullets, arrows drop fast. A five- or ten-yard mistake in estimating distance can make the difference between a hit and a miss. Sticks can be stuck in the ground to mark various yardages. Most of the time, however, trees, brush, rocks, and other natural features that are already present will serve as satisfactory distance markers. An accurate rangefinder can be a better alternative than pacing off distances because you won't leave as. much scent near your stand that can spook deer.

There is one more step in preparing a stand for the hunt. Since you want to be seated before first light, if possible, and stay until shooting light has faded, be sure you will be able to find your way to and from your post by flashlight. If you can do it with no aids, all the better. Consider marking some sort of a trail if you can't find your stand unaided.

Fluorescent tape is handy for marking trees. In some cases blaze marks can also be used. Light-reflecting tacks or tape are also good. Don't designate your route from where you leave your car all the way to your stand, however. Only use guideposts where necessary. Otherwise, you may have a number of curious hunters visiting during the day.

Proper mental attitude is involved in preparing yourself for the hunt. Mentally, you have to convince yourself that your post is the best position available in your area. Be confident and tell yourself that by being patient you will eventually get a chance for a shot. Staying put for only a few hours isn't enough. Unless, of course, you score quickly. A quick score can happen, but don't count on it. Plan on spending the entire day in your spot, if possible. If you can only handle a few hours at a time, spend the first few hours of the day, midday, and the last couple of hours in position. Most kills occur during those time periods.

Going hand-in-hand with a proper mental attitude is a good night's sleep. Don't stay up until all hours playing cards with the guys or drinking. A groggy mind can't be enthusiastic about anything.

The last point to consider is how to wait. Sounds simple enough, but there are a few points worth mentioning. Always be alert and ready to shoot. Listen for sounds and look for movements. Keep your gun, bow, or camera on your lap or gripped in your hands ready to shoulder, draw, or raise.

If at all possible, don't wear earmuffs or a hood, since these will affect your ability to hear or see a deer approaching.

After a time, familiarity will develop for how everything looks and sounds in the immediate vicinity. More often than not, anything out of the ordinary will be noticed immediately. Keep looking all around you, moving your head slowly from side to side.

Keep your personal noises to a minimum. Wrap food in material that isn't exceptionally noisy. Shifting positions regularly to maintain comfort is unavoidable. Always stay alert while doing it.

As far as smoking is concerned, if you are situated downwind from where deer are going to be, they probably won't notice it. Whitetails and mule deer are apt to notice the movements associated with smoking, however; so it is best to smoke as little as possible.

Scents designed to mask a hunter's odor will have little effect on hunting success if the hunter's stand is downwind of where deer are expected to show. When air currents are constantly shifting or deer approach from an unexpected direction scents can be advantageous. Try to use a scent that is natural for the area being hunted. Deer gland, fox or

It's a good idea to mark a trail to your stand to ensure that you'll be able to find it before daylight.

coyote urine, or skunk musk scents are the most versatile. Bucks may be attracted to scents made from the glands of does if the rut is on. Opened bottles of scent can be positioned in an elevated location at the hunter's stand or applied to a strategically placed ball of cotton. When using any type of deer scent, put it where you want an animal to stop for a shot, not on you or in your stand.

There are plenty of things to keep your mind occupied while you wait. Observing birds and animals other than deer can be entertaining. Sometimes they will warn you of an approaching deer. Every time a jay squawks or a squirrel chatters, you should wonder why.

A nearby shot, the snap of a twig, or the rustling of leaves may mean a deer is coming your way. Look for and identify the source of every sound.

I collected a nice ten-point mule deer in Colorado one fall by paying attention to rifle shots in my area. When I heard a group of shots over a ridge from me I knew that hunters had jumped some game and, if the shooters didn't connect, the animals should come uphill over the ridge. I kept my eyes glued on the skyline.

Within five minutes, not one, but seven bucks came over the top and into my lap. The ten-pointer I dropped was the biggest of the bunch.

Once a whitetail or mule deer is sighted, get ready as quickly as possible. If you are sure a deer is approaching, get your weapon up. That's one less movement you'll have to make when it comes in sight. If deer catch you off guard and are visible before you hear them, don't move unless the animal you want is on the move and will be out of sight shortly. Take the first opportunity for a clean shot when the buck has his head down or is looking the other way.

When that antlered deer goes down, you will be a confirmed stand hunter. Hunting in that fashion may take a lot of time, work, and patience, but it will be worth it when you walk over and inspect that buck.

6

Still-Hunting and Stalking

Still-hunting and stalking are difficult to separate because the same basic skills are required for each. The major difference is that while stalking, a deer hunter already has the quarry in sight. A still-hunter is searching for deer, but he or she may become a stalker as soon as he or she spots a whitetail or mule deer that must be approached before a shot is possible.

Still-hunting requires more activity than stand hunting. The hunter is on the move, but not constantly. When he or she is moving, it is at a very slow pace. A still-hunter actually takes many stands during a hunt, but occupies each one for brief periods of time compared to the duration a dedicated stand hunter often remains in one spot.

Normally, a hunter using the stop-and-go technique only remains motionless for a matter of minutes but on occasion will stay in place for as long as half an hour. It depends on the circumstances.

Stalking is simply a matter of decreasing the distance between a hunter and the quarry without being detected. The acceptable range depends on the weapon a hunter is using and his or her shooting ability. A bowhunter, for instance, may want to get within fifty yards of the target; a black-powder hunter or shotgunner might consider 100 yards the maximum range; and a rifle hunter using a .270 might feel confident of dropping a deer between 200 and 300 yards.

Obviously, deer hunters who use primitive weapons or shotguns will have to be more skillful at stalking than hunters who use modern rifles. Where open country is common, as it is in many of the western states, stalking ability can be an important skill for rifle hunters, as well.

Still-hunting and stalking can be employed successfully in most covers and terrains and under varying conditions. The only cover where stalking is seldom necessary is where visibility is fifty yards or less. Vegetation in these locations is often so dense that deer that are encountered are usually in range when spotted.

Stop-and-go hunting can be practiced most effectively in territory a hunter is familiar with. Knowledge of prime bedding and feeding areas and preferred travel routes allow a still-hunter to make the most of wind, terrain, and ability. When planning on still-hunting unfamiliar country, try to scout the area as thoroughly as possible before the season opens.

Contrary to what some hunters believe, still-hunting is not a technique that goes hand-in-hand with covering long distances and lots of terrain, especially in typical whitetail and blacktail habitat or when searching for mulies in timber. Covering a distance of 100 yards can take an hour. Where visibility is a couple hundred yards or more, a still-hunter may travel farther than he or she would in denser cover; not a great deal more, however, because the hunter should spend correspondingly more time carefully looking over every place a deer might be.

Still-hunting is not a casual approach to collecting a deer, either. Practicing it properly takes a lot of concentration, at least it does for me. I have to remind myself at regular intervals to move slowly and search every inch of the area around me. If I start daydreaming and forget about what I'm supposed to be doing, my pace automatically quickens and my eyes start bouncing from one view to the next with casual glances rather than the thoroughness necessary in still-hunting.

Admittedly, I'm not the best still-hunter. Nonetheless, I've taken a number of deer while hunting this way and have seen many more that got away. One advantage stop-and-go hunting has over hunting from a stand is that more deer are usually seen. But many of them are no more than flashes or waving tails.

The skills inherent in still-hunting can become second nature with practice. I've watched some still-hunters who are old hands at the technique and are regularly successful. Their movements are as instinctive and stealthy as the deer they hunt.

Beryl Jensen, a fellow Michigan deer hunter from Marquette, is a perfect example of a skillful still-hunter. We made arrangements to meet at my stand late in the morning one day. My post was in an old burn, and Beryl would have to cross an opening about 100 yards across to reach the spot.

I was watching for him as well as keeping an eye out for deer. When Beryl arrived, he appeared as suddenly as deer often do. He was a full twenty to thirty yards into the opening before I noticed him. I watched him closely as he approached.

It looked as though he floated across the remaining distance. He would take several short steps then pause and look around. The movement of his legs was almost imperceptible. I'm sure he saw me as soon as he entered the opening, but he advanced at his normal stop-and-go hunting pace. If there had been any deer in the vicinity, his presence certainly wouldn't have spooked them.

There are no hard-and-fast rules designating the perfect still-hunting pace. The terrain, visibility, ground cover and condition, and weather will dictate, to some degree, how to proceed. Each hunter will probably develop his or her own variations in pace.

As a general rule, taking from three to five steps between pauses is about right. Each advance often brings a new area into view or gives the still-hunter a different perspective on a piece of cover looked at minutes before. Try to check each shadow, clump of trees, brush, or tall grass carefully with your eyes. Deer can blend in surprisingly well with their surroundings.

Try to remember to look in all directions, behind as well as in front and to the sides. A still-hunter shouldn't move his or her head in quick, jerky movements, but in a slow, rotating motion. Also try to keep in mind the importance of focusing on the terrain as far ahead as possible. Don't expect deer to wait until you are almost on top of them. Their senses are keener than yours. To increase the chances of seeing them before they see, smell, or hear you, look as far ahead as possible.

Don't expect to see an entire animal. Try to pick out the deer's ears, legs, antlers, tail, or the horizontal lines along the back or belly. Subtle movements like a twitching ear or swishing tail can give a mule deer's or whitetail's position away, too. Once you home in on a part of an animal, the rest of its body will usually jump into focus, unless it is obscured.

If the deer you spot isn't the one you want, keep looking. There may be others with it, either to the sides or behind it. If you haven't been detected, try to remain motionless as long as possible, unless moving won't disturb the animal. Other deer will probably give themselves away eventually.

An effort should be made to get by deer that the hunter isn't interested in without spooking them. An alarmed deer may alert others in the vicinity.

When the rut is on and several does are encountered it can be worthwhile to watch them, or where they were, for at least a half-hour, on the chance a buck might trail them. I blew what could have been a perfect chance at a whitetail buck one time by not waiting long enough after seeing a doe.

I had stopped and was checking the cover ahead of me when the doe walked into view from left to right about sixty yards away. When she went

One or more bucks will often follow a doe when the rut is on, as shown here. Be sure to wait long enough, as much as a half an hour sometimes, after seeing a doe. Many times a buck will be some distance behind.

out of sight I got down in a sitting position with my rifle ready, on the chance a buck was following her. Nothing happened for several minutes, so I got up and slowly walked toward where the doe had been. When I reached her tracks, there was a snort off to my left as a buck whirled and hightailed it. There wasn't enough time for a shot.

Hearing is important to still-hunters, too. If you hear a nearby noise you can't identify, you should pause until you determine its source. The same goes for an unidentified movement. The disturbance may have been caused by a flitting bird or a nervous squirrel, but there is always a chance a deer is the source. Patience often provides the best means for a still-hunter to discover the source of what attracted his or her attention.

Some of the deer a still-hunter sees will be running, having been spooked by his presence or other hunters. These shots should be passed up, unless the animal's sex can be determined and there is an opportunity to put a bullet in a vital area.

You should keep several things in mind while still-hunting that can increase the chances of getting standing shots. Scent, sight, and sound, or the lack of them, are the three major factors that will make a difference. It is best to stop-and-go hunt into the wind. This eliminates the possibility of any deer ahead of you smelling you. A moderate to strong wind will also cover up some of the noise made by a still-hunter while walking.

Hunting across the wind is all right, too. Deer ahead of you still won't be able to wind you, nor will those on your upwind side. Any whitetails or mulies on the downwind side should be spotted before they are able to scent a hunter traveling across the wind.

A still-hunter's movement can be kept to a minimum if he or she takes short steps and swivels his or her head slowly. Visibility can be reduced by wearing camouflage clothes when possible. Additionally, still-hunters should avoid exposing their presence in the open by walking through fields or skylining themselves on the ridges. Try to skirt the edge of fields and openings. When crossing a ridge, keep a low profile.

Still-hunting along a ridge can often be productive, since deer don't usually expect danger from above and elevation gives the hunter an excellent view of the surrounding terrain. It is better, however, to walk just below the ridge rather than directly on top.

The amount of noise a still-hunter makes or doesn't make is a function of how light-footed he or she is, how thick the cover is, and how his or her clothes are made. The way you walk can be just as important as how much you walk. You should try to walk with most of your weight either on the toes or balls of your feet. Either portion of the foot should touch the ground first, then the rest of the foot can be lowered. This, in effect,

Still-hunting in such a way that you are above any deer you expect to see is as advantageous as when hunting from a stand, but try to avoid being silhouetted against the sky.

reduces the surface area making initial contact with the ground, thereby reducing noise. Before shifting your weight to the leading foot, however, feel for twigs that may snap. If you detect one, try to avoid it.

Still-hunters should also try to lift their feet clear of noisy ground cover rather than dragging their heels or shuffling their feet.

Outer garments of wool, Polar Tuff, fleece, and acrylic are the quietest clothes for deer hunting in cool or cold weather. Cotton is a quiet fabric, too, but since it isn't as warm as wool it is best suited for hunting in warmer weather. Many cotton-blend fabrics are as quiet as cotton.

Ground cover and conditions can have a significant impact on the effectiveness of stop-and-go hunters. Quietest ground conditions are grass, sand, and solid rocks, after a soaking rain, or when the forest floor is blanketed with soft snow or pine needles. Still-hunting can be excellent under any of these conditions. The technique is also worth trying in a strong wind, regardless of the ground conditions. Disturbance created by gusty winds is often enough to mask noises a hunter might make.

One noise hazard stop-and-go hunters should always be mindful of is brittle twigs and sticks that are sometimes hidden under leaves or snow. Try to avoid snapping these when you walk, but don't spend so much time watching where your feet are going that any deer up ahead might go

A blanket of snow provides one of the quietest conditions for still-hunting.

unseen. If a twig is broken it is a good idea to stop for a few minutes and then continue.

Dry leaves, crunchy snow, and loose rocks are the worst conditions to still-hunt in. Yet even in these noisiest of situations the stop-and-go method can be productive. Noise, in itself, doesn't alert deer, but the cadence or frequency does. Many hunters walk at a consistent pace. Animals pause frequently when traveling.

Mulies and whitetails know the difference. When they hear a stop-and-go hunter approaching they are apt to be more curious than afraid. As a result, they are likely to stay put and offer a shot. Deer and hunters are at an equal disadvantage when conditions are noisy since each can hear the other better than usual.

Still-hunters can reduce the amount of disturbance they make under noisy conditions by walking on logs, exposed tree roots, and pine needles.

One way for still-hunters to overcome noisy situations completely, turning them to their advantage, is to head for water. Shallow creeks, marshy areas, and rivers are perfect avenues to use to outwit whitetails and mule deer. Rubber boots are necessary for walking creeks or wet areas with water less than a foot deep. Hip boots or chest waders are a must for anything deeper. Hip waders are less cumbersome and noisy than the chest type.

A canoe offers the ultimate means for still-hunting rivers and streams. Gliding with the current in one of these streamlined crafts is much quieter than walking in water. Two hunters work best for still-hunting from a canoe: one steers and paddles and the other sits in the bow with rifle or bow ready. It is often possible to float within close range of bedded or feeding deer while in a canoe. Lone hunters can also float rivers in belly boats or inner tubes with seats.

Hunting on horseback is another form of still-hunting. Horse travel in deer country is most common in the West for mulies. Horses aren't as quiet as canoes, but deer don't seem to mind. Approaching them to within rifle range on horseback is possible. In the absence of conversation among riders, mule deer may mistake horses for elk.

One time when my brother Bruce and I were hunting mule deer in the Colorado Rockies with guide and outfitter Rudy Rudibaugh from Parlin, we rode up on a herd of deer that would have otherwise been difficult to approach. We were riding through willow brush above timber line when the group of five mulies, three of them bucks, got up from their beds about 150 yards away. They stood and watched us, seemingly more curious than alarmed.

Bruce dismounted and grabbed his rifle from its scabbard. Not wanting to take an offhand shot, my brother started crawling toward a pile of

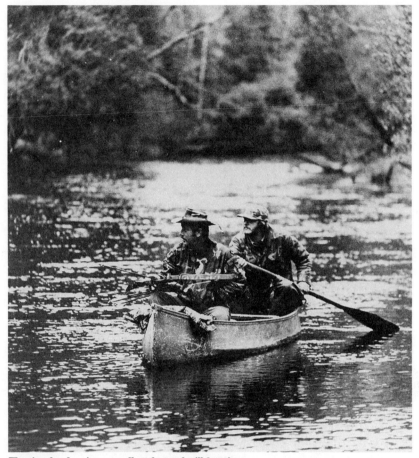

Floating for deer is an excellent form of still-hunting.

rocks where he could steady the rifle. As he did, the deer got nervous and started to move off. Bruce quickly got into a sitting position and tried two shots, but both missed their mark – a buck with four points on one side and three on the other. Bruce was forced to shoot too quickly. If a rest had been handy where he dismounted, that buck would have been his.

Horses are most useful in stop-and-go hunting mountainous terrain as a means of transportation from one observation point to another. A common and productive practice for locating mule deer is to stop at high points overlooking basins or valleys. Binoculars or spotting scopes are then used to scan the terrain for deer. Glassing properly can take several hours at each stop. Bedded animals are often difficult to spot, but they

Stalkers often use spotting scopes or binoculars to locate deer from high vantage points. These deer hunters are glassing for bucks while their horses graze.

usually get up at regular intervals to feed and can be detected then. Sometimes a deer will appear suddenly in a location where nothing was visible minutes before.

Once an animal a hunter wants to try for is spotted, a stalk is made. The cardinal rule for stalking in hilly terrain is always to approach from above. Deer seldom expect danger from above; consequently they spend most of their time looking downhill. If a deer is spotted above you while glassing or still-hunting, you should continue out of sight and hearing of the animal and climb above it before beginning a stalk.

Wind direction, hunter movement, and noise are just as important in stalking as in still-hunting. Any one of them can make or break the endeavor. The stalking hunter has an advantage over the still-hunter, however, because he or she has located the quarry. The hunter's major task is choosing the best course that will put him or her in range of a deer without alerting it to his or her presence.

Always go into or across the wind to stalk a deer. If there is much wind, its direction can be determined easily. When it is light to gusty try dropping sand, snow, or light blades of grass to see which way it drifts. The cool side of a wetted finger is also a clue to wind direction. A piece of thread tied to a bow or firearm and smoke from a lighted cigarette will aid hunters in determining air flow, too. When temperatures are below freezing, or close to it, a determination of air current direction can be made by exhaling and watching the vapor.

Even when great pains have been taken to stalk with the breeze in a hunter's favor the effort can be ruined by a change in wind direction, an unexplained gust, or a new current.

Try to be mindful of any change in wind patterns while stalking and, if necessary, make a change in course. If the only avenue of approach to a deer puts the hunter upwind of the animal, don't go after it if using a bow, shotgun, handgun, or muzzleloader. Hunters using high-powered rifles might be able to get within range before they are winded. If there is a possibility the animal will move to a more favorable position for a stalk or if the wind might change, it is best to wait.

If the breeze or air current is flowing downhill when above a buck, move down to the animal's elevation or slightly above, off to either side. When at an appropriate level, stalk across the slope at a downhill angle or on a line with him.

Hunter movement isn't a problem in stalking if done under cover or at the right time. Try to plan a stalk to take advantage of such terrain features as gullies, river beds, valleys, hills, trees, brush, and rocks — and always consider the deer's behavior. Let's look at deer behavior first.

Any deer is easier to approach when it is lying down rather than feeding. When on their feet, whitetails and mule deer are more alert than when bedded. Don't get me wrong; deer don't throw caution to the wind when they lie down, but they are more relaxed and less likely to detect a stalking hunter. An additional consideration for long stalks is that once bedded, deer usually remain in one place for at least an hour. A feeding deer can move surprisingly far during a long stalk, which increases the chances of losing track of it or spooking it.

In many situations it may be difficult or impossible to wait for a deer to bed down before trying a stalk. If time isn't a problem and a deer can be kept in sight without alarming it, try to wait until a deer beds before attempting a stalk.

If stalking a deer that is feeding where cover is sparse, try to restrict movements to the intervals when the animal's head is down. Keeping a low profile by crawling on hands and knees or belly is advisable in such a situation. Deer will raise their heads at regular intervals while feeding to look around. Be sure you are motionless when a buck or doe looks up.

When moving in on a feeding deer in a crouched or upright position, it is best to shuffle your feet if you are on grass or other ground cover that isn't noisy. It is possible to be caught off balance, standing on one leg, when lifting feet to close the distance on a deer.

The sun can be an advantage to a stalking hunter if you approach a deer with the sun at your back. If it is at the right angle, the strong backlighting can impair a deer's ability to spot a hunter. The same principle can be applied while still-hunting. Wind direction should be consid-

A deer hunter takes aim at a buck while a doe stands in the background. He caught the buck by surprise while still-hunting.

Mule deer like this one bagged by Jim Haveman are often taken by hunters still-hunting and stalking.

ered before sun angle, however, whether you are still-hunting or stalking.

Hunter movement isn't as important when stalking a deer from above as it is in other situations. Countless times members of my party and I have stalked deer from above in plain sight. If the animals had looked up they would have seen us, but few of them do. The advantages of moving in on deer from above can't be overemphasized.

Whenever possible, plan a stalk so you will be out of a deer's sight throughout an approach. The best way to close the distance unseen is by heading down a valley or gulley or by aligning trees, brush, or rocks between you and the deer. If the screening cover isn't high enough to walk upright, crouch or crawl. Before starting out on such a stalk, be sure to pick out landmarks to use as reference points so you will know where to come out of a valley and where the deer is supposed to be. Prominent trees, fences, ridge lines, or rocks should be noted carefully.

It may be possible to check on a deer periodically during a stalk. If not, be doubly sure you know where you are going or work out a system of hand signals with a partner who will be able to see the deer. Also, make sure he or she knows when you will want directions.

When I want directions in such a situation, I wave my hat. When my partner holds both arms up, it means the deer is still there. Just the right or left arm extended means the deer moved that way. A wave back is a sign that the animal spooked. Additional signals can be added to expand communication between a stalker and lookout. Just be sure you both understand what they are before starting a stalk.

Noise can be kept to a minimum in stalking by taking advantage of the same guidelines listed for still-hunting. Noise isn't usually critical until within 100 yards or less of a deer, depending on ground and weather conditions. Beyond that point, stalkers can move in as quickly as possible without much regard for disturbance from sounds they make.

7

Drives

At certain times and in certain types of cover neither stand nor still-hunting is productive. Deer that don't move from their daytime resting areas until dark make sitting at a stand all day a waste of time. The same holds for a still-hunter: many of the deer in the area may be too wary to get a shot at because they hole up in cover so thick that approaching them undetected is impossible.

When the two techniques are combined in a team effort, however, the chances of success improve and a third popular deer-hunting method evolves: the drive.

Some groups of hunters rely almost exclusively on this technique all season. Their success usually explains why. The first whitetails my brother and I claimed were taken on drives. I was a stander when I dropped mine. Bruce's was collected while he was a driver. Both standers and drivers have a chance to connect on drives, but the odds usually favor hunters waiting on post.

There were five of us the day my brother and I scored. Besides ourselves, there was an uncle, Leonard Yelle, his son Randy, and Jim Rankin, Leonard's brother-in-law. Our group size was just right for small drives. Leonard put Bruce and me on stands between fifty and seventy-five yards apart and instructed us to stay put until the drive was over. Jim also posted. Leonard and Randy made the push toward us.

It wasn't long before I heard something running toward me. A deer broke from cover, moving from right to left, about thirty yards away. It was a doe, but I had an antlerless permit. I shouldered my 12-gauge pump and fired. I was using slugs.

The deer showed no immediate sign of a hit, continuing at a fast clip without faltering. I assumed I missed, but before she went out of sight, she fell. I found out later my slug hit the deer in the heart. My excitement knew no bounds that day. I became a deer hunter.

On the next drive our group switched assignments. Randy and Leonard were standers; Bruce, Jim, and I moved through a piece of cover toward them. Moments into the drive there was a shot, and Bruce had his deer. The whitetail almost ran him down in an effort to get away from Jim. It tried to escape by going to the side rather than straight ahead.

Drives can be broken down into three categories: quiet, noisy, and dog-pack. The intent of all three is the same: to push deer from areas where they are resting or feeding, which are usually locations where their vulnerability to hunters is minimal, to standers. This is the only way hunters get a crack at some whitetails and mule deer.

Bucks that make it past the first few days of the hunting season often seek out the thickest patch of cover in their home range and stay there until the season is over. Travel is done at night, unless they are forced to do otherwise. Some deer follow these habits year-round, due to their age or the habitat they live in. For these reasons drives can be productive anytime during deer season if they are organized and carried out properly.

Only two hunters are necessary to make a drive, but a group numbering from five to ten is much better. Upwards of twenty or more hunters can be effective when driving large areas. Some states limit the number of hunters who may take part in drives. The time required to organize a drive, as well as the chances for a foul-up, increases proportionately with the number of participants, and this reduces hunting time.

To work effectively as a unit, drivers and standers should know the area being hunted. When new hunters are involved, an explanation of the lay of the land with the aid of a map will help. An attribute at least as important as familiarity with an area is that participants be able to follow directions. Worthy of equal attention is that there be someone to give directions and assign duties: a hunt captain, or leader.

The only difference between a quiet and a noisy drive, as the names imply, is the amount of disturbance made by drivers. On a noisy drive, for example, drivers sometimes blow whistles, beat on pans, shout, bark like dogs, and break branches in an effort to flush deer from hiding places and make them run to standers waiting ahead. On a quiet drive, drivers move toward standers without making an unusual amount of noise. They may advance as if they were still-hunting or as if going for a casual stroll, but not trying to conceal their presence.

Quiet drives are usually more effective than loud drives. The noise made by drivers sometimes has an effect opposite its intent. Instead of scaring deer into panicking and running blindly toward standers, the ani-

Drives take a lot of planning. Here a pair of drivers map their strategy.

mals may stay put, go out the ends, or between the drivers. This is especially true of the wise bucks who have survived one or two drives. Deer are tipped off to the positions of drivers by the noise they make, and the animals use the information to their advantage.

One season I hunted from a stand that was in a narrow section of woods. That piece of cover proved to be a favored area for drives by a group of hunters I didn't know. It was obvious a drive was in progress when a line of men moved toward me shouting, and barking like dogs.

I stayed put, hoping they would push a buck by me. They didn't. More to the point, however, was the fact that none of the drivers saw me, and they made the push three days in a row. I was wearing red and not as concealed as a deer would have been. Any deer in the area could have escaped detection as I did—by staying put. Most of them probably did.

The first two days the drive was conducted, there were no shots fired. I did see one deer, a fawn, that was a direct result of the drive. It came from the direction the drivers were moving after they passed by! The youngster didn't want to go the way they wanted him to and slipped through the line.

On the third day the drivers pushed the cover there were shots fired, apparently by a stander. From the shouting that followed I assume a deer was bagged; so noisy drives do work once in a while.

In fact, I've participated in some noisy drives since then that were very effective in Pennsylvania on Trout Run Development property near St. Marys. There is more than a 100-year tradition of drive-hunts on this large chunk of private property. Drives are well organized and generally very effective. For safety reasons, drivers do not carry guns on Trout Run hunts. Safety is also why noisy drives are conducted there.

Hunters who are posted know where drivers are by the noise they make and refrain from shooting toward them. Each driver also knows where his or her partners are and can maintain the desired formation and spacing while moving ahead. I have to admit that it is an advantage for posted hunters to follow the progress of a drive by listening to drivers. The level of excitement and anticipation never fails to increase as the line of drivers approaches your position.

Deer are always seen on noisy drives conducted on Trout Run property and whitetails are bagged on most hunts. It isn't unusual for a number of bucks to be tagged on some of the best drives.

The primary function of drivers — jumping and moving deer ahead of them — can sometimes be accomplished with more consistency on a quiet drive. Any deer in the drivers' paths will hear them as a twig is snapped or leaves rustled, but usually not enough to determine where they are at all times. This uncertainty is apt to make the deer nervous and move out.

Some deer may still hold tight or slip through the line, but the chances of its happening are reduced. Drivers on a quiet push should be looking carefully for deer as they go. They may spot one bedded or sneaking away from another driver. Noisy drives reduce the chances that drivers will get to shoot. I'm sure my brother's tag would have gone unfilled that year we both scored on successive drives if we tried to push the deer by intentionally making noise.

It isn't critical that standers be able to follow the progress of the drivers. Posted hunters should be alert from the time they get into position until the push is completed. On a quiet drive, drivers can signal standers if and when deer are jumped by shouting, "Here they come," or "Heads up," to make sure standers will be ready. Once the deer are moving, sound made by the driver that jumped them won't make much difference.

As far as drivers keeping tabs on one another, they should be close enough to see each other at intervals on the most effective pushes. When this isn't possible, they can whistle, hoot, or caw once in a while to maintain contact. Well-spaced whistles, owl hoots, or crow caws may be accepted as natural sounds by deer and not associated with hunters. On the other hand, they may not be. It is best for drivers not to make any sounds at all if possible. Drivers familiar with an area and their partners' paces should be able to progress properly without aural assistance.

More often than not, driven deer are far enough ahead of drivers that any shots fired by standers won't endanger drivers. To be on the safe side, however, drivers can move to the sides as they approach standers on the chance a deer may not show itself until the last possible moment. An alternative is for drivers to announce themselves by whistling or calling as they near standers. Drivers must be familiar with the driven area to use either technique.

Neither of these precautions should be necessary in my opinion. It goes without saying that drivers and standers alike should never take a shot in a direction that might endanger a partner. And above all else, hunters should be sure of their targets before shooting, regardless of the hunting technique used, but especially on drives where hunters can be in close proximity to one another.

No whitetail or mule deer, no matter how big, is worth wounding or killing a fellow hunter for. If it is considered unsafe for both drivers and standers to carry firearms or bows, drivers should leave their weapons behind until taking their turns at posting. The usual procedure is for drivers and standers to alternate duties. Hunters who have filled their tags join the ranks of the drivers for the rest of the season in our group. The fellow who quits hunting after bagging his deer is seldom invited along again, unless there is a good reason for dropping out of the hunt.

Terrain that you and hunting partners are most familiar with is the best to drive for deer. It is important to know where deer bed, feed, and travel in order to plan a drive effectively. This information should be readily available.

The smaller the area that can be isolated for a drive, the better. A swamp, valley, ravine, thicket, or wood lot that is a quarter-mile or less on a side is ideal. Cover that is narrower than it is long is best of all for a drive.

Areas larger than a quarter-mile can and are driven successfully, but the deer's chances of escaping increase as the size of the area increases. More area means more cover for deer to hide in unnoticed and wider gaps in the line of drivers for deer to slip through. A quarter-mile is simply a guideline, not a hard-and-fast rule. I have had my best success on drives conducted in areas within that size range. Another general rule is drives work well in the thickest cover around.

Any number of natural and man-made features can be used to isolate a driveable tract of land. Roads, rivers, lakes, ridges, power lines, railroad tracks, and such changes in cover as where swamps change to hardwoods, hardwoods to fields, timber to meadows, and sagebrush to aspens are examples of convenient borders. Cover that is very long, but narrow, might best be driven in stages.

If you can't think of suitable areas to drive in terrain you frequent or if you want to discover new possibilities, checking out a map or aerial photographs are good ways to locate suitable spots. Topographical or quadrangle maps are best for this purpose. All features of the terrain are clearly marked.

Once a location or two has been decided on for drives, selecting stands is the next step. This is where the chances of success for many drives disappear. The idea is not to choose stands where you want the deer to go, but where they want to go when jumped. Deer can seldom be forced to go where they don't want to. Few drives succeed in doing so. Hunters should use their knowledge of normal deer behavior and use of escape routes to determine where to place standers.

In the morning, deer generally move from feeding grounds to bedding areas. Many of them may already be bedded by daylight, especially after they have been hunted for several days. The trend reverses in the evening — deer move from bedding to feeding grounds. Deer will be bedded during a large part of the day.

Generally, drives should be made from feeding toward bedding areas in the early morning. Pushes at other periods will be through bedding grounds themselves. Bedded deer are the focal point of most drives I've been on.

For morning drives, if bedding and feeding areas are not far apart, say from a quarter to half a mile, standers should be positioned far enough beyond bedding locations (100 to 200 yards) so they won't spook any deer that are there when getting in position. When distance close to a mile separates the two key locations, the area can be driven in stages.

Deer jumped on a drive in the evening will not head toward feeding grounds as they normally would, unless that direction offers the most security. Their first reaction is to get away from what disturbed them. Bedding areas are often in thick cover; consequently, they mean safety to deer. A deer's dinner table, on the other hand, is often in open country, which whitetails and mule deer try to avoid during daylight hours when being hunted. This explains why deer will go toward bedding areas on morning drives but aren't likely to head for chow when driven in the latter part of the day.

Outside of early morning drives, then, standers should be located along escape routes. These routes normally lead from bedding areas toward the nearest patch of cover where deer hope to elude hunters. Escape routes may follow valleys or narrow necks of woods, or go over ridges.

If you have jumped deer from bedding areas before, you should have an idea which way they are likely to go. If not, do your best to anticipate routes driven deer are apt to take. Take the wind into consideration when doing so. Deer always try to move with the breeze in their faces so they can smell what is ahead. Sometimes they travel crosswind for a distance, too. If they are jumped going with the wind, they won't often go far in that direction. Due to variable wind conditions from day to day, deer may use different escape routes to best take advantage of their sense of smell.

Standers can avoid, or at least reduce, the chances of being winded by positioning themselves so their scent isn't blowing directly toward where deer are expected to appear. Elevated stands, where legal, are a great help in this respect.

Some of the best stands may be to either side of the line of drivers or, believe it or not, behind them rather than directly in front. Remember: deer go where they want to on a drive, not where the hunters want them to. Standers who connect will be covering locations where jumped deer normally travel when alarmed.

In the event deer were jumped and not seen by standers, an effort should be made to find out why. A lesson can be learned by failure of a drive if hunters are willing to take the time to do it. Most don't. An escape route a buck used successfully once will be used again if he is in the same area.

Snow makes the job of unraveling how deer made their getaway easier, but telltale signs can often be found under other conditions, as well. It is at least worth a try. If their escape route is discovered, be sure to have a hunter watching it the next time that area is driven. It may pay off.

Snow on the ground gives hunters a slight edge when making a drive. Any deer in the area, whether feeding or bedded, will have left tracks, unless the snow fell recently. One driver should be assigned to follow the tracks with the others to either side of him or her. Drivers to the sides should try to adjust their courses according to the tracker's progress.

The best way to accomplish this is to have the tracker whistle, bark periodically, or carry a bell so others can keep track of him or her. This is a variation of a noisy drive that can be very productive. Once the deer is jumped the odds of someone's getting a shot are good, whether it is one of the standers or the drivers to the sides.

Standers should be as quiet as possible when going to their posts, as well as once there. Too much noise can alert deer to their presence and whitetails or mulies will steer clear of them just as easily as they do of noisy drivers. If standers aren't cautious, they could spook deer out of an area before a drive begins.

The chances of running into a deer on the way to a stand shouldn't be discounted, unless it is dark. I bagged my first buck on the way to a stand preceding a drive. Deer may just as easily travel by standers on their own before a drive begins, so standers should always be alert.

Try to have standers in as many strategic positions as possible. Assigning them all to positions facing the drivers just because "that's the way a normal drive operates" is a mistake. If there are enough hunters, put some on the sides and behind the drivers. When a drive is made into the wind, bucks sometimes circle back through the line of drivers and think they are home free.

On drives made with the wind at the drivers' backs most of the standers should be to the sides and behind, unless the drivers are so close together deer aren't likely to get through. If deer are able to smell drivers, it has the same effect as a noisy drive. The animals are able to tell where the hunters are and will either stay put or circle back if they can.

The rear and sides can sometimes be covered best by still-hunters. Hunters on either side of the heavy cover should move with the drivers or

This buck was taken by a stander on the way to his stand before the drive began. Standers should always be alert for deer.

slightly ahead of them. Tail-end hunters should follow from 50 to 100 yards behind the drivers.

More often than not, drivers are started at prearranged times. Standers are given from fifteen minutes to a half-hour or more to get in position; then the drivers start. All watches should be synchronized for this purpose. Sometimes a car horn or whistle is used to signal both the beginning and end of a drive.

Instead of sitting in a vehicle or relaxing while waiting for standers to get in position, drivers should be standing on the edge of cover or just inside it until time to go unless, of course, it is dark. If standers do move deer on their way in, drivers may get shooting before starting out. I recall one time I should have done just that instead of passing the time in the car.

There were four of us that day. I was going to be the only driver because there was snow and the wind was right. Tracks would be easy to follow and I could get any deer moving that were in the piece of cover we planned on pushing.

Just after I started I found a lone, fresh track coming out. It was big, and I felt sure a buck made it. Those tracks were made by a deer my partners jumped when they reached their stands. The story was clear by the time I reached them. If I had been where I should have been I might have claimed an easy buck.

The standers didn't see any deer on that drive, of course. The animals had been alerted and moved out before I started in. This example points out the importance of standers' being as quiet as possible on their way to stands.

An important rule of drives is that standers stay put until the push is over. They should wait until hearing a prearranged signal or someone picks them up. If any deer are taken, everyone normally lends a hand getting them out of the woods. Following up a deer that is hit and runs off or dressing an animal should be postponed until the hunt is over. The same goes when drivers connect. They should mark the kill and go back for it later with other members of the group.

The use of dogs to drive deer is a tactic only practiced on whitetails in North America in limited areas. Hounds are not permitted to chase mule deer during the course of a hunt.

The only states where driving with hounds is now legal are in the Southeast. Deer hunting with dogs used to be practiced in northern parts of the country, but was outlawed there about 1900. In areas of the South where dogs are still permitted to hunt deer, the cover is so thick that canines are the best means of moving whitetails out of swamps to where hunters can get shots at them. Human drivers would pass by most deer without getting them moving in that terrain. Hounds can sniff the deer out.

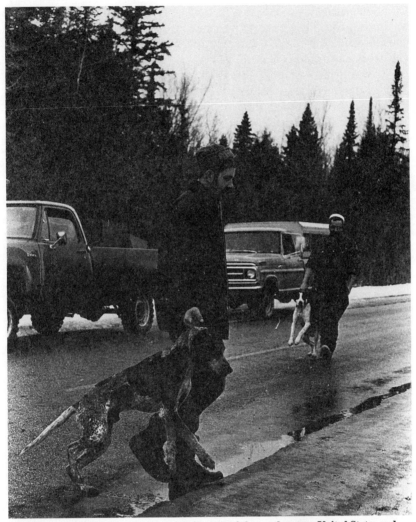

Hounds are commonly used to drive deer in parts of the southeastern United States and in Ontario, Canada.

Canada's province of Ontario also permits the use of dogs to drive deer.

A hunt with hounds is started by finding a fresh track crossing a road or by casting hounds in an area where they are expected to jump a deer. Either way, standers are positioned strategically in the location to be hunted before the chase begins. Standers are often positioned in a horse-shoe or S-shaped pattern.

Some members of the party usually try to stay with the dogs and serve as drivers, too. They help get deer moving and steer dogs toward posted hunters when starting out looking for a fresh trail. Once a chase is over, the drivers also catch the dogs.

Since a pack of dogs, usually numbering from three to six (some hunters use only one), often stays on the trail of one deer for some time, a chase may be stopped if they are on a doe. Some deer dogs reportedly prefer the track of a buck. Deer are easily able to stay ahead of dogs on such hunts. They are normally sneaking or trotting along 300 to 500 yards ahead of their pursuers rather than running flat out directly in front of them. The commotion created by driving dogs also moves deer that aren't being chased. For these reasons, standers must be constantly alert. A flicker of movement is often the only hint of an approaching whitetail.

Beagles and basset hounds are preferred by some hunters because they move whitetails at a leisurely pace and watchers have more of a chance at a standing or slow-moving target. Others prefer bigger black-and-tans, Walkers, or July hounds to keep deer moving at a steady pace. Purebred dogs are by no means the only types used for deer hunting. Mongrels are found in many packs. Dogs that only run the freshest track are preferred to those that try to follow a trail that is hours old.

Hunting deer with dogs requires as much coordination and planning as other types of drives, if not more. Hounds are not only useful to push deer to standers, but also to follow and find wounded whitetails that might otherwise be lost.

Much of the dog hunting in the South is done by organized hunting clubs. The best advice for hunters who would like to try this type of hunting is to contact the department of natural resources in a state they want to hunt for a listing of hunting clubs. States that permit hunting deer with dogs are Louisiana, Georgia, North Carolina, Alabama, Florida, Mississippi, and South Carolina. In many of these states hunting with hounds is only permitted in specific areas during specified times, not statewide.

8

Tracking

The general principles involved in hunting whitetails and mule deer by tracking them are simple: find a track in the snow, preferably fresh, and follow it. Hunters who stay with a set of tracks long enough will get the deer that made them.

Perseverance, physical endurance, and stealth are three of the qualities hunters who want to track deer successfully should possess. They must also feel at ease wherever deer lead them, free from worry about getting lost. A hunter preoccupied with that fear will not be able to devote the concentration to the tracking technique necessary to make it work.

Use of tracking to bag deer is usually restricted to the northern and mountain states and provinces where snowfall is common during deer seasons. The method would probably prove to be impractical in sandy areas under most circumstances.

Despite the fact that tracking as a hunting technique is restricted to certain geographical areas, all deer hunters should try to develop the skill. There are times when, despite how well a deer is hit with gun or bow, the animal will travel out of sight before going down. For this reason, hunters should be proficient at tracking deer under all conditions.

The hunting form of tracking can be practiced successfully in most terrains and covers; however, the chances of scoring are greatest in country that is predominantly hardwood-covered hills or mountains with scattered pockets and stands of evergreens. The odds also favor the tracking hunter in open bog country and similar terrain.

Visibility is greatest in these situations, which increases the chances of the tracker's spotting his quarry. The broken nature of hilly terrain makes it easier to move in on deer undetected. Another advantage common in this habitat is that deer densities are usually not high. This reduces the possibility of confusing the track of a deer being followed with those of other animals.

Fresh snow is ideal for this method of deer hunting, but not a necessity. Conditions that are best for tracking deer are after a heavy snowfall coats all trees and brush or in the fog. Sound doesn't travel far under these circumstances. Deer can't see far either. Wet or crusted snow is fair to poor for tracking.

There is an easy way to gauge how old deer tracks are in the morning, regardless of the snow conditions present. A friend of mine, Duaine Wenzel, uses this system all the time. He usually gets up at least once during the night and makes a footprint in the snow or flips a board, brick, or piece of wood over. Before leaving to look for deer tracks in the morning Duaine checks a fresh boot print against the imprint made during the night and has a rough idea what a fresh deer track will look like as opposed to one several hours old.

If it snowed during the night Wenzel will be able to judge a deer track's age by the amount of snow in it. On warm nights a track's age will be determined by how much it has melted. Prints made during periods of cold will freeze and sometimes ice crystals will form in them, depending on their age. It is often necessary to feel a print to assess how frozen it is.

Before going any further let's discuss what deer tracks look like. Whitetail and mule deer hooves are made up of two segments. There is a noticeable gap between the halves that widens near their tips. Each half is narrower at the front than at the rear, often almost pointed. The back end

This tracking deer hunter checks out a set of prints under ideal tracking conditions.

of each "toe" is more rounded than the front. A pair of dew claws are a short distance above the rear of each foot on the back of the leg.

When walking on solid ground in snow that isn't more than an inch deep, dew claws seldom show. Each print looks something like a pair of elongated drops of moisture side by side. Dew claws are usually visible when a deer walks on soft ground or in snow several inches deep, or when it runs. They appear as a pair of small depressions or marks behind or at the base of each "droplet."

The track of a running deer with dew claw marks visible.

Deer tracks look like this. Each of the two toes are pointed in front and rounded at the rear.

Bounding deer bunch their feet together. Prints from the hind feet will be imprinted forward of the front feet. Tracks of a walking deer will be almost in a straight line with the left and right footprints staggered either side of center.*

Duaine, like most tracking hunters, prefers to go after bucks, the biggest he can find. So he simply looks for the biggest, freshest track around. A few roads are checked by car, first, before daylight. If he doesn't find a good track that way, he zigzags through the woods until finding one. Through preseason scouting he usually knows what territory several good bucks occupy. When searching out big bucks in hilly or mountainous terrain the best procedure is to go up—unless heavy snows have pushed them off the summits to lower elevations.

There are ways to distinguish a buck's track from that of a doe. I know a pair of brothers, Jerry and Terry Weigold, who do it consistently. The problem is explaining the differences to another hunter. They weren't able to explain to me how they do it. Through experience they just know a buck track when they see one.

Duaine Wenzel is the same way. He told me, "There is a pace they make that I know is a buck. It takes experience to recognize it."

Generally, a buck is more likely to leave drag marks from his feet in the snow than a doe. Generally, bucks' prints point slightly outward rather than straight ahead like doe tracks. Generally, bucks will leave bigger tracks than does. Generally, two or three sets of tracks together, one adult and the others small, will be a doe and her young of the year.

The best advice I can come up with for choosing a track to follow that is likely to be a buck's is to do as Wenzel does: pick the biggest track possible. After following it a mile you should know for sure if you are on the track of a buck. By then they often rub their antlers on a sapling, scrape the ground and urinate in the area, or leave an imprint of the tips of their antlers in the snow while feeding. Sometimes only one or two tines will touch the snow when a buck lowers his head to pick up a morsel of food; so look closely for any telltale marks in the snow.

Tracks from a rutting buck will frequently lead the tracker to beds vacated by does, as the animal looks for prospective mates. Another sign to look for are drops of urine that fall as the deer walks. Occasionally a courting whitetail or mulie will get in a fight with another buck. The evidence of such a battle should be plain in the snow. If no positive indications of a deer's sex have been seen after covering a mile or more, it is best to stick with the trail unless a bigger print that is fresh has been seen.

---

*For more information on deer tracks and other sign refer to my book *Animal Tracks and Signs of North America* (Stackpole Books, 1982).

A tracking hunter checks the bed of a doe that a buck he was trailing led him to. A deer that frequently leads the tracker to other deer beds is usually a buck.

If the track a hunter is following is one of the biggest in the area, there shouldn't be any problem distinguishing it from others. On the chance a print of similar size might be encountered, however, hunters should look for anything unusual about prints made by a deer they intend to pursue, to avoid possible confusion. One segment of a hoof may be shorter than the other, for instance, or the toes may be rounded more than normal.

Tracking hunters should adjust their pace to correspond with the deer's gait that they are following. If the animal is walking at a steady pace, the hunter should try to do the same. Hunters should move as fast as they can after a deer that is running. When a buck is poking along feeding, a following hunter should slow down to a crawl and be "careful as heck," as Wenzel says.

Whitetails and mule deer usually start to feed before they bed down. While feeding they often loop back and forth nipping at browse. Deer usually eat the tips of plants, bushes, and young trees. The ends will be ragged where the tips are broken off by browsing animals.

Try to go as straight as possible when following a feeding deer. Look as far ahead as possible in an effort to sort out the track visually to avoid making all of the loops the deer made. It may take as long as five minutes to sort out the trail with your eyes, but it is usually worth it. Bedded deer

Tips of a sapling browsed by a deer.

A skillful tracker will catch sight of a deer in this position. This one doesn't have antlers, but trackers who pick the largest track in their area stand a good chance of spotting a buck.

don't think a hunter coming straight at them is as dangerous as one who is making every swing they did. A zigzagging hunter is also more visible to a deer that is bedded.

When moving in on a whitetail or mulie try to avoid making noise. Move branches and brush aside that may slap or rub against you or your weapon. It is best to detour around dense patches of cover that can't be negotiated quietly. Also try to avoid stepping on twigs that may snap.

All noises that might be made won't necessarily spook deer. The woods are full of noises. After making a sound that may alert an animal you are trailing, it sometimes helps to pause for several minutes before moving farther ahead.

Hunters should keep alert for any sounds deer might make. When not alarmed, whitetails and mulies sometimes make a lot of noise when feeding. They pull on brush and break twigs. It is even possible to hear them chew when they are close. The animals seldom feed continuously. They go "crunch, crunch, crunch"; then they pause for a look around. Hunters who hear a feeding deer ahead can move during the brief intervals the buck is noisy. When that close to a whitetail or mulie, it is usually best to stay put and wait for the deer to make the moves. If you are patient enough, it should eventually step into view.

Deer sometimes give their positions away by making noises while they are walking. When a tracking hunter hears an animal ahead of him, however, it is more often running or bounding than walking. A walking deer might snap a twig or slosh through mud hard enough to make a thudding sound. Brush-breaking noises often accompany the hasty departure of whitetails and mulies, too.

A hunter's eyes are usually more important than his ears for detecting the presence of his quarry. Try to concentrate your attention on the area ahead at a forty-five-degree angle left and right. Don't spend much time looking far left and right until the cover ahead has been scanned carefully. Stoop down and look low, too. Visibility is often better from this angle. It sometimes helps to divide the terrain into sections and scan them individually.

Deer other than the one being trailed are commonly seen; so when you see an animal, don't assume it is the one you have been after. Try to get a good look at it before deciding to shoot. Duaine has taken bucks other than the ones he was tracking on two occasions. My brother Bruce made a mistake one time while following a buck and shot a doe. He wasn't as careful as he normally would have been because his tag was valid for either sex.

Deer that are being trailed frequently go past other animals; then the deer stop and watch the animals' reactions to tip them off at the approach of a hunter. Tracking hunters who spot deer other than the one they are following should try not to spook them. If they are allowed to go on their way unalarmed, the animal being followed will frequently drop its guard.

Another trick used by deer that are being tailed is to stop after climbing a hill or crossing a clearing to watch for their pursuer. Savvy hunters can often get the drop on a buck by circling a hill or clearing to come in from the rear or side.

The stealthier a hunter is, the sooner he will get a look and maybe a shot at his deer. Even without stealth, a tracker who perseveres long enough will eventually get a chance at a buck being trailed. Whitetails and mule deer gradually come to accept the hunter and even get curious. They invariably make a mistake.

"If I could follow a deer four days, I could shoot it," Wenzel says.

Many times it is possible to score the first day a buck's track is picked up. Other times, it may take several days. Whitetail bucks have a tendency to return to their home area during the night after being trailed for miles; so their tracks can frequently be started in the same general area on successive days. Mule deer are less likely to do this. A big mule deer's track would probably have to be picked up where it was left the night before on successive days of tracking.

One time Wenzel jumped a whitetail buck from beds yards apart two days in a row. Duaine got several shots at the animal the first day when it jumped, but missed. He reloads his own rifle ammunition, but rather than take the time to pick up the brass, he hustled after the buck. He estimated he followed that animal eight miles that day without getting another crack at it.

Deer that are being trailed will often stop on a hill to wait for their pursuer. Trackers who are alert might be able to get the drop on a deer who tries this by circling ahead. *Montana Department of Fish and Game*

The next morning he returned to the place where he shot at the buck to pick up his brass. Just short of the spot, the buck jumped up. Caught by surprise, Duaine didn't get a shot. He eventually bagged the deer that day though. As the whitetail stood up from its third bed, Wenzel nailed him.

Shots frequently have to be taken in a hurry when tracking deer. Wenzel prepares for the season by practicing throwing his rifle to his shoulder and getting on target. He uses a six-and-a-half-pound .30-06 with a 1-4X variable scope. He fires 180-grain round-nosed bullets.

Like most experienced hunters who regularly track deer, Duaine is familiar with the areas he hunts. When trailing a deer he usually knows where he is and what lies ahead. This information sometimes helps him anticipate the route a buck will take. Over the years he has noticed that different bucks in the same vicinity have a tendency to travel through the same localities when pushed.

The novice tracking hunter can't expect to be as skillful as an old hand at the technique right away. It takes years to develop the familiarity with the lay of the land and the animals that live on it that Duaine and others like him have developed. Regardless of whether or not hunters who track deer connect, the experience is bound to be educational. Deer give their pursuers cram courses on what they eat, the habitat they prefer, their daily habits, and how clever they can be in staying out of sight. They don't give hunters lessons willingly, of course; those who want to learn must interpret buck sign left in the snow for hours and sometimes days.

All deer hunters, regardless of the hunting technique they use, should assume a whitetail or mulie they shoot at is hit. Most animals will give some indication of being struck, but not always. Deer that stagger, hunch up, kick, leap in the air, favor a leg, or break into a dead run after a shot are usually hit. Bowhunters can sometimes actually see their arrows strike deer.

If you know the deer you shot at is hit, that is usually good. A properly placed bullet or arrow will put a deer down in seconds, many times on the spot or within sight. It is the ones that are hit that make it out of sight before dropping that I will discuss here.

Try to make a mental note of where deer are standing when you shoot at them. This can be done after the animal has gone out of sight. Unless there is a good chance for another shot at a deer, it is best to stay where you shot from rather than immediately racing after a whitetail or mulie. If it is hit seriously, it may lie down just out of sight. A hunter who stumbles after a wounded animal right away sometimes reduces his or her chances of getting it.

Always try to watch a deer that has been shot at as long as possible. If it didn't show any signs of being hit at first, it may while in flight. Noting the course the animal follows will also make locating its trail easier.

Keep your ears open, too. A fleeing deer that is out of sight but within earshot makes a lot of noise. If the animal falls, you should be able to tell it and get a fix on the approximate location.

Once a deer that may be wounded is out of sight and hearing and you have the spot or spots marked where it was when you shot, walk directly there. It is a good idea to leave a hat or coat to mark the spot where the shot was taken from, unless there is a prominent identifying feature nearby. Bowhunters should look for the arrow if unsure of a hit. Archers using string trackers will know if they scored a hit and be assured of finding the arrow if it missed. Gun hunters should look for blood, hair, or anything between where they shot from and where the deer stood to determine if the bullet may have hit.

Archers who find a bloodied arrow know they scored a hit. If the search turns up a clean broadhead, the shot was a miss. A missing shaft might also mean the arrow was on target. Look for blood or hair if the arrow can't be found.

Tufts of hair or blood are sure signs of a hit. Look for these clues behind where the deer was standing, as well as at the spot. Firearms users who find a tree their slug hit before reaching a deer can almost count on a miss. It is worthwhile to check further before giving up in such a situation, though, especially if the tree or branch is close to where the deer was standing.

Location of a hit can often be determined by the color of hair or blood. Dark brown hair usually means the animal was struck in the shoulder or upper body. It will be light brown if the deer was hit in the chest or lower sides. White hair originates from legs and the belly area.

Pink, frothy blood means a dead deer—it was hit in the lungs. Dark, beet-colored blood indicates a liver wound. Bright red blood usually comes from an artery. Watery blood or none at all and food particles or intestinal matter are evidence of a hit in the stomach or intestines. Excellent deer hair and blood sign posters can be purchased from *Deer & Deer Hunting Magazine,* P.O. Box 1117, Appleton, WI 54912.

If unable to determine if a deer was hit by checking the area where it was standing, move along the course it took after the shot; but try to make as little disturbance as possible. Look for blood on the ground or bushes. Archers can also keep an eye open for a broken arrow lying off to the side. There shouldn't be any problem following a deer in snow or sand. In blankets of leaves or pine needles look for areas where leaves and turf have been kicked up by a running deer. Vegetation will be flattened and broken in fields and openings where a deer went through. Hunters who carefully watched the departure of deer they shot at should not have trouble following the animal's trail for 100 yards or more. There should be some sign of a hit discovered in that distance, but go as far as possible to be absolutely sure.

Bowhunters who find a bloodied arrow know they scored a hit.

Tracking wounded deer in the snow is often easy. This archer inspects spots of blood left by a deer he hit.

If it can be determined that a deer was hit in the lungs, there is no need to wait before following it. Enough blood should be present to easily follow the animal's trail the short distance it traveled. If it is raining or snowing there will be little choice but to follow up on a deer as soon as possible.

With a hit anywhere but in the shoulder area, it is best to wait before trying to trail a wounded deer. Don't worry if it is getting dark. As long as the weather stays clear you can go back and trail with a flashlight or lantern. Drops of blood often show up well under the illumination of a lantern.

When unsure of how badly a deer is wounded, waiting thirty minutes to an hour is usually long enough before picking up the trail. Try to hold off longer on paunch-shot animals. Five minutes can seem like a long time when you are anxious to follow a wounded deer; so it is best to try to do something to keep yourself occupied while waiting. If hunting with a partner or two it is a good idea to go get them to help trail. It will make the job easier. If alone, a walk to your car or camp is a good way to kill some time.

Hunters who have access to a dog that will track deer should consider getting it. Many states have laws prohibiting the use of dogs to trail deer; however, exceptions are often made in cases of wounded animals if a dog is restrained on a leash. Be sure to get an okay from a local game warden or department of natural resources official if unsure of the regulation pertaining to dogs.

Some states allow the use of dogs on leashes to track wounded deer.

Before leaving the spot where the deer was hit be sure you will be able to find it again. Leave a bright-colored hat or garment there or use ribbon to mark a course to the nearest road if the area will be difficult to relocate.

Try to start trailing a wounded deer from the point where it was last seen. If there is a moderate to heavy blood trail or snow, there shouldn't be any problem following the animal. Skill and painstaking care are necessary to unravel a trail with little or no blood. This is where a tracking dog can be a big advantage.

I examine blood on a leaf while trailing an arrowed whitetail.

Lacking a dog, scour every inch of the ground for the tiniest drops of blood and tracks left by a wounded deer. It is sometimes necessary to get down on hands and knees when searching for minute details. Wounded whitetails and mulies run more often than not; so the ground should be noticeably disturbed along the route taken.

Be sure to look at bushes and tree trunks that the deer may have brushed past. Blood will often show in these locations.

It is advisable to mark every spot where a drop of blood or track from a wounded deer is found. Plastic surveyor's tape is perfect for this purpose.

Flagging is a good way of marking where spots of blood are found when trailing a deer on bare ground.

White or orange ribbon, spools of string, or tissue will also work. Place markers on bushes or tree limbs where they can be easily seen. After several markers have been hung it is usually possible to get a general idea of the animal's direction of travel by looking back.

Try to circle ahead and to the sides when the trail is lost. It isn't unusual for deer to make abrupt changes in direction. Be alert for any deviations. If the trail is lost entirely, keep in mind that whitetails and mulies, if seriously hurt, follow a path of least resistance. They tend to go downhill rather than uphill, for instance. Additionally, wounded deer may head for nearby heavy cover or water.

Exhaust every effort possible to locate a wounded deer. Perseverance often pays off in this type of tracking, as it does when using the technique to hunt. If the animal isn't located, it probably wasn't seriously injured. While tracking a wounded deer, be ready to shoot again on the chance the animal isn't dead.

Deer hunters who are proficient with gun or bow and are conscientious about only taking the best shot possible can avoid unnecessary wounding. Because of variables involved in deer hunting, many of which hunters don't have control over, some wounding does occur. Few of these animals will go unrecovered if hunters follow the guidelines listed above for tracking them.*

---

*For detailed coverage on this subject, refer to my book *Tracking Wounded Deer* (Stackpole Books, 1988).

9

Calling Deer

At certain times it is actually possible to attract deer to a hunter rather than having to go to them or waiting where they might pass by. The techniques take advantage of the animals' mating instincts, curiosity, and in the case of whitetails, their territoriality.

There are two ways to bring deer to you. One method is rattling a set of antlers together to simulate a fight between two bucks. Mouth-blown calls also bring deer in if the circumstances are right. Most deer calls are designed to sound like the bleat of a doe or a fawn in trouble or the grunts of bucks and does.

The practice of rattling antlers to attract bucks originated in Texas and is commonly accepted there. It has been proven productive in other states, too, and is now widely used. The method merits more use in some areas. In Michigan, for example, rattling for bucks was slow to catch on, but it works there.

An Upper Peninsula resident, Dave Paquette, tried it for the first time during the fall of 1977 and got a ten-point buck for his efforts. Five to ten minutes from the time Dave started twisting tines together the whitetail came trotting into view. It was opening day of the state's November firearms season. He had practiced rattling on three occasions during the week before the season and brought another buck in on his last attempt.

I rattled in my first buck, a 3½-year-old eight-pointer, during 1986. I was using a Woods Wise Rattler Bag rather than antlers. Such a bag is easier to carry than antlers and sounds just as good as the real thing.

Rattling is most effective during the rut, which usually starts in late October or early November in northern states and December or January in the South. There may be other variations in timing of the rut from state to state. Deer in Florida, for instance, seem to breed at all times of the year with no peak breeding period.

The onset of cool weather in the fall usually triggers the rut, which can last for a month or more. Fights between bucks normally start over a doe that is ready to breed or when a buck catches a competing male in his territory. A third buck will investigate a fight out of curiosity — to join in if the squabble is in his stomping grounds or in an attempt to make off with the doe the fight might be over.

Mule deer don't establish territories like whitetails; so they aren't as responsive to rattled antlers. The technique still works on them, however. A mulie buck drawn to the sounds of a battle between two other bucks would be interested in any does that might be around or just curious.

The chances of rattling working in areas where there are a lot of does and few bucks aren't good. The same is true of locations where hunter densities are high. Under this circumstance the odds favor attracting other hunters rather than deer. Large numbers of hunters are seldom a problem during archery deer seasons. Bow seasons that coincide with the rut would be the best time to try rattling in many states.

Either whitetail or mule deer antlers will bring in bucks when rattled.

Whitetail bucks fighting.

The fresher they are the better, but an old set will do if that is all that is available. Check with a taxidermist or a friend who owns plenty of antlers if you don't own any. Generally, big racks are better than small ones, and the antlers should be as evenly matched as possible. Small, unmatched beams will work though.

To remove antlers from a skull, saw them off either below or above the burr. Also remove the brow tine and sharp tips of additional tines. A file can be used to smooth any ragged or rough areas. A carrying strap can be rigged for the antlers by drilling a hole through each base, putting a piece of leather or rope through them, then tying a knot in the ends of the material.

You might consider painting the antlers red or orange to be on the safe side, so there will be little chance of another hunter mistaking them for the real thing.

Early in the morning on a cool, quiet day is the best time to rattle. Any time of the day can be productive, however. Bucks are jittery on windy days, and the sound of antlers rubbed together doesn't travel far then.

The best place to try the technique is near a series of scrapes. The buck that made them isn't likely to be far away and won't take kindly to what he thinks are a pair of other bucks having it out on his doorstep.

Always try to approach a rattling location quietly. Don't slam car doors or talk if you are with another hunter. It is a good idea for two hunters to work as a team when trying to rattle in a buck. One should plan on doing the shooting and the other the rattling. The guy with the antlers should be as concealed as possible in a position next to a tree or in brush.

Also, try to select a calling site where an approaching buck will have some cover. They don't like to cross openings. Their tendency to avoid openings can be used to your advantage if a stand is chosen with a clearing downwind. Bucks coming to a fight will sometimes circle downwind. If there is an opening there, those that circle will have to expose themselves before they can wind you.

When two bucks fight they do more twisting and shoving than beating their antlers together. Keep this in mind when trying to imitate a battle. Bang the antlers together as loud as possible at first, then twist and turn them so the tines knock against each other and make as much noise as possible. Additional realistic sound effects can be made by pounding the bases of the antlers on the ground and raking them up and down a tree trunk or through brush. If gravel or rocks are common in your area scrape an antler through or over them. The object is to make noise; so don't be timid about it.

The procedure can be varied any way you like. Simply try to make the sounds realistic. It is a good idea to practice with the antlers at home to get a feel for how they should be manipulated.

Nick Sisley blows a grunt tube from a tree stand.

Nick Sisley with a nine-point buck he grunted in while on a Georgia hunt.

Make as few movements as possible during the process of rattling antlers. If a buck shows and sees you instead of what he is expecting, he won't hang around long. You will never know he was there if he sees you before you see him.

Antlers should be rattled for as long as a couple of minutes; then take a break from three to five minutes to look around. A buck may come charging in or he may sneak. Try to be prepared for either. Curious deer will sometimes stop on the edge of cover; so look closely.

After a pause, again go through the motions of two bucks trying to outmuscle and outmaneuver each other. If a buck doesn't respond in twenty or thirty minutes, there probably isn't one coming. Three or four series of antler clashing, ground pounding, and tree scraping should be enough in that span of time. Try not to rattle too much.

If a buck is seen approaching but looks unsure of whether he wants to come all the way, try touching the tines together lightly. A grunt might be enough to convince him the fight is for real, too.

When getting up to leave a calling site, do so cautiously. Look all around carefully for a deer that may have been hidden from view until then. One may decide to step in the open at the last minute.

Try rattling at locations that are from one-quarter to one-half mile apart. Don't expect to attract a buck at each spot. One may show at the first stand you take, or the tenth. If calling sites are chosen carefully during the peak of the rut, the odds of collecting a buck by having him come to you are good.

To prevent antlers used for rattling from drying they can be rubbed with linseed oil or lanolin.

I've had better luck attracting bucks to me with a Knight and Hale grunt tube than rattling. Bucks frequently grunt when trailing a receptive doe. Another buck who hears this sound frequently comes to investigate. Grunt tubes work best on bucks that are seen, but are too far for a shot or those that disappear before a shot is possible.

Mouth-blown calls will attract both bucks and does. Bucks respond best during the rut. Does are likely to investigate a call any time during the fall, especially to sounds of a fawn in distress. A buck in the rut expects to find a receptive doe when homing in on a call.

Deer calls are available commercially, or hunters can make their own. Some quail and predator calls available on the market work equally well on deer. I have called in several whitetail does while using a predator call. Alaska's sitka black-tailed deer are said to be receptive to quail calls.

The simplest deer call consists of a blade of grass. It is blown on while stretched between clenched thumbs. Homemade deer calls can be made from a rubber band and a couple of pieces of wood. The pieces

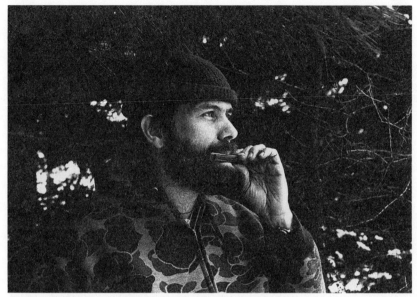

Jim Haveman blows a rubber-band-type deer call in Michigan.

should be about four inches long. Each should have matching, narrow openings in their centers. The elastic is held taut across the opening when the wood is fitted together. The ends can be taped or bound with strong thread. Indians get the credit for devising these two deer calls.

Calls will work any time of the day, but are most effective early and late in the day. There is more chance of a deer hearing the calls on a quiet day. Windy conditions are poor for trying to bring in deer with a call.

The same basic considerations discussed for choosing a stand for rattling apply when situating yourself to try a call. Whitetails or mule deer drawn to the sound may come on the run or sneaking. Try blowing the call at ten- to thirty-minute intervals. The technique can be varied, however.

One of the best ways to use a call is to have it handy while still-hunting. When deer are jumped and are running, a blast from a call can stop them long enough for a shot. It may even bring an animal back that has already gone out of sight, providing the buck or doe wasn't badly spooked.

A call can be used similarly while on stand. Deer that pass by without providing a shot may be lured back into view. Those that are running may be stopped by the sound of a bleat.

As with rattling, mouth-blown calls aren't likely to produce results in areas with high densities of hunters.

10

Weapons

There is no one best rifle or bow and arrow for deer hunting. There are a number of bests in each category.

Carrying it one step further, there is no one best type of weaponry for deer hunting. Rifles, both modern and muzzleloaders, shotguns, handguns, and bow and arrow all have their advantages and advocates.

There are, however, some in each category that are better for some or all forms of deer hunting than others due to trajectory, recoil, weight, and killing power. For these reasons, and others, some in each class are more suited for deer hunting than others. Those are the ones we will be discussing.

One of the major reasons for the diversity of "bests" for deer hunting is that both mule deer and whitetails are easy to kill. More important than a firearm's or bow's power, within limits, is the hunter's ability to place his or her shot accurately in a vital area. A firearm or bow is often chosen to meet the individual hunter's personal needs or desires rather than for its ability to kill a deer, since many can do this.

Another consideration in the line of best weapons for deer hunting is the varying types of terrain in which both mulies and whitetails are found. Rifles that are tops for deer in thick cover may be poor in open terrain, and vice versa. There are some that perform equally well under a variety of circumstances, however.

Obtaining a weapon adequate for deer hunting is probably the easiest part of the pursuit. The skills to use it properly and to be consistently in a position to shoot at deer with it are much more difficult to acquire.

There are a number of centerfire rifle calibers that will perform adequately for all deer hunting. They include the .243, 6 mm, .25-06, .270, .280, .284, .300 Savage, .300 magnum, 7 mm magnum, .30-06, and .308. Of those, the .270, .30-06, and .308 have to be rated the best of the lot.

My personal preference in caliber for a deer rifle is the .30-06. I bought my first one because my father had one and swore by it. Actually, that was only part of the reason. Dad said a rifle in that caliber would be satisfactory for hunting any big game in North America. What I read about the ought-six bore him out; so I was convinced. The hunting I have done with that first .30-06 and the others that followed has fortified my opinion of the caliber.

A .270 is just as good as a .30-06 for deer hunting. Some, usually hunters who own them, say it is better. The additional calibers mentioned don't rank far down the list from either of these two.

Some deer hunters may scoff at the thought of light calibers such as the .243 for all-around deer rifles. I once shared the opinion, but have since altered my position after seeing several in action on whitetails and mule deer. Their biggest advantage is light recoil, which often results in better accuracy, when compared with calibers that pack a more noticeable wallop. The .243, for instance, is a good choice for any deer hunter, but especially for women and youngsters.

A nice eight-point whitetail I bagged with a scoped .30-06.

Deer hunters shouldn't worry about the old myth that light, fast bullets are useless in brush. Such a bullet won't plow through twigs and branches that are in its way and drill a deer right where the shooter was aiming. Neither will a bullet from a rifle in any of the bigger calibers mentioned. The simple fact of the matter is that no bullet designed for deer hunting has the capability of busting through brush. Wait for an open shot and a .243 will kill a whitetail or mulie as dead as a .30-06 if the bullet is placed where it should be.

What about the .30-30, .35, and .44 for deer? They are all right for hunting in areas where shots are likely to be from 50 to 100 yards maximum. Their trajectories are poor at ranges beyond that.

There are characteristics or features of a deer rifle that are more important than caliber. Chief among these are length, weight, action, and sights. The type of terrain deer are hunted in and the most often used method of hunting them will dictate which features a hunter should consider when buying a rifle.

A still-hunter or tracker, for instance, who treads in cover where shots are less than 100 yards will want a rifle that is short, light, and fast-aiming and shooting. One that weighs between six and seven pounds or less, has an 18½-inch or 20-inch barrel, and iron sights. A peep sight is great for quick aiming. Some who like a scope and don't mind the extra weight might want a fixed-power model or a low-power variable. The action could be lever, pump, or semiautomatic.

The deer hunter who spends a lot of time on stands or hunts country where shots average from 100 to 300 yards will want a rifle that is as accurate as possible. Weight isn't as critical here; so a rifle that weighs more than seven pounds and has a 22-inch or 24-inch barrel is okay. A telescopic sight is almost a must. Any type of action would do, but bolt actions are a good choice.

An accessory deer hunters should seriously consider regardless of the type of gun they have or the preferred hunting method is a sling. The straps are helpful in steadying aim and for carrying a rifle over the shoulder while climbing or dragging a deer. Slings can also be used to hang a firearm on a convenient limb during a break rather than laying it on the ground.

Many deer hunters tend to use bullets heavier than are necessary. This is especially true in "brush country." Some hunters who frequent such cover in their search for deer incorrectly believe that the heavier the bullet they use, the greater their chances of hitting a deer on the opposite side of a thicket. Any bullet from a deer rifle that hits a branch or some other obstruction in its path will expand and deflect. Unless a deer is directly behind the obstruction that is hit, the slug is more likely to wound or miss the animal than kill it. Shots intentionally taken through branches with the

**A successful deer hunter inspects the buck he just dropped with a bolt-action .30-30.
This caliber is popular for deer hunting, but isn't one of the best choices.**

hopes of hitting deer are unsportsmanlike as well as a waste of ammunition. If an opening large enough to get a bullet through does not exist, hunters shouldn't shoot.

Slugs over 150 grains are unnecessary for deer hunting. Those weighing 180 or 220 grains often do not expand properly. There have been a lot of deer bagged with slugs 180 grains and larger. I have collected some myself. In many cases the projectile goes completely through the animal, inflicting less damage than a lighter bullet would. A second shot is sometimes required to finish whitetails and mulies hit with heavy bullets.

The amount of shocking power a slug delivers determines its effectiveness. A bullet that opens up and expends all of its energy inside a deer gives optimum performance. When a bullet passes through a deer, some of its shocking power is lost.

A disadvantage of heavy bullets in areas where long shots are common is their trajectory. They drop much faster than lighter slugs. According to Winchester's ballistics chart, a .30-06, 180-grain bullet drops about seven inches more than one of the same design weighing 150 grains at 300 yards.

Deer hunters who use .35s or .44s don't have any choice in bullet weight unless they handload. They are stuck with 200-grain and 240-grain slugs respectively in factory loads.

For the .243 and 6 mm, 100-grain bullets are tops. A 120-grain slug is good for the .25-06; 130 or 150 grains in .270; 140 grains in .280; 150-grain slugs are good for the .284, .30-30, .300, .30-06, and .308. Federal introduced a 125-grain, hollow-point, .30-30 bullet in 1977. This is not designed for deer hunting! It is for predator and woodchuck hunting.

Generally, soft-point bullets are the best for deer hunting. Pointed soft-points are better than round-nose bullets when shooting at moderate to long ranges. Pointed bullets have less wind resistance and drop less than blunt slugs. Round-nosed bullets are best for use in rifles with tubular magazines, though.

Try not to carry cartridges, not many anyway, in pockets where they will clank together. Shell holders that fit on the belt are good for carrying rifle shells. What I do is have a couple of extra shells handy, one in each pants or coat pocket. The rest of my ammunition stays in a pack I always carry when hunting.

Choosing a muzzleloading rifle for deer hunting is a different matter than selecting a modern gun. Percussion cap, replica muzzleloaders are best suited for deer hunting. Flintlocks are also used successfully by some deer hunters. Rifles are available in finished models or in kits that the hunter can put together.

Caliber choices vary, but the most popular for deer are .50, .54, and .58. The minimum required caliber for deer hunting varies from state to state. Most deer are shot with .50 or .54 caliber front-loaders.

Muzzleloaders can be obtained with either single or double triggers. On models with two triggers and one barrel, only the front trigger releases the hammer. The rear one is called a set trigger. When it is pulled back it reduces the amount of finger pressure required on the front trigger to fire the rifle. Double-barreled muzzleloaders commonly have a trigger for each barrel.

The newest type of muzzleloader on the market is the MK-85 made by Modern Muzzleloading, Inc. These rifles are indeed modern muzzleloaders. They are designed to shoot modern rifle bullets with sabots (pronounced say-bows), a type of plastic patch, in addition to traditional black-powder projectiles. The MK-85 has one other major feature that

Jim Haveman waits for whitetails with a modern muzzleloader during a December hunt in Michigan.

sets it apart from replica front-loading rifles. It has double safeties, which dramatically reduce the chances of an accidental discharge.

Besides saboted modern bullets, there are two basic types of projectiles used in muzzleloaders for hunting: round balls and bullet-shaped maxi-balls, or bullets. Thompson/Center makes a flat-based maxi-ball and hollow-point maxi-Hunter. Hornady manufactures Great Plains maxi-bullets with a concave base. Great Plains bullets are prelubricated and come in both hollow-point and solid-point versions. Maxi-balls and maxi-Hunters can be obtained prelubricated as well as unlubricated.

Hornady also sells boxes of modern bullets complete with sabots for use in modern muzzleloaders. Jacketed hollow-point .44-caliber bullets are available for use in .50-caliber MK-85s and jacketed flat-point .44-caliber bullets can be obtained for use out of .54-caliber models.

Any of the above projectiles are satisfactory for deer hunting, but their use may be restricted in some states or provinces during certain seasons. Some states only permit the use of round balls during special black-powder seasons, so be sure to check local regulations before deciding what to hunt with.

Round balls must be used with a patch. The conventional cloth patch must be lubricated. Cloth patches can be purchased dry or prelubricated. A commercial lubrication, such as Maxi-Lub available from Thompson/Center, should be applied to dry patches. Some musket shooters use

Crisco or Vaseline on their patches, but these preparations aren't recommended in cold weather.

The proper patch thickness to use with round balls is critical. A certain amount of pressure is required to start a properly patched ball down the barrel to insure a tight fit. If so much pressure is necessary that the lead ball is deformed, the patch is too thick. If the ball slips in easily, it is too thin. Most sporting goods dealers who handle muzzleloaders can recommend the proper size patch. There may be some variance from rifle to rifle, however; so if one thickness doesn't work right for you, try a different one.

Butler Creek Corporation from Jackson Hole, Wyoming, developed what they call a Poly-Patch as an alternative to cloth patches. They are plastic, cylindrical, and have a cup on both ends. I have test-fired round balls with Poly-Patches and got tighter groups than with cloth patches.

No patch is required with maxi-balls or bullets. Lubricant is applied directly to the bullet, unless it is prelubricated, and then it is seated on top of the powder charge.

A handy rule of thumb for determining a powder charge for hunting is to multiply your rifle caliber by two. With a .50 caliber, for instance, 100 grains of powder would be adequate. I've shot plenty of whitetails with that load out of my Thompson/Center Hawken with excellent results.

Poly-Patches are an alternative to cloth patches when shooting round balls out of a muzzleloader. My brother Bruce is shown loading a muzzleloader with a Poly-Patch.

Powder charges of 110 grains would be about right for .54 caliber muzzle-loaders. FFG black powder is satisfactory for use with all the calibers mentioned.

A powder designed for use in percussion muzzleloaders (it won't work in flintlocks) that isn't a true black powder has been developed. It is called Pyrodex. Pyrodex burns cleaner than black powder, resulting in less residue in the barrel after each shot. Pyrodex is generally accepted as a black-powder substitute, but may be prohibited during some muzzleloader deer seasons.

Loading a muzzleloader is easy. Before a front-loader is charged, a couple of percussion caps should be fired to clear away any grease or oil that may dampen the powder charge. Once this is accomplished, rest the rifle on its butt plate with the hammer at half cock. Then measure the desired amount of powder and pour it down the barrel. Strike the barrel several times with the heel of your hand to settle the powder in the chamber.

The projectile is next, either a patch and ball or a lubricated maxi. If using a cloth patch, try to be sure it is centered on the barrel and the grain of the cloth is facing the same way at each loading. Most round balls have a sprue mark, a spot of upraised lead, which should also be centered and face up.

Successful musket hunters drag their bagged buck. Both are carrying .50 caliber Hawkens made by Thompson/Center.

A starter is necessary to get a ball into the bore. Once it is several inches down the barrel, a ramrod can be used to seat it firmly, without pounding, against the powder charge.

The base of maxi-balls can usually be started in the muzzle with finger pressure. A starter can then be used to push the bullet a short distance down the barrel. The ramrod finishes the job.

Once a satisfactory hunting load has been determined, it is a good idea to mark the ramrod at the muzzle while it is resting on a seated ball or bullet; the mark will serve as a guideline for future loads to make sure all rounds are seated at the same depth. A piece of tape or a felt-tipped pen can be used to make the mark. A mark can also be scratched in with a knife.

Never use smokeless powder in a muzzleloading rifle or shoot one unless the projectile is seated against the powder. A muzzleloader can't be fired until a cap is placed on the nipple.

The safety features on modern muzzleloaders make it possible to have the hammer cocked and a cap on the nipple while walking or sitting. The hammer is the safety on most front-loading rifles.

The safest way to carry percussion-cap replicas while still-hunting is to have a cap on the nipple with the hammer uncocked. You will have to cock the hammer to put the cap in place, but then hold the hammer with your thumb while pulling the trigger to release the hammer. Always be sure the muzzle is pointed in a safe direction when doing this in case something goes wrong.

Once the hammer is released, ease it down slowly. When a shot is offered, cock the hammer to shoot. Practice uncocking without a cap in place so you will become familiar with the procedure.

Here are a pair of maxi-balls. The one on the left is unfired. The one on the right brought down a deer.

While hunting from a tree stand or ground blind with a replica muzzleloader, I have the hammer cocked, but no cap on the nipple. When a chance for a shot develops, a cap is put on the nipple. I prefer this procedure because it's safe as well as quiet. The hammer frequently makes one or more clicks when it is cocked and that noise can alert, if not spook, a deer that's close.

If a cap fits loosely on the nipple of your rifle, squeeze it to tighten the fit. Loose caps can fall off at the most inopportune moments. A knife blade is handy for removing a cap that fits too tight on a nipple to remove with fingers.

Unfired powder and ball can't be removed at the end of the day as conveniently as a modern cartridge. Actually, they don't have to be. In most cases, a muzzleloader is considered unloaded when the cap is removed. I have carried my muzzleloader with the same load in it for weeks without misfires. The rifle is always put in a case when I'm not in the woods and kept inside a cabin or house overnight.

A muzzleloader that needs cleaning or can't be stored safely between hunts should be discharged at the end of the hunting day, if possible. Be sure to shoot a muzzleloader at the end of the season. With the passage of time it can be difficult to remember if a load was left in the gun and an accident could result. If in doubt whether a muzzleloader is loaded, use your ramrod—which should be marked—to check. Don't fire a cap to test it!

Some parts of the United States require shotguns for deer hunting; and in other areas where cover is exceptionally dense and shots close, they are the most practical weapons. Without question, 10-gauge and 12-gauge scatterguns are the best shotguns for deer hunting. Sixteen- and 20-gauges are all right, but .410s are poor. Many states prohibit the use of .410 shotguns for deer hunting. Twelve- and 20-gauge shotguns that chamber three-inch shells are better than 2¾-inch types.

A shotgun for deer hunting should be as light as possible, within the gauge limitation. The action should be fast—either pump or semiautomatic—and doubles are all right. Many states require that shotguns for deer hunting be plugged to limit their shell capacity to three. Buckshot patterns best out of a full-choke scattergun, but buckshot is prohibited in some states. Open chokes, such as modified and improved cylinder, are better for slug use. Shotguns with barrels designed specifically for slugs are the best choice for the serious shotgun deer hunter. They come with iron sights and can be fitted with a peep sight or scope.

Slugs are the best choice in ammunition for shotguns used on deer. I've found Brenneke slugs to be the most accurate. Number one buckshot is best for hunters who are required or choose to use buckshot, where legal. The larger 000, 00, and 0 sizes are second, third, and fourth choices.

I pose with a buck bagged with a 12-gauge slug out of a Remington 870 with slug barrel. Shotguns account for many deer each year.

Buckshot is only effective at close ranges, forty yards maximum. For longer shots, slugs should be used.

Muzzleloading shotguns will bring a deer down, but aren't widely used.

Handguns present yet another category of firearm for deer hunters to choose from. Both revolvers and single-shot handguns suitable for deer hunting are available. Revolvers in calibers that have proven effective for deer are .44, .41, and .357 magnum. Single-shot models, such as Thompson/Center's Contender, can be obtained in .30-30 Winchester, .35 Remington, .44 magnum, 45/70 Government, and .375 JDJ.

Contenders are available with ten-, fourteen- and sixteen-inch interchangeable barrels. Faster velocities and more energy are obtained with the same bullets from the longer barrels. Barrels for the .375 JDJ are not available from Thompson/Center, but can be obtained from J. D. Jones of Bloomington, Ohio, who came up with that caliber and is with SSK Industries.

The .44 magnum revolver is the best of the lot because of the punch it packs. This caliber's heavy recoil and loud muzzle blast prevent some people from shooting it accurately. If groups from a lesser caliber such as the .357 magnum are more consistent and tighter than from the .44, it is the better choice for hunting. All of the calibers mentioned for single-shot handguns are good choices for deer hunting.

A hunter takes aim with a revolver at a deer.

Large-caliber handguns can be tamed somewhat by having vents put in the barrels. The process is called Mag-Na-Porting. The vents reduce muzzle lift and dampen recoil without reducing bullet velocity or increasing noise. For more information write or call Mag-Na-Port International, 41302 Executive Dr., Mount Clemens, MI 48045-3448 (313-469-6727).

A successful handgun deer hunter from Michigan, Ron Coleman, applies red fingernail polish to his front sight to make it easier to see.

Either soft-point or semijacketed hollow-point bullets are okay for deer hunting. The .44 is available in 240-grain slugs; the .41 in 210; .357 in 158 and 180; the .30-30 in 150-grain; the .35 in 200-grain; the 45/70 in 300-grain; and the .375 JDJ in 220-grain bullets.

It takes more practice to master a handgun than any other type of firearm I'm acquainted with; at least it does for me. Shooters who plan on hunting deer with one should familiarize themselves with their own and the gun's limitations before going afield. Shooting should be done from a steady position—sitting, prone, or resting against something—whenever possible.

Now, let's consider an entirely different weapon: the bow. Unlike firearms, bows are classified by pounds of pull rather than caliber. There are several types of bows available today: compounds, recurves, longbows, and crossbows. All are used for deer hunting, but compounds and recurves are the most popular. The vast majority of bowhunting for deer is done with compounds. Crossbows are illegal for deer hunting in all but a handful of states and Canadian provinces. A trend toward the use of longbows among archers is similar to the move toward muzzleloading firearms among gun hunters, but not nearly as widespread.

**A successful handgun hunter with
whitetail buck.**

Among the three basic types of conventional bows, longbows represent the earliest and simplest design. Compounds are the most recent, and the recurve falls in the middle. Bows have come a long way. Newer models have gone beyond the realm of the simple stick and string, although the principle remains the same.

Each advancement has improved the bow's efficiency for hunting. The step from straight bows to recurves wasn't as dramatic as the jump from recurves to compounds, but it was still a step ahead. Curved design of the limbs on recurves resulted in shorter bows. Both wood and fiberglass eventually went into the manufacture of recurves, making them stronger and more efficient than the all-wood longbows. With both of these styles of bows, their peak weight is reached at full draw.

On compounds, peak weight is experienced at the beginning of the draw. At full draw the archer is holding a fraction of the bow's peak weight. The reduction can be from 35 to 65 percent. From one-half to two-thirds of the way back the reduction can be felt at the bow's "breaking point." What happens at that point is the pulleys "roll over."

This feature reduces the amount of effort necessary to hold the bow at full draw, which is one of the biggest advantages of the compound over recurves. More accurate shots are the end result.

Arrows released from compound bows generally travel faster, have a

From left: compound bow, recurve bow, and longbow.

flatter trajectory, and have more penetration power than shafts shot from a comparable-draw-weight recurve. Another advantage the more sophisticated compounds have over any previous type of bow is their draw weight can be adjusted. Some can be adjusted over a range of ten pounds of pull; others can be varied by fifteen pounds.

Most compounds are fitted with two round or cam-shaped pulleys and an arrow rest in the sight window. Some of them, however, called overdraw bows, are modified with an arrow rest behind the sight window rather than in it. This modification allows the use of shorter, lighter arrows than possible with conventional compounds, resulting in faster arrow speeds and flatter trajectories. Release aids are recommended for use with overdraw bows because consistently smooth releases are a must.

Compounds with cam-shaped pulleys generate faster arrow speed than round wheels, but can be a little harder to draw because the string has to be pulled back farther before power cams roll over. Round wheel compounds are the smoothest and easiest to draw and that's the type I now use for hunting after using a cam bow for a number of years.

Hunters who get a compound bow and don't know how to tune it should have someone knowledgeable check it for them. A compound that is not tuned is difficult to shoot properly. While you are at it, have the draw weight checked to be sure it is accurate. The actual draw weight of a bow sometimes varies from what it is labeled as.

The limbs on most compounds are made of laminated wood and fiberglass, but some models have all-fiberglass limbs. Fiberglass limbs are not the best for hunting since fiberglass expands and contracts with changes in temperature. Ray Sischo, a local archery shop owner, explained that with fiberglass limbs "one day you might have a forty-pounder and the next a forty-two-pounder."

A compound that has a draw weight of at least forty-five pounds is more than adequate for deer hunting. Heavier bows up to sixty-pound pull are better yet, but I wouldn't recommend that a beginning bowhunter start out at fifty or sixty pounds. Shooting a bow is more physical than firing a rifle. Poor shooting habits can develop by starting out with a bow that is too heavy. Muscles used in drawing a bow are seldom used for anything else; consequently, they should be developed gradually.

A compound that can be adjusted from forty to fifty pounds or from forty-five to sixty pounds is perfect for the beginning bowhunter. Most states have draw-weight minimums of forty-pound pull. Forty-pound-pull bows will kill deer, but a forty-five pounder is a much better choice for hunters — with the exception of youngsters and some women who may have difficulty with that draw weight.

Recurves or longbows with forty-five-pound-pull draw weights and heavier are okay for deer hunting, too. Recurves had a couple of advantages over compounds when the newer bows first hit the market: they were less expensive and lighter than compounds. In many cases recurves can still be purchased for less than compounds and are lighter in weight, but these considerations aren't as important as they used to be. The advantages compounds have over recurves overshadow them to some extent. The only reason many recurves have retained lower price tags than compounds is because they wouldn't sell otherwise.

As with compounds, the laminated wood-and-fiberglass bows are superior to all-fiberglass models. Some recurves are available in take-down models. These are convenient for travel in airplanes or buses, or when packing into a remote area on horseback. Interchangeable limbs can be purchased for take-downs that vary draw weight. This feature is similar to changing weights on compounds, but it is closer to buying separate bows for each draw weight.

Recurves that are at least sixty inches long are better for deer hunting than shorter models. Recurves are usually unstrung when not in use. A bow stringer is best for this purpose. The through-the-leg method of stringing and unstringing bows is responsible for twisting bow limbs if not done properly. Compound bows remain strung.

Regardless of the type of bow purchased for deer hunting, be sure to get one to correspond to your draw length. An average draw length is twenty-eight inches. Some archers only reach twenty-six inches, however, and others come back thirty inches or more. Draw length depends on the individual's arm length. If interested in buying your first bow for deer hunting, try to get one from a shop where personalized service is given. An alternative would be to have a knowledgeable bowhunter help you pick out a bow suited to your draw length.

Arrows are designed to match the various draw weights of bows. The proper combination of arrow and bow is important. A rifleman wouldn't think of trying to fire a .30-30 round in his .30-06. Neither should an archer consider shooting an arrow designed for a sixty-pound-pull bow from his forty-five-pounder.

Shafts are made with a number of materials, including wood (cedar), aluminum, and carbon. Aluminum shafts are the most popular for hunting due to their uniformity, and they aren't subject to warping like wood. Quality cedar arrows can be shot with compound bows, but are most often used with recurves and longbows.

AFC is one of the major manufacturers of carbon arrow shafts and they have arrow selection charts to help hunters choose the correct size. Their chart shows that size 2200 shafts would be the best choice for use with my sixty-pound-pull compound. Arrows in size 2400 are recommended for hunters shooting sixty-pound recurves. Information about AFC shafts can be obtained by writing the company at Highway 52 South, Chatfield, MN 55923-9797.

Carbon shafts are slimmer than those made of aluminum, so hunters who will be switching to them may need a new quiver or have to adapt the one they already have. Those who have quivers made by Bear can obtain an accessory from the company that will make the switch quick and easy.

Easton has an arrow selection chart for aluminum shafts that clearly shows what sizes to choose for recurve and compound bows with respect to draw weight. The weight of broadheads you will be hunting with is also important in determining which arrows to use; this variable is also shown in Easton's chart. Most archery dealers have copies of this chart for their customers' reference.

A variety of broadheads are adequate for deer hunting. The trend is toward heads on which factory-sharpened inserts are used for all cutting edges. Examples of this type of broadhead that are good choices are Satellites, Savoras, Razorbak models 4 and 5, Rocky Mountain, and several models made by Bear Archery.

Among heads that require sharpening, I prefer the Bear Super Razor-head, Zwickey Black Diamond Deltas, and Rothhaar Snuffers. The first two have razorblade inserts, in addition to the main head, which has two cutting edges. Snuffers have big heads with three blades and should only be used with bows pulling sixty pounds or more.

Regardless of the style of broadhead you use, make sure it is *sharp*; sharp enough to shave the hair on your arm. Broadheads that rely completely on razor inserts will be sharp when purchased. Other types must be sharpened with a file or stone. At least one kit that is excellent for sharpening broadheads is on the market. It is manufactured by Razor Edge Systems, P.O. Box 150, Ely, MN 55731 (218-365-6419).

Some hunting heads perform better with one type of bow than another, so be sure to try those you intend to hunt with well ahead of the season. Arrows may fly differently with broadheads than with field points, so be sure your bow is sighted in with broadheads before hunting deer.

Plastic fletching is better for hunting arrows than feathers. Plastic doesn't get wet in rain and is also quieter. Plastic-fletched arrows must be shot from fingerlike arrow rests made of plastic or coiled wire. Feathers can be shot accurately from a shelf rest.

A quiver will be needed to carry hunting arrows. Back, belt, and bow quivers are the three basic types for hunting. I personally prefer those that can be attached directly to the bow by clamps or screws. Extra arrows are always at hand when needed. Whichever a bowhunter chooses, he should make sure the area where broadheads rest in the quiver is covered. This protects the cutting edges from getting dulled on brush and protects the hunter from accidentally cutting himself.

Bow shooters will also need an arm guard to protect the forearm from the occasional slap of the bowstring and to keep loose sleeves from interfering with the string. A shooting glove or tab for fingers with which to grip the string is required, too. Another of the target archer's innovations, releases, are used by some hunting archers. Mechanical releases are not legal for hunting in some states.

Mastering a bow and arrow takes more time and practice than mastering firearms. Nonetheless, the effort can be well worthwhile. Hunting deer with archery equipment can be more satisfying and challenging than hunting with any other type of weapon. Bow deer seasons are often longer than firearms hunts, which increases the hunter's time afield. One of the best ways to learn to shoot a bow and arrow properly is to read all you can on the subject and join a local archery club. Established shooters are always more than willing to give beginners pointers.

Bows don't normally require much attention to keep them in working order. The pulleys on compounds can be oiled occasionally, but that is about it. A light coating once a year should do the trick. Broadheads can be protected from rust by coating them with Vaseline.

The arrow this archer is retrieving after a miss will have to be sharpened before it is used again because it will have been dulled by rocks and sand. Note the back quiver this hunter is carrying. It is covered with deer hide to make it quiet.

Firearms should be cleaned on a regular basis, especially black-powder guns. The barrels of muzzleloading rifles pick up so much residue that loading them becomes difficult after they have been fired a number of times. Dirty bores aren't as much of a problem with modern rifles, shotguns, and handguns, but they still require care.

My dad impressed upon his two sons the importance of gun care as soon as they were old enough to hunt. After returning home from a day of hunting we had to look after our guns before anything else. If they had been fired, barrels were cleaned inside and wiped with an oily rag on the outside. Unfired guns were simply wiped down and then put away. The procedure took a matter of minutes.

I still believe it is a good idea to look after a gun each time it is used, especially if it is wet from rain or snow. After wet days in the field, barrels should be cleaned even if the gun wasn't fired during the day. Sometimes moisture gets in at the muzzle. A good way to keep rain and snow out of

I run hot water through a muzzleloader barrel, the first step in cleaning. The rag around the barrel protects my hand from the heat.

the barrel of a deer gun is to put a piece of tape over the muzzle. This doesn't affect accuracy and isn't dangerous.

To clean the bore of a modern gun simply run a wire brush with solvent on it through, then wipe clean with a couple of patches. Try to wipe all exposed metal parts with an oily rag before putting guns away.

Front-loading barrels must be cleaned with hot, soapy water (a mild soap such as Ivory is good). What I usually do is pour a pitcher of hot water down my muzzleloader barrel. That drains a lot of the black-powder residue. Then I submerge the nipple end in a bucket of soapy water and work a 12-gauge shotgun-cleaning rod with a patch up and down. Once the barrel is clean I use two or three patches to dry it completely.

A light coating of oil goes on the exterior surfaces of the gun. After cleaning is complete, I usually snap a couple of percussion caps to make sure the barrel is dry.

When deer hunting away from home, try to remember to bring a gun-cleaning kit along. Rusty Duck manufactures a perfect kit for hunters, with brushes and patches for cleaning both rifles and shotguns. The kits come complete with solvent and lubricant.

11

Sights

Sights are an integral part of any gun and many bows used for deer hunting.

For firearms there are two basic types of sights: iron and telescopic. Scopes are the most widely used because of their adaptability for many hunting situations. They have several advantages over iron sights: target and sights are visible on one plane; the target is usually magnified; and scopes have the ability to gather light under low light conditions. Most scope eyepieces are circular, but wide-field models that are oblong are also available.

The field of view a hunter has through a scope decreases as its magnification increases. For this reason low powers from 1.5X to 4X are best for close shots and finding running deer in the glass. Higher magnifications are best used for medium- to long-range shots and looking for antlers on deer that can't be seen clearly with the naked eye.

Telescopic sights are available in either fixed power or variable models, with a selection of reticles. Variables are the most versatile. The selection of variables includes 1.5X-4X, 2.5X-7X, and 3X-9X. For hunters who do a lot of still-hunting and tracking or want a scope for their shotgun, the low-power variable is tops. Stand hunters who frequent open country would be better off with the higher magnification variables.

When hunting it is best to keep variables on the lowest power. If a deer is spotted that you want to get a better look at, crank up the power then. Try to remember to crank it back down after the higher magnification is no longer needed. I made the mistake of not doing that one time and missed a buck because of it.

While on a stand I spotted a deer about 150 yards away. I cranked the power on my scope from 3X all the way up to 9X to look at its head. It was a doe. Some time later a buck came hot-footing by me no more than thirty yards away. My field of view was so small at that range with the scope still on nine power I couldn't find him in it. He was out of sight before I realized what the problem was.

Fixed-power scopes are generally less expensive than variables. Good choices for rifles or shotguns are 2X, 2.5X, or 4X. Handgun scopes come in 1.3X, 1.7X, and 2.5X.

Crosshairs are the most popular scope reticle. The duplex or tapered variety ranks on top, followed by coarse crosshairs, and dot types. Fine crosshairs are difficult to see in poor light, which makes them a poor choice for deer hunting.

Scope covers are a must for rainy or snowy days. I prefer see-throughs that permit aiming with them in place. I leave them on all the time. A magazine article I read said using clear lens covers is a bad idea, however. It said they reduce image clarity and light gathering qualities of the scope, and more important, change the point of impact. I haven't noticed any problems with my scoped rifles on which the caps were used; maybe because they were sighted in with the covers in place. Hunters should test the accuracy of their scopes both with covers on and off to see if there is a difference, if they wish to use clear types. In the event poorer results are achieved with covers in place, plan on removing them to shoot whenever possible. Remember: clear caps are not made for quick, easy removal.

Lens covers for scopes that are designed to flip up and out of the way with the touch of a finger are the fastest to remove. They are manufactured by Butler Creek Corporation, P.O. Box GG, Jackson Hole, WY 83001. These aren't available in a see-through style.

The type of rifle or shotgun a scope is put on dictates whether it will be mounted on the side or on top. Beyond that, there are mounts that flip to the side, those that are mounted high so iron sights can be seen under them, low mounts, and those that can be detached quickly. One mount is as good as another as long as it is solidly anchored and the shooter can see through the scope properly.

I use low mounts that can't be detached quickly because I have faith in the scopes on my rifles. They have never let me down. The incident mentioned earlier about not getting a shot at a buck because my scope was on high power was my fault, not the scope's. The only situation I've encountered where a scope would have been useless if a shot were offered is when looking directly into the sun. I always avoid putting myself in a position where aiming at a deer into the sun would be required.

I will admit scope mounts that provide for quick conversion to iron-sight use have their place. If something happened to a scope on a hunting trip rendering it temporarily or permanently useless, such a mount would prove invaluable. Fortunately, I haven't been in such a situation. On deer hunting trips away from home I sometimes carry a spare rifle.

Scope users who have flip-over or quick-detachable mounts should make sure that after using iron sights the scope is flipped back or remounted the way it originally was. If it isn't aligned properly, the point of impact will be changed and the next shot taken with the scope probably won't go where it ought to. Marks of some sort can be used as guidelines to make sure the scope is always repositioned properly.

It is best to have a gunsmith or dealer mount a scope unless you have done it before. Set screws must be cinched down tight so recoil won't jar them loose. If you do the mounting yourself, use a screwdriver that fits the screws properly. Also, put some Loctite or varnish on the screw threads just before putting them in as added insurance against their loosening.

A number of years ago, one of my brothers-in-law, Bruce Dupras, bought a new rifle and scope. I advised him to have a local sport shop mount the scope. He didn't listen. Bruce went through more than a box of shells on his first trip to the range trying to sight in his rifle before he realized the scope was loose.

Most rifles and handguns come with iron or open sights. Hunters who can't afford a scope are stuck with them. They are not all that bad, though. Some deer hunters even prefer iron sights over the telescopic variety. A rifle is lighter with iron than glass, and in many cases can be aimed faster. Iron sights are not made for long-range shooting, however. They perform best on deer at distances under 100 yards.

In my opinion, a receiver or peep sight is superior to the conventional rear sight for deer hunting. The eye automatically centers the front sight in the aperture for accurate, quick sighting. Since the peep is close to the eye, it will be out of focus, as it should be; and the shooter will have only two planes to try to focus on (the front sight and target) as opposed to three points of focus when a conventional rear sight is used. Additionally, peep sights don't block parts of deer from the shooter's view as other rear sights do.

It is best to unscrew the eyepiece on peep sights and use the larger hole for hunting.

Rear sights that are standard equipment on rifles and handguns vary, but most are notched in the shape of a U or V. The U on some sights is squared off; others are rounded. I prefer a notch as small as possible in the round-bottomed U. Rear sights that have a triangular-shaped mark on the surface facing the shooter make it easier to find the center for aligning the front sight.

Front sights come in bead, blade, or post varieties. I like the bead. Some front sights are hooded to block out side lighting. I don't like them

Here are two types of receiver or peep sights. They are great for quick aiming.

A hunter takes aim at a target range with an iron-sighted handgun.

because they reduce light in low-light situations. Hoods are also distract-
ing to me. They can usually be slipped off easily.

When buying a gun with iron sights, try aiming it to see if the sight
picture is satisfactory. If not, look for a different firearm. Regardless of the
other qualities a rifle, handgun, or slug-barreled shotgun may possess,

its effectiveness will be minimized if the sights are less than adequate for your use.

Some bowhunters don't use sights. They shoot instinctively in a fashion similar to the way a shotgunner points his gun, or the tip of their broadhead is used as a point of reference for aiming. Many archers use sights, however, as evidenced by the increasing variety of bow sights on the market. There are pins, scopes, peeps, rangefinders, and lighted sights.

As a gun hunter turned archer, I prefer a sight on my bow. It helps me to pick out a spot on a deer rather than shooting at the whole animal. Sights are especially valuable for shooting at distances beyond thirty yards. Some bowhunters shoot instinctively at ranges under thirty yards, but rely on a sight for longer shots.

Due to the poor trajectory of an arrow as compared to a rifle bullet, multiple aiming points are available on most sights. A series of pins is the most common and, I think, the best for deer hunting. The pins are usually set for distances in increments of ten yards. If a bowhunter restricts his shots at deer to within thirty yards, he may only need one or two pins.

Pendulum sights have one pin that is designed for use from tree stands. The sight swivels to adjust for the downward angle of shots.

A rear sight isn't necessary for aiming with a bow. Archers draw to the same anchor point (a corner of the mouth is the most commonly used) for every shot, which results in a consistent sight picture. Some bow shooters do use peep sights. These sights fit between strands on the bowstring. Peeps make precision shooting possible and are used primarily by target archers.

Nocking points are another feature on bows that allows for a consistent sight picture. Metal "stops" are clamped on the string, usually at a point from three-eighths to one-half inch above the arrow rest, to mark nocking points. Arrow nocks fit on the string directly under the nocking point.

Telescopic sights made for bows were also designed for target shooters, but can be used for hunting, where legal. They come in two, four, and six power. Rangefinder sights are helpful to bowhunters if they have difficulty estimating distances accurately in the field. Sometimes there isn't time to use them, though. Lighted bow sights are advantageous for seeing point-of-aim under poor light conditions, but their use is prohibited in some states.

As with any other type of sight, try to choose one for your bow that you will be happy with. Test several varieties if possible. Sights that can be securely fastened to a bow with screws are a better choice than those that must be taped in place.

Sights have to be aligned so the bullet or arrow hits where it is aimed

The best type of bow sight for hunting incorporates a series of pins that can be set for various yardages. The sight with rings is a rangefinder model and the single pin in the middle is a lighted sight.

before they will do the gun or bowhunter any good. Most iron sights are reasonably accurate as they come from the factory. Scopes mounted by dealers are usually bore-sighted. Nonetheless, be sure to shoot the rifle, shotgun, or handgun yourself to adjust the sights for your eyes and desired sight-in distance. Do it as far in advance of the opening of deer season as possible, especially in the case of a brand-new gun. Problems with guns and sights don't develop often, but if they do they should be recognized as soon as possible so they can be corrected.

One year a friend of mine ordered a deer-hunting rifle on which the firing pin broke after several rounds were fired. Fortunately, he got it months before the season and was able to get a rifle to hunt with to replace the faulty one.

Hunters who don't have access to a regular range to sight in their gun should select a location with an adequate backstop. State and provincial departments of natural resources or fish and game usually have certain areas designated for target practice. Targets can be pinned to cardboard boxes. I usually use a paper plate for a target. If shooting a scoped gun, a circular aiming point is colored in the center with a crayon or felt-tipped pen. A heavy cross is used as an aiming point for iron sights. The front sight often completely covers a circle.

When shooting a gun or sight you are not familiar with, do not start out with the target far away. If the sights are way out of whack, your bullets may hit off the paper at those distances. It is best to fire the first rounds at a target no farther than twenty-five yards away. Once the gun is on target at close range it can be fine-tuned for longer ranges.

Always shoot from the steadiest position possible when sighting in a rifle. The same goes for hunting. A benchrest where the shooter can sit down and prop his gunstock on sandbags is best. Trees, vehicles, or posts are also helpful in steadying a rifle or handgun. Try to use something such as a firm cushion, tightly rolled sleeping bag, or sandbag to rest the gunstock on when shooting from a vehicle. The prone position with a rest is also good for accurate placement of shots. A notched cardboard or wooden box makes a good rest for shooting prone.

Slings increase accuracy from a sitting or offhand position. To get into a sling if you shoot right-handed, slip your left arm through with the rifle pointed upward and bring the strap as far back as it will go under your arm. As the rifle is lowered twist the left hand back and through the sling again. Grip the forend so the strap lies across the back of the hand. The strap should feel tight across the chest. If it is loose, pull the left hand back. When using a sling in a sitting position, legs should be spread so elbows can rest on knees.

Some sort of ear protection, plugs or muffs, is invaluable for target practice.

When sighting in a firearm, sight adjustments should be made on the basis of three-shot groups. The center of the group should be the point of correction. Telescopic sights are the easiest to sight in. The simplest way to align the crosshairs is to move them to the center of the group by turning windage and elevation knobs. To do this, the gun must be resting solidly on sandbags, lying in a notched box, or clamped in place.

Gun and scope should remain in the same position throughout the process. First, fire three shots with the crosshairs on the bull's eye. Then check to see where the center of the group is. If magnification of the scope isn't great enough to see the center, darken the spot with a pen or crayon. Next, turn windage and elevation knobs while looking through the glass so the crosshairs move across the target to that point.

Once the adjustments are complete, another group should be fired to test the accuracy of the new setting. If the procedure is done properly, slugs should hit close to where they are aimed.

To get consistent groups, try to squeeze the trigger on each shot. If shots are erratic, one of several things are probably happening. Either the

Two hunters sight in a rifle for deer hunting using a steady rest and ear muffs.

With his scoped rifle in a notched cardboard box, this hunter is moving crosshairs to the center of his three-shot group to sight it in.

shooter is jerking the trigger, his or her position isn't steady, or the scope is not mounted solidly. Set screws can work loose from the recoil of one or two rounds if they aren't installed properly. It sometimes helps me to get the feel of a trigger by dry-firing a gun several times before loading the firearm.

When holding a scoped gun in a steady position isn't possible, sight correction will have to be determined by measurements. Once a group has been fired, measure the distance from its center to the center of the target. Then scope adjustment dials can be turned an appropriate number of clicks or marks. Each calibration usually represents a shift in point of impact of an inch or less at 100 yards. How the dials are calibrated is usually specified inside dial covers, on the dials, or in the instructions that come with the scope.

Some scope adjustments are calibrated in minutes of angle. Don't let that confuse you. If each mark moves point-of-impact one minute of angle, at 100 yards the point of impact will be shifted one inch. The shift will only be one-half inch at 50 yards and one-fourth inch at 25 yards.

Let's look at an example. Say the center of your group was two inches high and 3½ inches to the right at 25 yards and your scope adjustments are calibrated in half-minutes of angle (that means each mark moves point-of-impact one-half inch at 100 yards). At 25 yards the shift would be one-fourth of that, or one-eighth of an inch. To adjust the crosshairs the elevation knob would have to be turned 16 clicks down (eight per inch) and the windage dial 28 to the left.

Iron sights are most often adjusted by moving the rear one whether it is a peep or the notched variety. Many types are designed to make changes to both windage and elevation easy. Set screws often control them. Some older styles of iron sights (there are still plenty of them in use) simply made allowances for shifts in elevation. Much effort was necessary to adjust for windage by pounding them (either front or rear right or left) with a punch made of copper, brass, or nylon and a soft mallet. Shims of varying widths were required under one side or the other of some peep sights to change their right/left alignment.

It isn't as easy to determine exactly how far to move open sights as it is with scopes. The best approach is to shoot a group and make moderate corrections if any are necessary. If the next group is still off, the shooter should have a good idea how much to move the sights a second time to finalize adjustments.

Point-of-impact will shift the same direction the rear sight is moved. If the center of a group is high, for example, the rear sight must be lowered. When grouping to the right, the rear sight should be moved to the left. A change in the front sight will move point-of-impact the opposite direction. If the bead is moved left, bullets will hit farther to the right than

Gene Lengsfeld practices with a Golden Eagle bow. "Follow the arrow" when adjusting bow sights.

they did before the adjustment.

Aligning a bow sight works the same way as adjusting the front sight of a gun. The general rule is to "follow the arrow." In other words, if your arrows are grouping to the left of center, the sight should be moved to the left. Point-of-impact will be moved to the right. If arrows hit high, raise the sight and the shafts will strike lower.

Bow sights can be moved accidentally or jarred out of place easier than gun sights. I have found that it is beneficial to mark the positions of pins once they're set for desired yardages. Then if they are moved, they can be easily repositioned.

Peep sights for bows are situated on the string in a position that will conform at full draw to the shooter's eye.

Most guns or bows only have to be sighted in once, as long as the same loads and shafts are used. Alignment of the sights should be checked every year before hunting season, however, just as a precaution. Your eyesight may have changed in the course of a year or something could have happened to the sights.

Always sight a gun or bow in with the same shells, load, or arrows you will be hunting with. A change in brand, bullet weight, powder charge, shaft composition, or type of broadhead will change the point-of-impact.

Deer rifles used in brush country should be sighted in for 50 or 100 yards. Flat-shooting rifles can be sighted in for 200 to 250 yards by adjusting sights so bullets hit about an inch high at 100 yards. Shotgunners who use slugs, black-powder shooters, and handgunners may want to sight in for 50 or 75 yards. Maximum yardages most bowhunters ready sights for are from 50 to 60 yards. They will also have pins set for closer distances. Gun hunters should know where their bullets, round balls, or slugs hit at a variety of ranges, too. Ballistics tables available from ammunition manufacturers give shooters a good idea how much bullet drop to expect at distances beyond 100 yards if test-firing at those yardages isn't possible.

Hunters who use buckshot in a shotgun with a simple sight plane may laugh at the idea of sighting in with their loads. True, sight adjustment isn't possible, but some shotguns pattern high, low, left, or right of center. If so, the situation can be compensated for when shooting at a deer. Buckshot users will have to try their loads on paper to determine what kind of a pattern they are getting. Several types of buckshot should be test-fired at targets to see which one gives the tightest pattern.

All deer hunters should be aware that shots taken at an uphill or downhill angle are different from those taken on a level. Bullets and arrows have a tendency to hit higher than normal when shooting either up or down. Exactly how much higher depends on the circumstances. It is a good idea to try some shots uphill or downhill to get a feel for the situation.

One of the first mule deer I shot was at a steep downhill angle. The buck was bedded about 200 yards below me. To compensate for the angle, I held the crosshairs low on his shoulder and squeezed a shot off. He jumped to his feet at the shot, apparently untouched. I held lower on the second shot and could see daylight between my crosshairs and the bottom of his shoulder when I touched it off. That one broke his back!

The time taken to learn where a gun or bow will hit at various distances and under different circumstances gives deer hunters confidence that will help when a shot is offered at a whitetail or mule deer. There won't be a bull's eye or X to mark a spot to aim at, though. Hunters will have to know what point of the anatomy to try for: the spot where a hit will bring the surest, cleanest kill.

Without question, the best all-around hit on a deer is in the lungs. This is because they are vital organs, present a relatively large target, and their location is easy to determine. A deer hit in the lungs with a projectile from any of the weapons discussed in this book is not going to go far.

The lungs fill a large part of the chest cavity. On broadside to slightly angling-away shots, aim for a spot directly behind the front leg, in the

A lung shot is the best for sure, quick kills on deer. An X marks the spot for a lung hit. The heart is low in the chest where the circle is.

middle of the body. Even if the shot strays one way or the other, the hit will be fatal. A bullet or arrow that enters behind the front leg will ruin no meat. Shot placement on whitetails or mule deer that are angling away at a sharp angle should also be placed in the middle of the body and behind the front leg, on a line with the opposite shoulder.

Gun hunters should try for the back of the neck on deer facing directly away from them, unless the hunter is in an elevated stand. From a tree, hunters should attempt to hit between a deer's shoulder blades in the middle of the back. The backbone will be broken if you are on target; the lungs are to either side. This type of shot is not recommended for bow-hunters because the potential of making a non-fatal hit is high due to the presence of heavy bones.

Ground-based gun hunters can bring a deer down by hitting between the hams below the base of the tail. This shot is only recommended for long guns with good penetration power.

My brother Bruce dropped a dandy eight-point whitetail with a rear-end shot one year. Bruce missed an angling shot first, but when the buck turned straight away he was on target. His 150-grain .30-30 slug piled the

Here is where to aim on a deer angling toward you.

deer up on the spot. The bullet ranged forward into the lungs. There wasn't a speck of meat ruined, either.

Hunters faced with shots at whitetails or mule deer angling toward them should try for the area between the shoulder and chest.

When a deer is facing the hunter, aim for the base of the neck. A shot that goes high will very likely break the animal's neck. An arrow that strikes too low might hit the brisket, which could cause little or no damage. It is a different story if the shaft slips in on either side of the brisket. A low hit with lead isn't as critical as with an arrow.

A heart shot is always fatal, but in contrast to the lungs, the heart is a small target. The heart is lower in the chest than most hunters realize, too.

This buck won't go far, if at all, if hit behind the shoulder where the X is. This hit will not ruin meat.

A hit at either of these spots should bring this buck down for keeps.

There is a crease of skin on the back of the front leg where it joins the body that is a good aiming point for those who want to try for the heart.

Properly placed neck shots kill immediately. The only problem here is that the strike zone is narrow. A hit to either side of the vertebrae can wound.

Intentionally aiming at the head is worse than trying for the neck. A deer's brain is small, the potential for wounding great.

Whenever taking a shot at a deer, do so from the steadiest position possible. If there is time, use a rest. At least try to shoot from a sitting position. A sling helps steady aim.

If your sights are on, if you know where to aim, and if you can hit where you aim, you will get that whitetail or mule deer. Each of these considerations is equally important. They all must come together to make consistent kills.

Hunters should always be sure a deer that is down is dead before dropping their guard. If the whitetail or mulie shows any signs of life, shoot again. If you are close to the animal, a neck shot is best. It is better to be safe than sorry. I've heard too many accounts of supposedly dead deer getting up and running off. A dead deer's eyes will be dull, lifeless, and open.

12

Cameras

An adequate camera and lens can make deer hunting a year-round pursuit. There are no seasons, bag limits, or sex restrictions when you are after deer with a camera. Camera "hunters" don't even need a license.

Camera hunting is a logical offshoot for bowhunters or gun hunters interested in "shooting" deer during winter, spring, and summer. A camera is the only "weapon" available to people who want to bag whitetails and mule deer without killing the animals.

Deer hunting with a camera is every bit as challenging as trying for one with bow and arrow. Best results with both are obtained at close range. For this reason the camera user often has to be a skillful hunter, at least when after wild deer. Penned, caged, or tame whitetails and mulies are fair game for deer-fancying shutterbugs, too. Hunting skill isn't necessary to get within range of these animals.

Single-lens reflex (SLR) 35 mm cameras are the best choice for photographing deer. The photographer sees exactly what he or she is shooting with a 35 mm because viewing is done through the lens. It is similar to looking through a rifle scope. Most other cameras have viewfinders offset from lenses. These will be discussed later in this chapter.

Twin-lens reflex (TLR) cameras can also be used for capturing deer on film. As the name implies, these cameras have two lenses. One is for viewing and focusing, the other for taking photos. Twin-lens cameras are generally heavier, more awkward, and slower than 35s.

SLR and TLR cameras have one feature in common that makes them suitable for hunting deer: they can be fitted with a variety of lenses. Lenses

I take a break from photographing a one-antlered buck at a feeder.

range from wide-angles to telephotos. Wide-angle lenses make subjects look farther away and smaller than they do to the naked eye. Telephotos increase the size or magnify subjects and bring them closer. A normal lens is the same magnification as the human eye. In other words, a subject viewed through a normal lens will appear approximately the same as it would without looking through a camera.

Normal lenses for 35 mm cameras are usually 50 mm. A 25 mm wide-angle would decrease the size of subjects by one-half. Such a lens will also make the subject look twice as far away as when viewed with a normal lens. A telephoto that is 200 mm will magnify subjects four times and make them look closer.

Cameras other than SLRs and TLRs usually come with unremove-able lenses. They are often wide-angle or normal magnification. Telephoto lenses are musts for obtaining satisfactory photos of deer. The most popu-lar sizes for "shooting" deer are 135, 200, 300, and 400. Lenses can be purchased that have either fixed magnifications or a range of magnifica-tions. The latter types are called zoom lenses.

Before getting into lenses further let's take a closer look at 35 mm SLR cameras in general. To beginning photographers, especially those familiar with Instamatics, SLRs often look complicated. The various numbered dials give them that appearance. Actually, 35s are not difficult to use. In fact, many of the new 35 mm SLRs are as easy to use as Instamatics, but it's still important to understand how an SLR functions.

It sometimes helps to consider the lens and camera body as separate entities. The only operation to worry about on the camera body itself, besides advancing the film and pressing the shutter, is setting shutter speed. Shutter speed is controlled by a dial with numbers on it that generally increase by a multiplication factor of two: 2, 4, 8, 16, 30, 60, 125, 250, and 500. Some cameras go as high as 1,000, or more.

These numbers represent the fractions of a second it takes for the camera shutter to open and close. A setting of 60, for instance, represents a shutter speed of 1/60 of a second and 250 is 1/250 of a second. The larger the number, the faster the shutter speed. Which setting to use depends on the subject, assuming there is sufficient light. A moderate shutter speed of 60 or 125 is fine if the subject is stationary. Faster shutter speeds, 250 and 500, are useful to stop the action when the subject is in motion.

There are two adjustments that must be made on camera lenses in preparation for taking pictures. The first is setting the diaphragm opening. Diaphragms can be opened or closed to adjust for varying light conditions. There is a moveable ring around each lens that controls diaphragm openings. Each aperture is designated by a number on the ring called an f-stop. The smaller the number, the larger the diaphragm opening will be.

Sixteen, for example, indicates a small opening. On the other hand, the number 1.8 reflects a large aperture. In effect, the amount of light present will determine what f-stop should be used. Small-numbered f-stops are best for days when light is poor and large-numbered stops are appropriate for bright days.

The other adjustment necessary on lenses is focus. Focusing is accomplished by looking through the viewfinder and turning the focus ring until the image is clear.

With camera body and lens together, taking a picture can be broken down into five steps: 1, cock the camera; 2, set the shutter speed; 3, adjust the f-stop (most SLRs have light-metering systems to enable the photographer to select the proper f-stop); 4, focus; 5, release the shutter. Fully automatic 35 mm SLR cameras now available will take care of four out of those five steps automatically. All the photographer has to do is press the shutter release after the subject is in the viewfinder.

There are a variety of reliable SLR cameras and lenses on the market. I use Canon bodies and Canon or Tamron lenses. Pentax, Nikon, and Minolta are other good makes. Good deals can usually be obtained on used equipment. When buying a new camera don't expect quality performance from the cheapest one on store shelves.

Now that the basics of using SLRs are out of the way let's get back to telephoto lenses. As the lenses increase in magnification, their light-

Telephoto lenses magnify subjects and make them look closer. Always try to focus on a deer's eye.

gathering ability usually decreases. The light-gathering ability of a lens is determined by the smallest number f-stop the diaphragm will open to.

Fast lenses will have a maximum diaphragm opening of 2.8 or larger. Slow lenses may not open any farther than 5.6 or 4.5. Fast lenses can be used in situations where light conditions are poor, and the lighting has to be good where slow lenses are employed.

My two favorites in telephotos are the 135 and 300. My 135 is an f 2 lens and my 300 is an f 2.8, both of which are made by Canon. Some photographers who regularly shoot deer swear by 400s, and even 600s.

Lens extenders called doublers can be used to double the magnification of telephotos. Doublers fit between the camera body and regular lens. Those I have used yielded poor results. Extremely good light is necessary to use lens extenders because they reduce the light-gathering ability of lenses. Best results are obtained with extenders made by your camera's manufacturer.

The weight of telephoto lenses increases in proportion to magnification. A 300 mm is generally heavier than a 200 mm, and a 400 mm is heavier than either of the others. This is an important consideration when it comes to taking photos of deer. The heavier a lens, the less likely it is that a photographer will be able to take good pictures when holding camera and lens by hand. Weight induces wobbling, which blurs pictures.

Fast shutter speeds are often enough to offset the jiggles caused by hand-holding a telephoto. It is even better to rest a camera mounted with a long lens against a tree, fence post, car, or anything else to steady it. A tripod is better yet for shooting with telephotos. Tripods enable camera deer hunters to get satisfactory shots of deer with a telephoto at low shutter speeds that are sometimes necessary in the morning and evening when light is poor.

A couple of general rules that apply to shooting deer with a camera are to use a tripod whenever possible and shoot at the fastest shutter speed the available light will allow. Try to press the shutter release smoothly, too, as you would squeeze the trigger of a rifle. Punching the release will increase the chances of camera movement, which can blur pictures.

Always try to focus on the eyes of a deer before taking its picture. The eyes are the center of attention. If they are in focus, the photo will be acceptable. And above all else, take a number of exposures of your subject, if possible. Don't be satisfied with one or two shots. Those extra exposures can make the difference between mediocre and excellent results. It only takes one good shot to make a photo session with deer worthwhile in terms of getting a "trophy." The one you didn't take may have been the best.

Vary your exposure, too. Light meters sometimes read the background rather than the subject. This is especially true when shooting with snow, water, or sky in the background. If time permits, take a couple of exposures on what appears to be the right setting; then take a couple each at one stop over and one stop under that. This is called bracketing. It almost guarantees that at least a pair of shots will be properly exposed. Sometimes underexposed or overexposed subjects produce interesting effects. Silhouettes are prime examples of underexposed photos that can be appealing.

A beginning camera hunter shouldn't expect to get topnotch results the first time out. Becoming proficient with a camera takes practice, just as proficiency with a gun or bow and arrow does. Zoos are perfect practice ranges for deer photographers. Try to expose several rolls of film at a zoo before heading into the field. It helps to jot down f-stops and shutter speeds used during practice sessions to evaluate the results when the film is developed.

Silhouette of a whitetail buck in Michigan.

Overexposed pictures are the result of too much light striking the film. Underexposures mean there wasn't enough light. Fuzzy or blurred photos are the result of poor focusing or camera movement caused by a too slow shutter speed or an unsteady lens.

Unlike hunting with gun or bow, success with a camera is subject to the user's interpretation. Deer successfully bagged with a bullet or arrow are dead. There is no in-between. Images of deer shot with a camera are imprinted on film. The images can be distant, close-up, in focus, out of focus, fuzzy, sharp, underexposed, overexposed, or a combination of these.

From my point of view, I would consider a photo of a whitetail or mule deer that is in focus, properly exposed, and reasonably close a successful shot. Anything else would be a miss. I can remember times, however, when I was happy with any image of a deer on film.

The quality of a photo isn't the only factor that determines its value to the photographer. Memories that go with it add their special appeal to exposures of deer. A photo or slide that is poor quality may be valuable (a trophy) if it brings to mind pleasant or humorous memories of the circumstances under which the shot was obtained.

Film is rated according to ISO (it used to be ASA), which refers to its light absorbing properties. Low-numbered ISO films require more light to expose properly than high-numbered ISO films. Low ISO films exhibit less grain and usually give better quality enlargements than high ISO films.

Color slide film is the best choice for photographing deer. It is less expensive to have processed than print film. Additionally, prints, both black-and-white and color, can be made from good slides. Kodak slide film comes in ISO 25, 64, 200, and 400. The 400 film can also be used at 800 ISO ("pushed") under poor lighting conditions to enable you to simply take a photo or to obtain faster shutter speeds than would normally be possible. If you push your film to a higher ISO, be sure to tell the lab so it can be properly processed.

Kodak film is about the best made. They make Kodachrome and Ektachrome slide film. Kodachrome accents reds. Ektachrome is a blue film. Kodachrome comes in ISO 25, 64, and 200. The Ektachromes are available in 64, 200, and 400. I use Kodachrome 200 more than any other type.

Fujichrome 100 is also a good slide film. It can be pushed to 200 ISO.

The ISO dial on 35 mm cameras should be set to correspond with the film being used. This adjusts the camera's light meter.

Try to load film in your camera properly. Instructions that come with the film will explain how. Before closing the camera cover make sure the film advances as it is supposed to by pressing the shutter and cocking the camera. The rewind knob should turn when advancing the film after taking several exposures. If it doesn't, the film isn't advancing.

Hunters who are successful in bagging a deer during the fall hunting season frequently want to get pictures of themselves with their kill. SLR 35s with a normal or wide-angle lens are fine for this use. Other cameras, such as Instamatics and rangefinder 35s, can also be used in these situations.

It isn't possible to look through the lens or interchange lenses with rangefinder 35 mm cameras. Otherwise their use is similar to SLRs. Some rangefinders have automatic lighting adjustments and crude focusing systems, too.

Instamatics and fully automatic 35s are the simplest cameras to use, even though some models are rather sophisticated. All there is to do with these is center the subject in the viewfinder and shoot. Polaroid cameras are also easy to use, but they seldom function properly outside, except when the weather is warm.

The best deer-kill photos are available immediately after the kill; so hunters should try to carry a camera with them. The happy expression of a successful deer hunter is bound to be more appealing at that time than a forced grin later. A natural setting also adds a great deal more to such a picture than a cluttered yard, basement, or a deer-on-the-car pose.

Try to get in close for photos of hunters with their deer. Close-ups are often more dramatic than exposures taken from a distance that lack detail. Too much background can detract from the subject. Before taking close-ups, remember to make sure the deer's tongue is in its mouth. Wiping off excess blood will make the photo look less gruesome, too.

Due to the poor light conditions whitetails and mulies are frequently shot in, it is a good idea to carry a flash attachment if your camera doesn't have a built-in flash. Without a flash it might not be possible to capture that happy moment on film.

Deer hunters who are alone when they make a kill can still get photos. Some Instamatics and most 35s have self-timers. Simply set the deer up where you want it, leaving room for yourself in front of or behind the animal. To frame and focus the photo, use a stick with a hat on it as a dummy for yourself. The camera can be set on a tripod, a backpack, a rock, or a stump.

I used a self timer to take this photo of myself and an eight-point buck I had just dropped.

Focus either on the deer or hat, then get in position. Self-timers usually give the hunter at least five seconds to get into position from the time the shutter release is pushed. For best results, I use a slow shutter speed, which allows a small lens opening, and focus on the downed deer's eye. This allows enough depth of field so that the hunter is usually also in focus.

Several things to keep in mind when taking shots of yourself are to make sure no obstructions such as grass or twigs obscure any part of the deer or yourself; when wearing a hat or cap, tip the brim up so it doesn't shade your face; and take a number of exposures at different f-stops to make sure the exposure will be correct.

13

Clothing and Equipment

Your effectiveness as a deer hunter will be determined in part by your comfort, which is directly related to the clothes you wear. The type and amount of clothing a deer hunter wears will be dictated by the weather and the type of hunting that is to be done.

Temperatures can be warm to downright hot during early fall hunts. Outer garments of cotton or cotton blends are best for such situations since cotton is light and quiet. Camouflage clothing can be purchased with shirt and pants separate or as a one-piece suit—either is perfect for bowhunting. Hunters can wear fluorescent-orange vests over the camouflage if hunting with firearms. A bright-colored cap or hat is also a good idea for warm-weather gun hunters. Camouflage hats are fine for archers, but if you buy a camo cap with a brim, it may be best to wear the hat backwards so it won't interfere with your draw.

A shirt and pair of pants or jeans can be worn under the camo outfit if it isn't too warm. Long underwear should be considered if you are hunting early mornings and evenings when temperatures are cool, especially when spending most of your time on stand. Still-hunters or drivers probably won't need longjohns until daytime temperatures are consistently cool.

There are at least four types of long underwear: fishnet, polypropylene, cotton knit, and heavy insulated. I wear knit underwear most often, but many deer hunters prefer the fishnet weave. It is a matter of personal preference based on weather conditions and hunting technique. To see which is most comfortable for you, try different types. Insulated underwear is best for cold-weather use. In extreme cold these are sometimes worn over knit or fishnet underwear.

Always try to dress in layers for deer hunting. Bring along enough garments to keep warm in the coldest weather. If it is warmer than expected, some layers can be shed. Hunters unprepared for cold thermometer readings can't put on layers they don't have.

Tennis shoes with a light pair of socks are fine for still-hunting or stalking early in the season. If thorns or cactus are a problem in your area, a light pair of leather boots might be a better choice. Rubber footwear is the ticket for walking in wet terrain. Whenever I wear out a pair of waders, I cut off the heavy boot and wear these deer hunting early in the fall. There are no laces to worry about and they are durable and light. Wool or cotton socks are satisfactory for use in early fall.

Outer garments of wool, Polar Tuff, or fleece are great for cold-weather deer hunting. Wool insulates you from the cold even when wet, and it is quiet. Polar Tuff and fleece are water resistant. Trackers, still-hunters, and drivers who won't be standing in one place long may do fine with a set of longjohns for an inner layer below the waist. Three layers should be considered for the upper body. A shirt, sweater, or light sweatshirt can be worn over a longjohn top followed by a coat or hooded sweatshirt. Outer layers should be bright-colored (red or orange is common) when gun hunting. If you are hunting in a state that requires wearing orange and your clothes are red, simply wear a fluorescent vest over the sweatshirt or coat and a fluorescent hat on your head.

Some provinces, including Saskatchewan, have specific clothing requirements, such as wearing full suits of white, red, or orange. These successful hunters chose to wear white.

Stand hunters need maximum protection from the cold, since they won't be moving. I know because I spend a lot of time on stands in cold weather, sometimes when temperatures dip below zero. My legs are covered with one or two longjohn bottoms, a pair of jeans, and wool pants. On the upper part of my body I wear a longjohn top, a shirt, a sweater, one or two sweatshirts, and a heavy coat. I sometimes top off my outfit with a snowmobile suit. The number of layers varies in accordance with the weather conditions.

When hunting with bow and arrow in snow I wear a pair of white coveralls or Realtree snow camo for camouflage. Realtree camo in either the brown or the gray pattern is worn when no snow is present. All of the outer garments I wear deer hunting are purchased in sizes that permit wearing several layers underneath. If normal-size outer layers are obtained for deer hunting, they will be tight and make it difficult to move comfortably.

I do not wear all of my clothes when walking to a stand. If I did, heavy perspiration would be inevitable and the chances of getting chilled once situated would increase. A portion of my heavy clothes are carried in

Polar Tuff garments like those I'm wearing here are great for cold weather hunting along with polar fleece and wool.

White coveralls, snow camo, or other patterns will do for camouflage when hunting in snow.

a pack until I reach my destination. I try to start heading for a place I want to sit early enough so there is no need to rush.

Something to cover the head is as important as warm clothes when sitting in cold weather. A lot of heat escapes via an uncovered head. I prefer a wool knit hat or short-billed hat, but any type will do that you are comfortable with.

A flap of wool sewn to the back of a cap or hat prevents snow from falling down a deer hunter's neck when the white stuff covers trees. As far as I know, El Harger of Munising, Michigan, originated the idea. The cap modification was explained to me by a friend of his, Andy Tingstad.

Another way to keep snow from falling down your neck is to wear a scarf. Scarves protect the front and back from cold breezes, as well as snow.

Don't wear a hood over your head if at all possible. The material covers your ears and dulls your hearing.

Some deer hunters use suspenders to hold up their pants, but I prefer a belt. I usually carry a sheath knife on it and can use my belt to drag a deer if I forget a rope. A tracking hunter I know wears a belt from six to eight inches longer than usual so he can tuck shed layers of clothes under it when he is moving on a track.

I often wear a snowmobile suit over other layers when on a stand in cold weather.

Andy Tingstad is wearing a cap with a wool flap sewn on the back to prevent snow from falling down his neck while deer hunting in snow-covered woods.

Raingear may be necessary on some deer hunts. Ponchos are fine in many cases. Two-piece outfits will keep you drier than ponchos. An orange vest should be worn over the top of raingear during gun seasons unless the raingear is orange. Wool or Polar Tuff clothing will keep hunters dry during periods of light rain or snow.

Boots with felt linings are the best I've found for keeping my feet warm in cold weather. I wear the leather-top, rubber-bottom variety. The felt absorbs perspiration. My boots, like my clothes, are purchased at least one size larger than usual to accommodate plenty of socks. I wear from three to five pairs of heavy socks to fill out my boots. After a day of hunting, be sure to remove the felt liners to let them dry. An extra pair of liners can also come in handy. Air-filled "Mickey Mouse" boots in white or black are the best for use in extremely cold weather. These boots can usually be obtained at Army/Navy surplus stores.

Rubber or leather boots are okay for deer hunting in situations where you won't be staying in one place long, such as still-hunting or tracking. Those that are light and fit snug will make it easier to "feel the ground" better, increasing the ability to walk quietly.

Hands need protection during cold weather. I wear light cotton gloves whenever possible. They are not bulky, so I can easily handle a gun, bow, or camera with them on. I usually carry two pairs in case one gets wet. I frequently stick gloved hands in my pockets to keep them warm during long waits in cold weather. Hand warmers can come in handy, too.

Bowhunters who use a three-fingered shooting glove can keep that hand warm by cutting the middle fingers off a cotton glove for that hand.

Ponchos are handy to have along on deer hunts when rain is expected.

"Mickey Mouse" boots are the warmest available for cold weather use. Note the valve for adding air.

The shooting glove can be strapped on over it. I now wear a full-fingered golf glove on my shooting hand.

Proper clothing; a gun, bow, or camera; ammunition or arrows; and a hunting license are the essentials for deer hunters. Before venturing into the field, however, hunters should slip a few additional items in pockets or a small pack. One item no deer hunter should be without is a compass. Don't just buy one, try it out to make sure it is accurate and you know how to use it.

Before going in the woods, mountains, desert, swamps, or wherever, try to take a compass reading to determine which way you are heading in and which way you will have to go to get back out. It only takes a couple of seconds.

Metal from a gun will sometimes throw a compass off, so set your gun down when taking a reading and walk a few steps away from it. When deer hunting, it is also a good idea to look at a map or carry one that shows all roads, powerlines, railroad tracks, lakes, and streams in the area you will be hunting.

When disoriented in areas that have roads or identifiable features on all sides, simply use a compass to head in one direction. You will eventually come out to someplace familiar. If you ever become totally lost in an area where the potential for finding familiar ground in one or more directions isn't likely, the best thing to do is stop where you are and build a fire. Wandering aimlessly is a waste of energy and will only make matters worse.

Deer hunters should always carry a compass and know how to use it.

To build a fire you will need matches or a lighter, which are other essentials every deer hunter should carry. Book matches are fine, but carry some in a waterproof case on the chance those in a pocket get wet. Aluminum match cases are available in sporting goods stores. I use spent shotgun shells (plastic) to keep my matches dry. Twelve-gauge and 16-gauge cases fit together snugly. It is a good idea to include a striker in a watertight container with matches. A space blanket will help hunters who are forced to spend a night in the field to stay warm. They are small when folded and lightweight, so they are handy to carry.

If the woods are wet when you want to start a fire, use the inner bark of birch trees, small twigs that grow under dense-needled pine trees, birds' nests, or unraveled threads from a sweater for tinder. The tissue or paper towels you should have with you can also be used to start a fire. Tissue can be used in other ways, too. It comes in handy if nature calls, to blow your nose, or to dry a scope lens. Paper towels can be used to wipe the inside of

These are some of the things deer hunters should carry with them. They include high-energy foods such as raisins or candy bars, a lunch, a knife, tissue, a small rope for tag, flagging, a camera, waterproof matches with a striker contained in empty shotgun shells, a flashlight, a plastic bag, a compass, and stout rope for dragging or hanging a deer.

a dressed deer carcass or bloody hands after the chore is done. Rubber gloves can be included in your gear if you want to keep hands clean and dry while dressing a deer.

Don't forget a knife to dress a whitetail or mulie with. Either pocket or sheath models are fine, as long as they are sharp. A stone or kitchen sharpener can be included with your gear if you expect to skin a deer in the field. A folding saw or hatchet is useful to open the pelvic area or quarter a deer.

A plastic bag will be useful for holding the heart and liver from that dressed buck or doe.

You should carry a flashlight to help you see before daylight or after dark. I like the two-cell models, but some hunters get by with small penlights. Carrying two lights makes sense in case one malfunctions. Regardless of the type used, be sure it has fresh batteries. It is a good idea to carry spares, too, along with extra bulbs. If you have a flashlight reserved for use during deer season, try to remember to remove the batteries or turn one backwards after you are done hunting for the year so they won't corrode.

A length of stout rope is another item you don't want to be without. It will be useful to hang or drag a mulie or a whitetail. Thin rope or a piece of wire should be included to fasten a tag to that buck or doe. A spool of string or roll of surveyor's ribbon will be useful to mark your way to or from a stand, the trail of a wounded deer, or the route to take to reach a deer left in the woods overnight.

High-energy snacks such as candy and granola bars, raisins, and brownies should be carried while deer hunting. A Thermos of coffee, bouillon, or soup can be a great pick-me-up on cold days. Also try to pack a lunch if you plan on being in the field most of the day. If you are operating out of a car or camp, you may want to return to it for lunch. If so, Thermos and sandwiches don't have to be carried with you, but try to make it a point to carry candy or raisins with you in the woods. Then you will always have them in case you don't get out of the woods when expected.

An optional item you might want to carry is a camera. Photos of a bagged buck, scenery, and camp scenes will bring back fond memories in future years. Try to remember to bring a flash unit, too. Many of the best exposures on a deer hunt will be possible in low-light situations.

Binoculars or a spotting scope are also optional, but they can be a tremendous aid in any type of deer hunting, especially in open country. Trackers should consider bringing sunglasses to wear, since staring at snow for long periods can be hard on eyes.

Bowhunters may want to include a stick of camouflage coloring for application to their shiny faces or a hood that pulls down over the face. I prefer stick camo. Visibility isn't impaired as it sometimes is with a hood. The face paint washes off without any trouble after a day of hunting.

An arrow sharpener can also come in handy in the field. A file or kitchen-knife sharpener will do for a quick touchup on heads that missed their mark.

If the weather is so warm that ticks, mosquitoes, and biting flies can be expected, insect repellent should be brought along on a deer hunt. I've

A pair of binoculars can also be useful to deer hunters.

used Ben's 100 with excellent results. The makers of this repellent manufacture mesh clothing called Bug Armor, which helps keep bothersome insects away. For more information contact the Tender Corporation, P.O. Box 290, Littleton Industrial Park, Littleton, NH 03561 (800-258-4696).

A piece of thread tied on a gun or bow, or at a stand will serve as a constant indicator of which way the wind is blowing. The least little breeze activates it. I always have a piece of thread tied to my bow quiver. A strand can be attached to the trigger guard on a gun.

Deer or predator calls can be useful at times while hunting whitetails or mule deer. A blast on them will sometimes stop a running buck long enough for a shot. Deer calls are discussed in chapter 9.

Slingshots often come in handy when hunting brushy draws. Bedded deer can be tricked into showing themselves if you flip a stone into a thicket from an observation point.

All of these items aren't necessary on a deer hunt; however, it is a good idea to get in the habit of carrying some of them for precautionary reasons. These include a compass, waterproof matches, lighter, flashlights, and raisins, candy, or granola. A rope, knife, flagging, and tissue paper are also basics for the deer hunter. You may not need these things most of the time, but the one time you do need them and don't have them, you will kick yourself.

A compass is something I seldom use unless hunting unfamiliar country. Even in new territory I often manage to get by without using one. Nonetheless, I always carry one when in the field. One morning I needed it when I least expected I would. I was hunting in familiar country, terrain I could say I knew intimately, when I got disoriented. The problem was caused by a heavy snow the night before. I simply couldn't get my bearings without my compass because many of the landmarks I normally used to navigate were blotted out by the snow.

Small day packs or fanny packs are excellent for carrying some of the extra gear deer hunters should have with them. When hiking into a remote location in cold weather, I frequently carry a large backpack and frame to accommodate extra clothes and gear. On most deer hunting excursions, though, a medium-sized, frameless pack made of Polar Tuff is adequate. Hunters who hunt by tracking will want to travel as light as possible, fitting essentials in coat and pants pockets.

14

Guides

I learned some lessons about how to choose a guide for deer hunting the hard way.

Colorado used to have an early-season rifle hunt in high country wilderness areas primarily for trophy mule deer bucks. The season was in August, so the buck's antlers were still in velvet. Due to the remoteness of the terrain, coupled with my lack of experience hunting mulies at the time, I decided to hire a guide and outfitter.

It took me three years and a lot of money to find an outfitter who offered what I wanted. The first one I signed up with took as many hunters as he could fast-talk into booking with him. Consequently, his camp was overcrowded and service was lousy, but he was in a good area.

The second year I had a guide who limited the number of hunters in his camp and was conscientious about the care of his clients; however, his approach to finding deer at that time of year wasn't adequate. I can say that now, but didn't know it at the time. The territory he hunted had a low density of deer.

Year number three, everything fell in place. I hired an outfitter who restricted the number of hunters in his camp, knew how to hunt deer extremely well, and was in a good area. The man's name is Rudy Rudibaugh of Parlin, Colorado. He operates the 711 Ranch when he isn't in the high country. I hunted with Rudy for a number of years with both gun and bow and took a nice buck each time. The reason I mention Rudy's name is that truly good guides like him are hard to find.

If I knew then what I know now, I probably never would have booked with either of the first two outfitters. The first fellow I signed up with offered the cheapest rate of any I contacted. He also guaranteed me a buck with at least four points on a side.

The saying "you get what you pay for" is as true for guides and outfitters as anything else. Good guides aren't inexpensive. When a hunter pays for a cheap hunt, that is exactly what he gets. I should have also questioned my bargain-priced guide's guarantee of success. A 100 percent chance of success is unheard of, with the possible exception of hunting preserves or game farms, on any deer hunt I know of that is run on the up-and-up.

After my first experience with an outfitter, I was happy to locate one the second year who told me how many hunters would be on the hunt and leveled with me about my chances of scoring. My mistake this time was not comparing the area this guy operated in with others in the state.

Permits had to be obtained to hunt in his area. The number of permits was limited. Additionally, only bucks with four points on a side were legal. These factors indicated the territory had a limited surplus of deer. The restrictions were imposed to prevent an overharvest.

There were other locations in the state at the time that had healthier deer populations, which were also reflected by hunting regulations. No restrictions were placed on the number of hunters who could try their luck in Rudy's area, for example. And any antlered buck was legal.

The problems I encountered finding a satisfactory guide were my fault. I simply wasn't careful enough in making the selection at first. For that reason I suggest that deer hunters interested in securing a guide or outfitter try to investigate all the angles thoroughly before committing themselves. The only way the selection process can be done properly is to start looking well in advance of a hunt: from six months to a year or longer in many cases.

An alternative is to use the services of a reputable booking agent. They often know first-hand who offers the best hunts and can make the selection process easier. One booking agent hunters can contact is North American Adventures, 12301 Whitewater Dr., Suite 220, Minnetonka, MN 55343, (800) 228-0531.

Planning is a must for hunters interested in trying their luck in states such as Wyoming, to make sure licenses are obtained. Applications have to be in well before the season, by March 1, when a drawing is held to fill the quota of nonresident licenses. Hunters have to be assured of getting a license in Wyoming and states like it before securing a guide or outfitter.

Even though a commitment can't be made to a guide or outfitter in Wyoming, for example, until the hunter knows he or she will have a license, tentative arrangements should be correlated with deciding on where to hunt because a specific region has to be indicated on a license application.

I should point out here that deciding on an area with the highest possible density of whitetails or mule deer in any given state isn't a prerequisite to enjoying a successful guided hunt, although it should be considered. Good guides can usually get their hunters into deer regardless of their abundance because they are familiar with the country and the animals' movements within it.

There are a number of ways to get the names and addresses of reputable guides and outfitters. Some outfitters advertise in the classified sections of outdoor magazines such as *Outdoor Life, Field & Stream,* and *Sports Afield.* Some are mentioned in magazine articles, too. Additional listings are carried in The National Rifle Association's hunting annual. State and provincial departments of fish and game plus guide and outfitters associations can also provide contacts. Chambers of commerce are good contacts in Texas, for one, to get a line on deer-hunting services. Addresses of state and provincial agencies that provide information on guides and outfitters can be found in chapter 3.

Word of mouth is another source of information on guiding outfits. Acquaintances who have gone on guided hunts can provide a name or two along with a recommendation or a word of caution.

Here is a list of contacts for guides and outfitters with their addresses and phone numbers:

For a current Alaskan guide/outfitter register, send $5 to Department of Commerce and Economic Development, Division of Occupational Licensing, 3601 C Street, Anchorage, AK 99503 (907) 465-2542.

Colorado Outfitter Licensing Board, 1525 Sherman St., Room 606, Denver, CO 80203 (303) 866-3898.

Idaho Outfitters & Guides Association, P.O. Box 95, Boise, ID 83701 (208) 376-5680.

Montana Outfitters and Guides Association, P.O. Box 631, Hot Springs, MT 59845 (406) 741-2811.

New Mexico Council of Outfitters and Guides, 160 Washington SE, No. 75, Albuquerque, NM 87108 (505) 243-4461.

Oregon Guides and Packers Association, P.O. Box 10841, Eugene, OR 97440 (503) 683-9552.

Washington Outfitters and Guide Association, P.O. Box 95229, Seattle, WA 98145-2229.

Wyoming Outfitters Association, P.O. Box 2284, Cody, WY 82414 (307) 527-7453.

For a directory of Quebec fishing and hunting packages contact Tourisme Quebec, CP 20000, Quebec, Canada, G1K 7X2 (800) 443-7000 from the eastern U.S. or (800) 361-6440 or (312) 427-0240 from Ontario and the Atlantic provinces.

Saskatchewan Outfitters Association, P.O. Box 2016, Prince Albert, Saskatchewan, Canada, S6V 6K1 (306) 763-5434.

For a Saskatchewan Outdoor Adventure Guidebook contact Tourism Saskatchewan, Saskatchewan Trade and Convention Centre, 1919 Saskatchewan Drive, Regina, Saskatchewan, Canada, S4P 3V7 (800) 667-7191.

As names and addresses of operators are obtained for the area you want to hunt, write them an introductory letter. Make it as brief as possible. Tell them what type of hunt you are interested in and the weapon you plan to use. Some guides only handle bowhunters, or those who use firearms. Also ask for information on their rates, services, past success, and references from recent seasons (names and addresses of hunters who have used their services).

Some guides operate out of comfortable lodges and use vehicles as the principle means of travel to and from hunting areas. Others get into backcountry on horseback and tent out with their hunters. Drop-camp arrangements are also possible. In this situation an outfitter provides a fully equipped camp and leaves hunters on their own, then picks them up at a later date. Hunters who have a complete line of camping gear may simply want an outfitter to transport them and their gear to and from a remote campsite.

Some guides or outfitters may be eliminated by their initial response or lack of one. The next step involves corresponding with the references mentioned by operators who reply. If one or two guides look more promising than others, check out their references first.

To increase the chances of replies from an outfitter's past hunters, try to ask for brief answers and provide a stamped, self-addressed envelope. The more convenient it is for them, the more likely they are to provide the desired information. Following is a sample letter that could be sent to references.

Dear Mr. or Ms. ____ :

I am considering a hunt with (*guide's name*) and was given your name as a reference. Any information you can provide about your experience with him as a guide or outfitter would be appreciated. Answers to the questions below will help. A return envelope is enclosed for your convenience. Thank you for your assistance.

When and where did you hunt with the person mentioned above?
_____

Were you successful? _____
Size and sex of deer, if successful: _____
Other deer seen? _____
Was the guide easy to get along with? _____
Were services adequate? _____
Which ones weren't, if any? _____
Did the guide seem to know what he was doing? _____
Would you hunt with this guide again? _____
Why? _____
Do you know the names and addresses of other people who have hunted with the guide whom I can contact? _____
Please list:
_____
_____
_____
_____

Additional Comments:
_____
_____
_____
_____

Sincerely,
(Your Signature)

If replies aren't received from hunters you want input from, try calling them. Some people don't like to fill out questionnaires no matter how simple the query may be.

Comments from past hunters should give you a good idea who the best guide or outfitter is. Beware of guides who hesitate to give references, unless it is their first year in business. The final selection shouldn't be made until you find out, via another letter or two and maybe a phone call, what

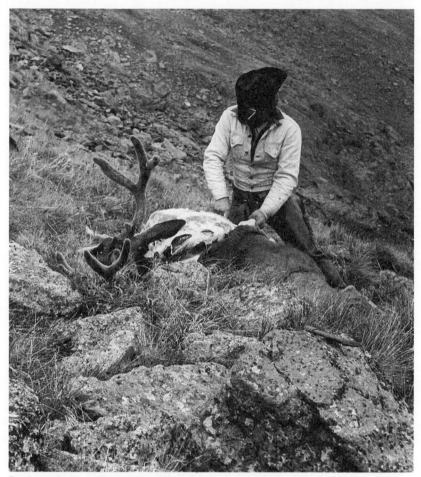

Be sure to find out what services a guide provides. Here Rudy is skinning a buck I took.

openings they have for the upcoming season, how many hunters will be along, and what the total cost will be for the type of services they provide. Also, make sure you know exactly what equipment they will be providing and what they expect you to bring.

Don't be afraid to ask questions. You are going to be shelling out good money for a hunt. Try to make sure you will be getting what you pay for. On the other hand, don't expect your guide or outfitter to be a slave. Help out with camp chores whenever possible, and don't try to tell him or her how to run his or her business.

Some guides operate out of tent camps; others use motels or lodges as the center of operations.

Be sure to ask if there are any special hunting regulations you should know about. Some states require proof of completion of a hunter safety course even if you have been hunting for years. Others have stringent restrictions on the weapons that are legal.

It won't hurt to ask about what weather can be expected, too, so you will know what types of clothing to bring. Some states and provinces have special clothing requirements, so it's a good idea to ask about that, too.

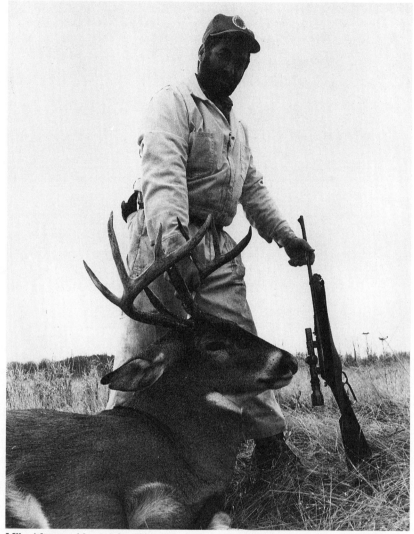

Mike Aftanas with a trophy whitetail in Saskatchewan. He wore white to comply with provincial regulations.

Once dates for the hunt have been decided, the guide or outfitter may ask the hunter for a deposit. This is a common practice, but make sure you get a receipt for it. Also find out if it is refundable if you can't make the hunt.

A guided hunt can be one of the most pleasurable and successful you will ever go on, but it can also be the worst. The difference is often determined by the amount of screening the hunter does before deciding on a guide or outfitter.

Other guides I've enjoyed pleasant deer hunts with are Dick Rinta-maki in Wyoming, Mike Aftanas in Saskatchewan, and Hayward Simmons in South Carolina. Dick and Mike are no longer guiding, but Hayward manages a hunting club. His address and phone number are Rt. 1, Box 166W, Allendale, SC 29810 (803) 584-4785.

Gun deer seasons open August 15 in Hayward's area, which provides a unique opportunity to hunt whitetail bucks in velvet.

15

After the Kill

Once a deer is down, the hardest part of a hunt is over. At that point the successful deer hunter can turn his or her attention to care of the carcass. Proper handling from the time a whitetail or mule deer is dropped until the meat reaches the freezer will insure a supply of tasty venison for months.

A supply of venison is a bonus of deer hunting that my wife, Lucy, and I always look forward to. The meat is delicious, high in protein, and better for us than domestic meats such as beef and pork. A deer on the meat pole represents an economic benefit to us. Venison meals reduce the amount of money we have to spend at the supermarket for domestic meats. In fact, most of the meat we eat is from wild game such as deer. Frankly, without venison from the deer I bag each year to carry us through the winter, our budget would be strained farther than we would like to admit.

Some hunters insist on considering the cost of firearms, bows, other equipment, and hunting expenses such as gas, guide fees, and plane fares as the price paid for venison. The dollar value per pound of venison can be high in many cases using this rationale, much higher than meats available at the butcher shop.

But I think the money I spend on deer hunting buys me the opportunity to hunt deer, nothing more. I don't have to shoot a deer to get returns on the money invested in deer hunting. I buy recreational value, a commodity that is difficult to put a price tag on. Countless times I feel I have gotten more than my money's worth on a deer hunt even though a deer wasn't collected.

Many people spend money to watch football and basketball games for the recreational value involved in watching the teams play. The price of admission doesn't include a meal; neither should deer hunting. That is why I feel venison is a bonus of any deer hunt rather than an economic benefit.

I can honestly say I haven't had any bad-tasting venison from whitetailed or mule deer, regardless of the animal's age, if the carcass was cared for properly. Distasteful meat is often the result of poor handling somewhere along the way from the time it was shot until it was cooked. There is no excuse for either.

Once a deer is dead, it should be dressed (the viscera removed) as soon as possible. Before starting to dress a deer, your tag should be affixed to the carcass. There is no need to "bleed" a whitetail or mule deer by cutting its throat. Most blood that hasn't drained out of the wound will be in the body cavity and will drain during the cleaning process. A cut in the hide on the underside of the neck is definitely not recommended if you think you may want to have your deer head mounted.

One of the first things a hunter should do after getting a deer is to tag it. This successful hunter is punching his tag.

When dressing a deer, its head should be uphill if on an incline.

If a deer is on an incline, position the carcass so the head is uphill.

Penis and testicles on bucks can be removed before opening the body cavity. Simply cut the skin around them and they can be pulled away from the body. To start a cut in the skin around the sex organ, pinch a fold of skin between thumb and forefinger then slice it. Opening the skin this way prevents unnecessary cuts in the meat.

A tube is connected to the penis at the rear. Don't cut it. Pull back testicles and penis with tube attached and lay them on the ground behind the carcass. The tube should be cut only after the bladder is removed, which will be a final step. (Some states require that proof of sex remain intact on a deer carcass. In that case these steps should be eliminated.)

To start the dressing process, make a horizontal cut in the belly area while standing over the deer facing toward its head. This cut doesn't have to be long; about three inches is fine. Try to cut in the center of the belly where there is little or no hair. Keep the knife blade, which should be sharp, level when making the cut, and take it easy. Make short, slicing strokes. Do not stab a knife blade into the belly to start a cut. As obvious as it may sound to most deer hunters, I know some beginners who have done so. The intestines or stomach may be ruptured by stabbing a knife blade into the abdominal cavity, which is not desirable.

Several layers of muscle and tissue lie beneath the skin. All have to be cut through to reach the body cavity.

After the cut is completed, insert middle and index fingers of the left hand (if right-handed) under the skin and lift it up and away from the viscera. Now you can start a cut toward the head, working the knife blade between your fingers.

Cut at least as far as the rib cage, farther if possible. Most heavy-bladed knives that are sharp will cut through ribs. You can use both hands to hold the knife to cut ribs if necessary. There is nothing that will rupture in the chest area. The ribs can be cut as far as the brisket. If, however, you are considering mounting the head, you should stop cutting just behind the front legs.

A better way to open the body cavity is to make the initial opening just behind the rib cage. With a deer resting on its back, there is a space between skin and internal organs here. Therefore, the chances of accidentally rupturing anything are reduced.

Once an opening is cut, use the middle and index fingers to elevate the skin and guide the knife blade toward the rear. The cut can be extended farther forward by going back to the starting point and slicing ribs.

Now that the carcass is open, intestines, stomach, and liver can be rolled out on the ground. Use your knife to cut any tissue connecting this material to the sides or back of the body. Kidneys and fat may remain along the back. These can be easily removed by pulling on them.

There will be a thin, muscular membrane across the body cavity in front of where the stomach was. This is the diaphragm. It should be cut free along the ribs and back.

The heart and lungs can be removed next. They can be pulled out once the windpipe is cut. The windpipe is all the way forward in the chest cavity. It is circular and semirigid.

Next, cut completely around the anus so the lower end of the digestive tract and bladder can be pulled forward and discarded. This step is much easier if the pelvic arch is split open. An axe or saw works best for this, but a sturdy knife blade can be used if you exert enough pressure. Splitting the pelvis isn't necessary to remove the lower digestive tract, though.

Whichever method is used to remove the lower digestive tract, make sure all material is removed from the anal passageway so blood from the body cavity can drain through it. A cleared passageway will also speed cooling of the meat.

To keep hands clean while dressing deer, some hunters wear rubber gloves. If hunting in exceptionally cold weather where temperatures are below zero, wearing gloves is a good idea. Bloody hands get cold quickly after field dressing is complete.

If intestinal matter got on any part of the meat as a result of cleaning or from wounds, try to wipe it off with leaves, grass, a clean handkerchief, or paper towels. An alternative is to cut away a thin layer of the affected meat.

Some hunters remove the glands on the back legs of deer as well as the entire windpipe. I have found neither practice to be necessary.

Once cleaned out, a carcass can be elevated to help it drain. As examples, it can be propped up against a stump, on bushes, or draped over a log. Most blood can be drained by simply lifting the front quarters off the ground.

Be sure to salvage the liver and heart from your deer. They are great eating. If you don't want them, it probably won't be hard to find someone who does. The tongue and kidneys of deer can also be eaten. Carry these items in a plastic bag.

Some hunters prepare and eat the liver from a deer the same day it is bagged. I do the same thing with the tenderloins. They are narrow strips of delicious meat on either side of the backbone. Each one is about a foot long. I usually wait until I get home to cut these delectable pieces of meat out. They can be pulled out once an end has been freed with a knife blade.

Left: **Tenderloins as they are found against the back on the inside of the body cavity.**
Right: **Tenderloins after they have been removed.**

Ideally, a whitetail or mule deer should be skinned and butchered the same day it is shot. This is a must when hunting in warm weather, but isn't as critical when temperatures are in the 30- to 40-degree range. Some hunters recommend aging deer carcasses. This is difficult to do properly, except under controlled conditions. I have found that venison tastes better when butchered as soon as possible.

When a deer carcass won't be processed promptly, it should be hung so it will cool. It can be hung with the head up or down. A deer that isn't

A deer that is to be caped should be hung head down.

drained should be suspended head up. If the whitetail or mule deer will be caped, hanging it with the head down is best.

I sometimes hang my deer from a tree in the woods if getting it to camp or home isn't convenient right away. This isn't possible where there are no trees, of course. In such a situation, prop the body cavity open with a stick, then roll the carcass over so it rests on its chest, and spread the legs. The carcass should be in shade if possible. Body heat won't be able to radiate properly from a carcass lying on its side; consequently, the meat in the area that is on the ground could spoil if left for any length of time.

If a deer must be left outside in warm weather, flies can be kept away from the meat by sprinkling pepper over the inside of the carcass and on any exposed flesh. Flies will lay eggs on unprotected areas otherwise. When you have shot a deer in warm or hot weather where flies are a problem, it's actually better to put off dressing the carcass until it can also be skinned and butchered or put in a cooler. This should be done as soon as possible, of course, keeping the carcass in the shade until it can be processed.

Coyotes and bears won't often bother a deer carcass that has been handled by humans and left in the woods. A shirt, coat, or some other article hung nearby will help discourage them. If human thieves are a problem in your area, you might try marking the carcass by notching the ears. Or try putting a business card, slip of paper with your name on it, or some other identifying article in the mouth of a dead deer. If your tag is on

In warm or hot weather, wait to gut deer until they can also be skinned and put in a cooler or butchered.

a whitetail or mule deer, that should be proof enough who the animal belongs to. The local sheriff or conservation officer should be notified of the theft of a deer and what to look for in identifying the carcass.

There are a number of ways to get a deer out of the woods. Probably the most commonly used method is dragging. This is the best way if there is snow on the ground or there isn't far to go on hard-packed ground. Bucks come complete with handles (antlers) for dragging. If there is a hunter for each side and there isn't far to go, this approach works fine.

A successful rifle hunter drags a whitetail buck by the antlers.

A better method for dragging either bucks or does is to use a rope. The animal's front legs should be folded on top of its head then a rope should be tied around the neck and legs. The rope can be tied at an end or the middle. If the middle of the rope is secured around the deer's neck there will be two pieces, one each for a pair of draggers. If there is only one dragger, each of the two pieces of rope can be tied to a stick to rig a makeshift harness.

Yoke arrangement for dragging a deer with a rope.

When the end of a rope is tied to a deer for dragging, it can be adapted to allow two hunters to pull by attaching a sturdy stick or pole to the tag end. The pole should be long enough to extend across the pullers' chests and work like a yoke. When pulling alone, a short stick can be tied to the rope to serve as a handle. This is easier on the hand than gripping the rope.

If for some reason you don't have a rope, a belt will do to drag a deer.

Handle arrangement for dragging a deer with a rope.

If at all possible, get help to drag a deer rather than do it yourself. Hauling 100 pounds or more of dead weight, whether on bare ground or snow, is strenuous. It is difficult enough with two people, let alone one. Make it a point to take frequent breaks when dragging a deer, even if there are two of you. There shouldn't be any rush to reach camp or the nearest road. Overexertion can quickly turn a successful hunt into a tragedy. More than one deer hunter has suffered a heart attack while trying to muscle a carcass to car or camp.

If darkness is approaching and you want to get out of the woods, hang the deer where it is and go back for it in the morning. But make sure you will be able to find it. Hang a bright-colored coat or vest in a prominent position near the carcass and mark a trail to a road if you are in unfamiliar territory. Blaze marks can be cut in trees, tissue or surveyor's tape hung on branches, or feet scuffed along the ground to mark the route.

Deer shouldn't be dragged over sand or mud, nor should they be dragged for long distances. If they are, there is a good chance the meat will get soiled and bruised. Alternatives to dragging a carcass are carrying it yourself or transporting it by horseback, boat, canoe, motorcycle, all-terrain vehicle (ATV) such as a three- or four-wheeler, or snowmobile. There are restrictions on the use of motorized vehicles in some states during firearms deer seasons. Be sure to check before using an ATV or snowmobile to retrieve a deer.

This pair of hunters have tied a strap to the middle of this deer so each has a piece to pull.

Two hunters load a mule deer onto a pack horse in Colorado.

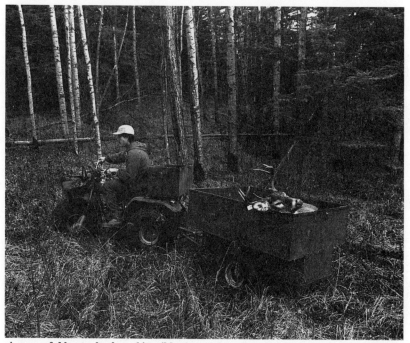

A successful hunter hauls a whitetail buck out of the Canadian bush with a three-wheeler.

I have saved myself some long hauls with deer carcasses by dragging them to a nearby river and retrieving them with a canoe. Deer should be carried in a boat or canoe whenever possible, but when there isn't enough room they can be pulled in the water. The carcass will float just below the surface. Hair on a deer's hide is hollow and will hold the carcass up. If this is attempted on a river try to go downstream, since the submerged deer creates a lot of drag. The inside of a carcass that is dragged in the water should be wiped out thoroughly once your destination is reached. This will remove dirt and speed drying.

I have carried a few deer on my back, and it isn't as bad as it may sound. The best way to do it is to cut the carcass in pieces, either halves or quarters. If a deer is small it can be carried whole, but for safety reasons this isn't recommended during firearms seasons. It can be done safely during archery hunts, though. Just the same, a brightly colored vest or garment should be attached to the carcass.

If you are interested in having the hide tanned or the head mounted, the deer should be skinned before it is butchered. One of the biggest mistakes deer hunters make when caping a deer head that is to be mounted is not allowing for enough hide. It is better to give the taxidermist too much than not enough.

To cape a deer, make a cut through the hide that extends completely around the body behind both front legs. The skin can then be sliced

Canoes or boats provide an easy means of transporting deer to camp or car when water is available.

around the front legs where they join the body. A second major cut should be made perpendicular to the first, in the middle of the back. The cut should extend up the back of the neck to a point just below the base of the antlers, providing the deer is a buck.

From there a short slice can be made to the base of each antler. On antlerless deer, make the cut up the back of the neck to a point just past the ears. With these cuts made, the hide can be peeled forward.

The best place to start separating skin from flesh is on the deer's back at the intersection of the two major cuts. Once started with a knife, the skin often peels away from the carcass by pulling on it. After the cape has been skinned as far as the base of the neck, turn your attention to skinning the rest of the hide. You want to leave the cape attached at this time to protect the front quarters from dirt.

The only cuts necessary to complete skinning are on the inside of the hind legs. Once these are completed, the skin can be worked free on the legs and the remainder of the carcass, one side at a time. Skin remaining on the front legs will have to be removed, too. Skin the legs only to the knees. The lower portions can be cut off at the knees.

To skin a deer that isn't to be caped, simply extend the cut that was made to dress the animal to the head at the throat. Make the cut up the middle of the chest and the underside of the neck. Then slice the hide up the inside of each leg from the cut running the length of the deer's body. The hide can then be slowly separated from the carcass, working on one side at a time.

The skinning process is more awkward when a carcass is on the ground rather than hanging, but it isn't difficult if done a step at a time. The operation is easy with two people working together.

The carcass can be quartered and the head removed after the hide is separated from it. This should be done while the carcass is lying on the skin. A saw will be necessary to separate the quarters. To quarter a deer, cut the carcass in half across the backbone, then separate the front and rear portions in half again by sawing down the middle of the backbone. If you don't have a saw or want to reduce the amount to carry, simply remove front legs and shoulders, hind legs, and loins from the carcass. These pieces represent at least 90 percent of the meat on a deer and they can all be removed with a knife. Cut between shoulders and ribs to remove them, with front legs attached. Hind legs, or hams, can be removed by cutting the hip joint.

The loins are boneless strips of meat on both sides of the backbone. Make cuts along each side of the backbone to peel loins away from the carcass. By removing meat from the carcass this way, it isn't necessary to carry most of the bones out of the field. They will be eaten by scavengers.

The quartered meat should be covered with the hide or cloth meat bags to protect it while it is carried. A bright coat or vest should be draped over the deer head and hide.

Pack frames are best suited for carrying a quartered deer. The meat can be tied to frames with rope. It is a good idea to distribute the load between two hunters, especially if the deer was big. Each can take half. If alone, two trips may be necessary to transport a large deer.

Hunters who don't care about saving their hide or cape can halve or quarter their deer with the hide intact. Skinning can be taken care of later.

Deer that are to be transported by vehicle can be tied on the car top or over the trunk, or put in the bed of a pickup or in a trunk. Don't put a deer over the hood where heat from the engine will increase the chances of spoilage. If the weather is consistently warmer than 40 degrees Fahrenheit and you will be on the road for several hours, use dry ice to keep the meat cool. Quarter the carcass before leaving on a long drive. Then put a chunk of ice between the front and rear quarters and cover them with blankets or canvas for insulation. Ice will have to be replenished on long drives.

Some states require that deer be transported visibly and in one piece. Here again, try to be familiar with the regulations in the state you are hunting.

If a deer wasn't skinned and caped in the field, it must be done at camp or home. A carcass that is hanging is easier to work with. For caping, a deer should be hung upside down. To remove the entire hide, the carcass can be hung either way.

A stout branch or piece of wood should be inserted through the gambrels of both hind legs to suspend a deer with its head down. Gambrels are on the back of the legs just above the joint. There is an area of skin here between a heavy tendon and the leg bone. This skin can be cut to allow a stick to pass through. Be careful not to cut the tendon.

While the deer is held in position — with the hind legs straddling a beam, pole, or limb — the stick can be passed through the gambrels so it rests on a support. To hang a deer with the head up, a rope can be used to fasten the carcass to a support. One end of the rope should be around the deer's neck or base of the antlers. If you plan to have the head mounted, hang a buck by its antlers. If hung by the neck, hairs will be broken that can't be repaired.

Slice the hide in the same fashion as mentioned earlier for either caping or skinning once a whitetail or mule deer is hung. The hide can often be peeled off the carcass by pulling downward. A knife will be necessary to start the skinning, however. The underside of the tail should be split so the tail bone can be removed.

A head or hide that is to be preserved should be taken to a taxidermist as soon as possible. If more than a day (a few hours if the weather is warm) will elapse from the time a cape or hide is removed from the carcass until it can be delivered to the taxidermist, salting or freezing the hide will be necessary. Before a cape is salted or frozen, it should be removed from the head by completing the skinning unless you have a freezer big enough to accommodate head and cape, or it's below freezing outside. The best way to skin the head is to invert the hide over the skull.

Cut the ears off close to the skull. A dull instrument, either a spoon or a screwdriver, is best for prying the skin loose from around the base of the antlers, but a knife blade will do. A pair of pliers can also be used to pull hide from the base of the antlers, but take it easy to avoid tearing the hide. Extreme care should be exercised when the eyes are reached. Use a sharp knife to cut the skin flush with the eye socket. The tear duct is on the forward side of the eye. Be sure to continue separating the skin as close to the skull as possible in this area. Caution is required in skinning the nose and lips, too.

The cape can be put in a freezer once skinning is complete. For salting, the earq must be skinned after the cape is removed from the head. Slowly and carefully invert the skin on the back of each ear over the inner cartilage until you reach the tip.

Before the completely skinned cape and hide are salted, remove any fat or flesh that is clinging to the skin. There is usually a thick layer of meat around the lips. Try to trim as much of this as possible without damaging the skin. Ordinary table salt is fine for applying to capes and

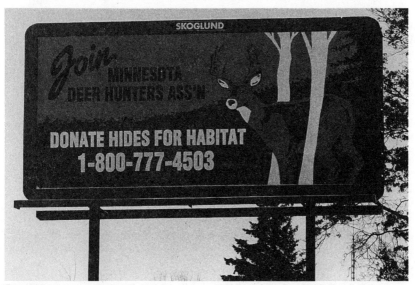

Deer hides can prove valuable if they are channeled back into deer habitat as is done in Minnesota.

hides. Don't be stingy; pour lots of salt on and rub it in all over with special attention to lips, nose, ears, tail, and edges of the hide.

Never send a deer hide through the mail enclosed in a plastic bag. After the salted skin dries put it in a paper bag or gunny sack, then wrap it for mailing. Do not salt a cape or hide you plan to freeze. The salt will prevent freezing.

Do not throw deer hides away. They can be sold for a few dollars or made into gloves or a coat. If nothing else, donate them to state organizations such as the Minnesota Deer Hunters Association, which uses the money from deer-hide sales to buy deer habitat.

The antlers from your deer must be brought to a taxidermist along with the salted or frozen cape. Since he won't need the skull, the antlers can be sawed from it. Start sawing on the back of the skull so the saw blade passes just below the tops of the eye sockets and complete the cut on the bridge of the nose. Taxidermists will remove antlers from skulls for hunters who don't care to do it.

Hunters who shoot a buck with a set of antlers they want to save don't have to go to the expense of having the entire head mounted. The antlers and skull plate can be mounted on a plaque with a piece of felt covering the exposed bone. Antlers mounted this way make attractive decorations. Kits are available with the necessary materials for mounting.

The meat from a deer, like the hide, should be processed as soon as possible. It may be best to care for the venison first if there is a chance of spoilage. I used to bring my skinned deer to a local butcher and he cut the carcass while I waited. Any odds and ends were ground into hamburger. At home, my wife and I packaged and labeled the venison, then put it in the freezer. All hair and fat was removed from the meat and damaged portions trimmed as we wrapped it. Now I do the butchering myself, unless pressed for time. All fat and bones are removed. The boned, trimmed venison that results takes up a minimum amount of space in the freezer and is ready to cook, once thawed.

The process takes time, but proves to be worth it when we enjoy delicious meals of venison. If venison is frozen with the fat intact, the quality of the meat will deteriorate.

Butchering your own deer also saves money. Most establishments that regularly butcher deer charge high fees. For this reason, among others, hunters should know how to cut up their deer. The procedure is simple.

A couple of sharp knives are all you will need to butcher a deer. A work bench or covered kitchen table will do to work on. Use freezer paper or aluminum foil to cover a table, not newspaper. The carcass must be quartered for butchering.

First, separate the leg and shoulder from the rest of the quarter. This section can be cut away with a knife by slicing between the shoulder blade and the body. I remove all meat from front legs and shoulders for use in stews, casseroles, or burger. The shoulders can be used as roasts.

The neck can be cut next. Meat from the neck is used for roasts, stews, or hamburger. I usually trim meat from the neck for burger.

Stew meat or hamburger can be obtained from the upper and lower ribs. The brisket is best suited for stewing or making burger.

Steaks, chops, and roasts are the primary cuts from the hind quarters, with the exception of the flank and shank. The flank is a thin muscle in the belly area and the shank is the lower portion of the hind leg. Meat from these locations can be used for stews or hamburger.

The loin is a tubular piece of meat that runs along the backbone. This can be cut out and sliced into steaks or chops. From that point everything else can be cut into steaks or roasts. I remove muscle from the leg bone, separate large muscles from one another, then cut into steaks or leave them as roasts.

Hair and fat should be removed from cuts before they are packaged. Use freezer paper or heavy-duty aluminum foil to wrap the meat. A felt-tipped pen can be used to write the type of meat, the cut, and the date on freezer paper. Make labels out of masking tape when venison is stored in aluminum foil.

Butchering a deer may seem like an endless task the first time it is attempted. This is only because the steps are unfamiliar. The chore will become less tedious in future attempts as you become more proficient at butchering and realize that the dividends of your labor will be delicious meals of venison. It helps to have at least two people working together on a carcass. If at all possible, have someone who has butchered a deer before show you how.

The procedure I have listed here for butchering deer is by no means the only way it can be done. Many hunters develop their own routine for reducing a carcass into the cuts they like.

Try to be conservative when discarding bloodied meat that looks like it is beyond salvage. Saltwater is great for getting blood out of meat. Cuts that look bad may be able to be saved by soaking them overnight in a saltwater solution in a refrigerator.

Many hunters have beef suet mixed with ground venison. My wife and I seldom do this. We use ground venison in spaghetti, meatloaf, and casseroles, and it tastes great. Another option for ground venison is to have it made into sausage. Some meat-processing plants regularly make venison sausage for hunters.

16

Antlers

Antlers are important to most deer hunters. They are symbolic in many ways, but primarily serve as mementos of successful hunts.

Large sets of antlers are accorded special recognition. Those that meet certain standards are listed in one of two national record books, depending on what type of weapon was used to bag the deer that wore them. The Boone and Crockett record book lists outstanding racks taken with firearms. Pope and Young classifies record deer heads collected by bowhunters. Some state record-keepers recognize both gun and bow kills.

Many hunters share the desire to shoot a deer with a record rack, but few succeed in doing so. White-tailed and mule deer wearing antlers that meet record-book standards are hard to come by because they simply are not abundant. Those that do exist usually spend their time in remote, lightly hunted terrain, in refuges, or on private property.

Numerous trophy bucks are bagged each year. The definition of "trophy buck" varies from one hunter to another. The first buck I shot was a trophy to me at the time, and it only had spikes. Now it would take whitetail and mule deer bucks bigger than those I have hanging on my living room wall to be classified as trophies. My best whitetail has eleven points and an inside spread of about nineteen inches. The mulie has nine points with a spread comparable to the whitetail. Neither is exceptional; many larger racks have been taken, but I am happy with mine.

Something unique about my mule deer head is that the antlers are in velvet. I shot this particular buck during a special early hunt in Colorado while hunting with outfitter Rudy Rudibaugh of Parlin. Ken Asbury was my guide.

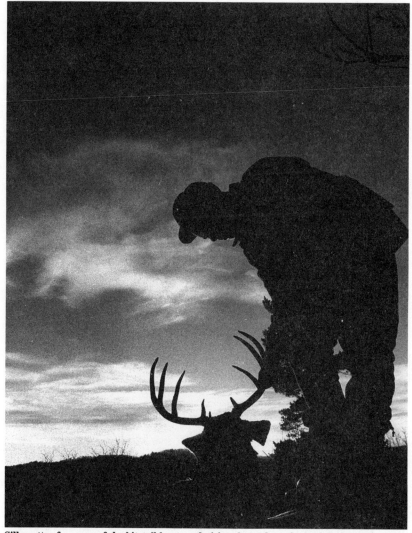

Silhouette of a successful whitetail hunter admiring the antlers of a buck he bagged.

There are two popular methods of classifying the number of points on a set of antlers: Eastern and Western count. In some parts of the West the brow tine or eye guard isn't considered a point, and only the side with the most tines is specified. Using my mounted mule deer as an example, one antler has three points, and the other four, discounting the brow tines. My buck is a four-point by Western count.

Every tine over an inch in length is considered a point by Eastern count. In my opinion this system is better. It coincides with the classification used by Boone and Crockett and Pope and Young. The other method can be confusing because it doesn't give a total picture of what a rack looks like. A four-point buck by Western count can have four points on one side and two, three, or four on the other. The rack may have eye guards or it may not.

It is usually possible by Eastern count to get an accurate idea how a set of antlers is proportioned. An eight-point normally has four on a side; a seven-point generally has four on one side and three on the other. Occasionally a buck will have an odd rack with two points on one side and four on the other, but not often.

On the chance you shoot a buck with a rack that might qualify for Boone and Crockett or Pope and Young, you should know how to measure the antlers to see if they will qualify. The procedure is relatively simple. All that is required to score a set of antlers is a quarter-inch, flexible steel tape for measuring (any tape would do for rough measurements) and a piece of paper and a pencil to jot down figures.

Both whitetail and mule deer racks are classified into two categories: typical and nontypical. As you might guess, most sets of antlers fall into the first classification. Typical racks exhibit tines branching from the top of the main beams in an orderly fashion, although there may be one, or several, abnormal points.

There is a slight difference between typical whitetail and mule deer racks. Whitetails have unbranched tines. Points on mule deer antlers beyond the brow tine normally fork.

Nontypical antlers are characterized by numerous points sprouting at odd angles from the main beam and tines, in addition to normal points. Racks of this sort commonly have twenty points or more. Incidentally, for any projection to be considered a point, the distance it extends upward or outward must exceed the length of its base in addition to being at least an inch long.

The steps in measuring whitetail or mulie antlers for record classification, regardless of the category, are similar. Let's take a typical whitetail rack to start with.

To keep track of figures in an orderly fashion allow for three vertical columns on a sheet of paper. Two are for figures obtained from each antler, and the third is for differences in measurements from one antler to the other. Any discrepancies between sides will detract from the total score. Symmetry is an important characteristic of record-book heads.

There is one measurement required for scoring that won't fit into any of the three columns: inside spread of the main beams. It can simply be written to the side or at the bottom of the paper and added to other figures later.

The first lengths we want to measure are the main beams. These are taken from the lowest outside edge of the burr (circular formation at the base of the antlers where they join the skull) over the outer curve of the antlers to the tip of the main beam. The tape measure should follow the center line of the antler. Beams can also be measured by laying a string or cable along their length and then measuring the string.

It may be necessary to obtain this figure in stages since most beams are curved. A control point should be marked each time a change in direction of the tape is required. All figures should be to the nearest eighth of an inch.

This is how to measure beam length, although the actual measurements might have to be done in stages to prevent kinks in the tape.

Enter the measurement for the right antler in the appropriate column and the same for the left. If one beam is longer than the other, enter the difference in the third column. (See sample score sheet for further guidance.)

Now, measure the length of each normal point on each antler. To arrive at an accurate score, the tape should extend from the nearest edge of the main beam to the tip over the outer curve of the tine. Tips of main beams are not measured as points. These are considered in the figure for the antler lengths.

Measurements of corresponding points on each antler are then compared and any difference is written in the appropriate location. Typically, a record whitetail buck will have from eight to fourteen normal points; however, a greater number is possible.

Beam circumference at four points is next. The first one is gauged at the smallest point between the burr and first tine. Jockeying the tape around in that area may be necessary to locate the smallest circumference. The smallest circumference between the first and second points is consid-

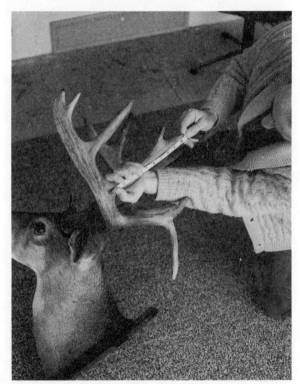

Length of tines is measured along the outside edge.

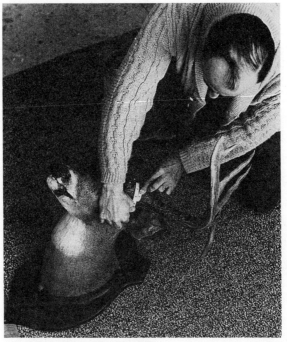

Circumferences are measured at several locations.

ered next, followed by a like position between second and third and third and fourth. In cases where the first point or brow tine is missing, the first two measurements can be taken at the smallest point between the burr and second point. On beams with four points, measure the last circumference halfway between the beam tip and third tine.

The next step is tallying the total length of abnormal points. These should be measured from their base, whether on the main beam or a tine, to the tip along the outside curve. On a typical whitetail head any points that jut out at odd angles from the main beam or branch from any of the tines are abnormal.

Occasionally, a point coming off the top of the beams may be considered abnormal. Let's look at an example. Say one antler has six points and its mate, seven. The extra tine is between the second and third points and is only four inches long. Point number three on the opposite antler is ten inches long.

If the four-inch tine were considered normal, it would become the third point and scored with its longer counterpart. This way six credits would be lost, and there would be no mate for the fifth point on the side with the most tines and additional credits would be lost. So consider that extra point abnormal. Only four points would be lost that way.

Sample Score Sheet for Rough Scoring Deer Heads

Example: Typical Whitetail

	Column 1	Column 2	Column 3
	Right Antler	**Left Antler**	**Difference**
1. Length Main Beam	23²/₈	22⁷/₈	⁵/₈
2. Length First Point	5⁶/₈	5⁶/₈	—
3. Length Second Point	7¹/₈	7³/₈	²/₈
4. Length Third Point	9	8⁷/₈	¹/₈
5. Length Fourth Point	8⁶/₈	8⁵/₈	¹/₈
6. Length Fifth Point			
7. Length Sixth Point			
8. Circumference between Burr and Second Point	5³/₈	5³/₈	—
9. Circumference between First and Second Points	4⁷/₈	4⁶/₈	¹/₈
10. Circumference between Second and Third Points	5	4⁷/₈	¹/₈
11. Circumference between Third and Fourth Points	4⁶/₈	4⁷/₈	¹/₈
12. Total lengths of Abnormal Points (on typical heads this figure is subtracted from score, but is added to nontypical tally)			3²/₈

Inside Spread of Antlers: 21¹/₈

Total Column 1:	73⁷/₈
Total Column 2:	73³/₈
Spread Credits:	21¹/₈
	168³/₈
Column 3:	4⁶/₈
Total Score:	163⁵/₈

Final score for this head is 6³/₈ points short of the minimum qualifying tally (170) for a typical whitetail in the Boone and Crockett Record Book. However, it would easily surpass the minimum for Pope and Young (125).

The length of abnormal points is added to the score of nontypical heads, but subtracted from typical racks.

Enter the figure obtained from abnormal points in column three.

The final measurement that affects the score of a rack is the inside spread of the antlers. This must be assessed at right angles to the center line of the skull and can be taken at the widest point between beams.

If the figure obtained is greater than the longest main beam, the difference must be entered in column three on the tally sheet. A number less than or equal to the length of the longest main beam can be written in as credit for inside spread.

For instance, let's say the inside spread of the head on the sample score sheet came out to be an even 25 inches, instead of 21⅛. In that case it would be greater than the longest main beam, which was 23⅖. So their difference, 1⅝, would go in column three and spread credit would be 23⅖.

An official scorer for Boone and Crockett or Pope and Young would jot down several additional measurements that simply indicate the conformation of the rack. They don't affect the score. These are the number of points on each antler, tip-to-tip spread, and the greatest outside spread.

Once all of the necessary measurements are determined, the final score can be totaled. To tally this figure add all the numbers in columns

Here is how to tape the inside spread of a rack.

one and two plus the inside spread. Then subtract the total of column three from that total.

Minimum qualifying score for a typical whitetail rack in Boone and Crockett is 170. Pope and Young accepts scores of 125 or higher.

If a rack is close to or exceeds these minimums, it should be taken to an official scorer for verification. However, sixty days must have elapsed from the time the head was collected until it is officially measured. This allows for drying, during which time some shrinkage occurs.

During early hunts in some states deer antlers may be in velvet when collected. Velvet must be removed from the rack of an animal taken in this condition that is to be measured for record-book consideration.

The same procedure as above can be followed for scoring a nontypical whitetail rack. However, the total length of abnormal points is added to the score rather than subtracted. Tally of abnormal points should be listed as a plus figure along with inside spread, rather than placing it in column three as before.

Minimum score for nontypical whitetails taken with firearms is 195, and 150 for bow and arrow.

The guidelines for measuring and scoring mule deer racks is nearly the same as the technique for whitetails, with a couple of minor exceptions. Mulies usually have fewer normal points than whitetails, often four per beam, not including the beam tip. There is no limit to the number of normal points that may be present.

Due to the difference in structure of mulie racks, circumferences must be taken accordingly. As with whitetails, the first two circumferences are measured between the burr and first point and the first and second. The

A whitetail buck with a nontypical rack carrying twenty-two points.

third one, however, is gauged between the main beam and tine number three. The final circumference is assessed between the second and fourth points, always at the smallest place.

Minimum Boone and Crockett scores for typical and nontypical mulies are 195 and 240, respectively. For Pope and Young qualification they must be 145 and 160.

A list of official Boone and Crockett scorers in your area and other information can be obtained by writing to Boone and Crockett Club, 241 S. Fraley Blvd., Dumfries, VA 22026. Pope and Young information can be obtained from Glenn Hisey, Box 548, Chatfield, MN 55923. The departments of natural resources and fish and game in each state might also be sources for contacting official scorers in your area.

Photos of a trophy head, front and sides, plus a $25 registration fee must be sent with official score charts that are to be considered for record-book entry.

Deer antlers are not true horns. Unlike antlers, horns such as those worn by sheep and pronghorn antelope are not shed, although an outer sheath is on pronghorns. Deer shed their headgear every year. Most antlered whitetails and mulies are bucks, but occasionally a doe will sprout a set.

Bucks normally shed their antlers early in the winter, after the rut is over. Both beams may be lost at approximately the same time, or there could be a week or more lag from the time one antler is lost until its mate

The buck that grew these antlers at 2½ to 4½ years of age obviously didn't have the genes for growing a big rack.

drops off. The timing varies from deer to deer. All of the bucks in a given area won't lose their racks at the same time, either. The health and age of individual animals makes a difference. Severity of the weather is also thought to affect the length of time deer sport their antlers.

In my home state of Michigan, bucks start dropping antlers toward the latter part of December. Yet, a few will be seen still wearing headgear as late as March. In Florida, bucks' antlers are reportedly lost and grown with no pattern, due to the relative consistency of the weather.

Circular patches of raw skin called pedicels are visible on a buck's head for a day or two after his rack is shed. They heal quickly. A new set of antlers starts to sprout in the spring, by late April or early May in my part of the country. The growth rate of antlers is tremendous, especially on large-racked deer. Their development is complete by August, which is late summer in the northern states.

While the antlers are growing they are covered with what is called velvet or moss. It is true skin. All of the tissue is soft and generously supplied with blood during the development stage. If the delicate antlers are damaged or the deer itself injured while they are growing, one or both sides of the rack can become malformed. This is how some nontypical

The buck that grew these antlers had a fork as a yearling, but each year after that from 2½ to 5½ the antlers carried the same number of points and had the same general structure. The only major change was an increase in beam circumference.

These five antlers were grown by a buck when 3½ through 7½, from bottom to top. A forked brow tine was grown from age 4½ on. A second tine also forked at age 7½.

antlers result. Bucks with hormonal imbalance or permanently damaged sex organs may produce nontypical formations year after year.

Once antlers are completely developed the supply of blood to them stops and the tissue dies. Then the velvet is rubbed off, leaving hardened antlers. Antler coloration varies from bleached white to a deep brown. My theory is that a buck living in open country where his antlers get a lot of exposure to the sun will generally have a lighter-colored rack than a buck that spends most of his time in heavy cover where the sun seldom penetrates.

Some claim that antlers are stained by dried blood when the velvet is shed. Others feel that antlers derive their color from the trees they are rubbed on when polished. A combination of these factors may play a role in antler coloration.

The size rack a buck grows is dependent upon three factors: heredity (genetics), nutrition, and age. Deer that grow outstanding headgear have to be in good health, at least several years old, and genetically disposed to antler growth. Even yearling bucks can have respectable heads sporting eight or more points, providing their diet and parentage is right. Yet, some bucks can be healthy and old, but sport mediocre racks because the right genes aren't there.

In the presence of many mature bucks this yearling grew sub-legal antlers despite having plenty of high-quality food.

Interestingly enough, a buck's antlers will form in the same general pattern year after year. The number of points may increase the first couple of years, but the general shape and features of the rack will normally remain the same.

John Ozoga, a wildlife biologist with the Michigan Department of Natural Resources, showed me several series of antlers shed by the same bucks over a period of years. The deer were in an enclosure and could be monitored closely. The resemblance of the racks from one year to the next for each animal was remarkable. In many cases the only change over a span of years was an increase in the circumference of beams. John could identify individual bucks during his observations by the shape of their racks.

Another fact the biologist learned from his studies of penned deer is that antler growth in yearling bucks can be adversely affected by an abundance of older, mature bucks. In situations where big-racked bucks were common, a percentage of the yearlings in the population grew sublegal antlers, less than three inches in length. Food wasn't a limiting factor here since the deer were on a high-nutrition diet.

17

Deer Management

Strictly from a management point of view, it would be better if whitetail and mule deer bucks didn't grow antlers, or if both sexes did.

An adequate harvest of antlerless deer (does and young-of-the-year bucks) is difficult to achieve in parts of the United States due to the traditional stigma many deer hunters associate with shooting deer that aren't wearing antlers. If both sexes of deer did or didn't have antlers, the problem wouldn't exist.

I believe part of the reason a percentage of deer hunters resist harvesting does is due to their poor understanding of deer management. Since it will be easier to try to get hunters to understand and accept the need for shooting both bucks and does than developing a strain of antlered does or antlerless bucks (maybe), let's get on with it.

It would be nice if deer herds could continually increase by simply protecting does, but unfortunately that isn't how things work. Each deer range has enough browse to feed only a certain number of deer throughout the year. Available deer food is scarcest during the winter and other severe weather. So the maximum number of whitetails or mulies that can be supported in any given habitat without reducing its quality (its carrying capacity) is determined by the amount of food available to them then. Drought, floods, and heavy snows limit the amount of food available to deer. In many cases the winter deer range is only a fraction of the size of the summer and fall ranges. Mulies and some whitetails have traditional wintering areas, which they use year after year. Their nutritional needs must be met within that limited area.

While drought and floods are seldom predictable, winter is. The key to a healthy deer herd is maintaining its winter population at or below the carrying capacity of its habitat. A herd that comes through the winter in good shape will produce a maximum yield of fawns. By fawning time, deer will have dispersed throughout the summer range where there is an abundance of food, enough to sustain the increased population. Before winter returns, the number of white-tailed and mule deer in an area has to be trimmed to correspond with the limited food supply.

That is where hunting comes in. The purpose of the fall hunting season is to reduce the population to the level the winter range can sustain. To do this, the number of deer that were produced for the year (as close to it as possible) must be shot. Both bucks and does can and should be harvested to reach that goal.

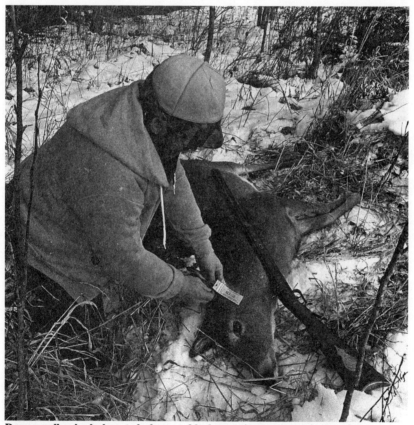

Does as well as bucks have to be harvested by hunters in many areas for best deer management.

After all, both sexes were fawned. More of each sex than were reproduced would have to be removed from the population before there would be a net decline. Looking at it another way, some does can be shot and the herd will still increase if fewer are harvested than were produced for the year.

The number of births and deaths in a deer population have to balance with the food supply. Imagine a platform balanced on a central pivot like a teeter-totter. Births and deaths are on each end and food is in the center as the fulcrum. The scale may tip one way or another for a time, but will eventually return to a balance.

If a deer herd is well below the carrying capacity of its range, allowing the herd to increase is good management. This can be done by protecting does entirely for a time or harvesting a fraction of those produced each year. Does can't be protected indefinitely, though, if that route is chosen. An increasing population will reach its limit, then must be maintained at or below that level. To do that, the annual increase of both bucks and does must be removed each year. A herd at a level that is below the capacity of its habitat is preferable to one at the limit. It is like having money in the bank.

Populations of whitetails or mulies that have gone beyond the carrying capacity of their range are the biggest problem in deer management. In order to bring them back in balance, more deer have to be removed than are produced each year. Many times it is difficult to achieve a large enough kill.

Overpopulations reduce the habitat's ability to sustain deer. More deer food is consumed than is produced. Some food sources are killed off by overuse. The number of deer their habitat will be able to support in future years will decline for each year the herd population exceeds its range's carrying capacity.

If hunters are unable or unwilling to reduce a deer herd on a year-to-year basis, the health of the population suffers. In stress situations created by extremes in weather, such as winter, some of the excess whitetails or mule deer will die of malnutrition. Those in weakened condition will be easy prey for predators.

The worst side effect of an overpopulation of deer, one that few hunters are aware of, is their reduced capability to reproduce.

A biologist said it better than I can: "Reproduction is a luxury. That animal (doe deer) is geared for its own survival. If there isn't enough food, deer just won't reproduce. A doe may become pregnant, but the young will be aborted or some other means will be used to get rid of it."

In such a situation, too many does are usually the problem. A doe left to live under these circumstances can be a detriment rather than an asset.

Ground hemlock is a preferred deer food. When deer overpopulate they reduce this to . . .

. . . this. With proper management, such situations can be avoided.

Many fawns born to weakened does will be dead at birth or die shortly afterward. Some of the young will live, but only a fraction of those that would have survived if the herd were healthy.

As odd as it may sound, more fawns will be produced by fewer does in a healthy condition than twice as many winter-weakened females. Research has shown that on properly managed deer range 30 percent of six-month-old does will produce a fawn, 90 percent of the yearlings will fawn (some with one and others with twins), and adult does will usually produce twins.

In contrast, adult does on poor range will average from .4 to 1 fawn each. Younger does in such a situation are nonproductive.

Simply looking at birthing figures among adult does, the advantages of maintaining a balance between range and herd size become apparent. Ten healthy does can be expected to have twenty fawns. Twenty poorly nourished does will reproduce a maximum of twenty young.

Going one step farther using the same reasoning, deer hunters can harvest more whitetails and mulies annually from a properly managed herd than from one that is out of balance with its habitat, even though there are fewer animals carried through the winter in the first instance.

Sounds simple on paper doesn't it? It is, really. But how do deer managers know what the carrying capacity of habitat is, how many deer are using it, and how many of each sex should be harvested?

In the field there is no way to account accurately for every deer. However, their numbers can be estimated with reasonable accuracy. This is done in a variety of ways. One method consists of counting groups of deer pellets on randomly chosen plots. It sounds far out and maybe a bit ridiculous at first, but think about it for a minute. When scouting for deer, one of the signs hunters look for is droppings. The frequency with which they appear provides a rough index to what extent the area is being used.

When done scientifically, the number of pellet groups in an area actually does represent the number of deer in an area. Biologists know through studies how many times a deer defecates in a day. This information, combined with random sampling and statistical probabilities and calculations, provides a reasonably accurate estimate of populations. The entire procedure is too sophisticated to detail here, but it has proved to be one of the best ways to determine deer numbers.

There are other methods of estimating deer populations, such as marking individuals, aerial surveys, and others. Each is based on sound information and involves complex mathematical computations. The important thing to keep in mind about deer-population estimates is they allow for error. Figures reflect upper and lower limits rather than a single, cut-and-dried number, even though they may be listed that way.

A whitetail doe with twin fawns in Michigan. Healthy adult does will produce twins.

As an example, the deer population of the two-square-mile wintering area near where I live was recently estimated. Researchers concluded that from 361 to 543 deer wintered in the yard. The same thing is done for individual management units and entire states.

The carrying capacity of an area is determined in a fashion similar to the way some deer-population estimates are conducted. Random plots are chosen, then edible browse is cut and weighed. Mathematical computations are used to complete the survey. It is important to realize that when estimating the amount of browse that will be available in wintering areas, only the material that will be within reach of whitetails and mulies is considered. Much of the food hunters see in the fall will be covered with snow in winter or is too high for deer to reach.

Population and browse estimates are used to determine how many deer of each sex can be harvested. The number of hunters expected and harvests achieved in previous years are also considered. Additional variables deer managers try to take into account are deer losses to poachers, predators, and automobiles. Another important consideration in western states is competition between livestock and deer for available food supplies.

States are usually divided into a number of different management units because of varying conditions often present within each. Harvest goals are normally determined for each unit.

It is seldom difficult to get a desired harvest of bucks. To encourage the take of antlerless deer, hunters are sometimes offered them as a bonus to the regular limit. Some areas have a two-deer limit and one of the animals must be antlerless. Others offer camp or party permits that can only be filled with a doe or young-of-the-year buck. Another option is hunter-choice permits. A hunter holding one can shoot either a buck or doe. Additional possibilities exist and are in use.

Some years the hunt goes as expected and an appropriate number of deer are harvested. There are others, however, when not enough or too many whitetails and mule deer are bagged. Variable hunting conditions and hunter densities may make animals more, or less, vulnerable than expected. The deer range is surveyed every year to keep tabs on its status. Part or all of the deer killed each season are examined as well to determine their physical condition. If wintering areas are overutilized more deer will have to be removed from the population the next season through liberalized regulations.

Malnourished deer in the winter are a sure sign of too many animals. Biologists can determine the condition of dead deer by breaking open a bone on a hind leg and looking at the bone marrow. A healthy animal will have white, tallowy marrow from the fat contained in it. Malnourished deer will have exhausted much of the fat in bone marrow, leaving it red and gelatinous.

Underutilized wintering areas usually result in restrictive hunting regulations to allow herds on such range to increase.

Habitat changes and reduction are also major considerations in deer management. Even though a herd is maintained at or below the carrying capacity of a particular range, its capacity to support as many deer as it formerly did may be reduced as the vegetative growth, usually trees, matures. Forested areas with numerous openings, both grassy and logged types, are ideal for deer. Habitat such as this will support a maximum number of deer. As trees crowd into grassy fields and they grow up out of reach of deer, the habitat's deer-supporting capability is reduced. The same thing happens when habitat is flooded or developed in some way that makes it no longer useful to deer.

When the habitat is lost the white-tailed or mule deer that formerly occupied it have to move to other areas or, if there isn't room elsewhere, they will be removed from the population, preferably by hunting. Remember: the birth-and-death rate of a deer population has to balance with the food supply.

Habitat that is maturing is not a lost cause in many cases. It can be brought back to maximum deer production and maintained there through manipulation or improvement. Logging is one of the best ways to keep a necessary portion of deer range productive. Controlled burns, natural fires, and herbicide use also improve living conditions for deer.

When logging is utilized to improve habitat, trees should be cut every five to ten years. Obviously, this can't be done to the same group of trees that often. Most take much longer than that to mature. The practice that is used to manage forests, both for deer and timber production, involves keeping as much of the habitat in mixed-age stands of trees as possible.

In an ideal situation a percentage of the trees in an area will mature at five- to ten-year intervals. For example, consider a forty-acre stand of forty-year-old aspen. It can be cut on a forty-year cycle. A ten-acre clear-cut could be made every ten years. By the time the last ten acres were cleared, trees on the first area cut would be mature again. When done on larger acreages a continuing patchwork of openings can be maintained.

This illustrates how habitat management works. It would be great if all deer range were suitable for such a scheme. There is so much diversity, however, that individual management plans have to be developed for each range. Unfortunately, a large percentage of deer habitat across the U.S., much of which is privately owned, isn't managed at all. State lands suitable for deer production are usually managed under the guidance of foresters and wildlife biologists with the departments of fish and game or natural resources.

Deer hunters who own land that isn't currently managed may be able to improve the habitat and realize an increase in deer on their property, which would result in better hunting. State game biologists, foresters, and county extension agents are usually available to help develop a suitable management plan. Private landowners can realize financial benefit from timber sales for habitat improvement as well as increased deer numbers.

A way to increase benefits of cutting to deer is to cut in the winter when natural browse is scarcest. Felled treetops represent tons of nutritious food to whitetails and mule deer. This is a form of feeding deer, but it is beneficial, unlike the artificial feeding of corn, hay, and pelletized food that is practiced in some areas.

Artificial feeding does more harm than good. First of all, the digestive systems of many deer cannot handle a rapid change in diet. Bacteria are present in their stomachs to aid in the digestive process. The type of bacteria varies, depending on the type of food that is being eaten. Deer that have been feeding on woody material, for example, cannot adequately utilize corn or hay given them when there is a shortage of natural food. In the case of corn, kernels that are eaten by hungry animals lie undigested in

Cutting in the winter provides immediate food for hungry deer.

the rumen where they ferment and form a poisonous ammonia gas that can kill them.

This problem does not exist when whitetails or mulies eat the felled tops of trees, their natural food.

Deer can use artificial food adequately during the winter when fed these rations throughout the season. Their digestive systems will adjust to it. This type of artificial feeding builds an artificial herd, if done on a continuing basis. Deer numbers will go higher and higher and the quantity of food necessary to feed them will increase steadily, as will the food bill.

While the herd is building, its winter habitat will deteriorate. Its capacity to provide natural browse will reach low levels. Although the artificially fed deer herd that has overpopulated its winter range may not need the browse, deer will eat whatever is available.

Eventually, a point will be reached when not enough artificial food can be provided. The inevitable then happens: deer die. If rations are drastically reduced or eliminated, a major decline in the population occurs. Liberalized hunting regulations are necessary to harvest the number of deer required to avoid great death tolls under these circumstances.

Live-trapping the animals would be too costly and impractical in most situations.

The only way an excessive build-up of deer can be avoided in an artificial feeding situation is to crop the herd's annual production every year. Sound familiar? This practice is the same as maintaining a herd within the carrying capacity of its natural food supply. Artificial feeding simply is not necessary if the habitat is healthy and the deer population using it is in balance with the natural food supply. If there are too many deer in an area, removing the excess number or improving the habitat to accommodate them are better alternatives than artificial feeding.

An artificial deer-feeding situation that proved to be a problem existed in a national park in upper Michigan: Pictured Rocks National Lake Shore. The affected area is known as Beaver Basin. Deer that wintered in the basin were artificially fed for years while it was privately owned by the Michigan-Wisconsin Pipeline Company. The company spent thousands of dollars every year to sustain the whitetails.

The herd was well in excess of the carrying capacity of its range when the federal Park Service acquired the land. It has a policy against the artificial feeding of any wildlife. Rather than halt feeding altogether, rations were reduced while a special hunt was planned to thin the herd. Some local residents opposed the hunt because they felt estimates of the herd size were too high and there was enough natural browse to sustain it in the winter. As a result, no special hunt was held and the herd died off at a rate of more than a hundred per season. This was with supplemental feeding. There would have been a dramatic crash had the feeding been stopped entirely.

Winter-starved fawns are common problems in areas with poor deer management.

Hundreds of deer that could have been harvested by hunters died. In the process the habitat was damaged further. Because of this, it will take more years for that wintering area to rejuvenate to the point a herd of any size can be maintained than if hunters had removed the surplus. If the hunters who opposed the hunt had a better understanding of deer management, those animals could have been put to better use than as food for predators and scavengers.

As an offshoot of poor deer or habitat management, predators are often wrongly blamed for declines in deer populations. In Beaver Basin, for example, a number of deer were killed by coyotes and bobcats, a higher number than would have been susceptible if the herd were healthy. Winter-weakened deer that may die anyway are easy prey for predators.

Loss of fawns is often attributed to predators, too. In reality, many does on poor range simply don't produce living fawns.

Such predators as coyotes, bobcats, wolves, and mountain lions certainly kill deer, both young and adults, from healthy populations. Their kills, however, are usually not responsible for the decline of a population any more than hunter kills are. As mentioned previously, deer managers take predation into account when setting harvest goals for hunting seasons. As long as total deer mortality is the same or less than reproduction for any given year, the population will not decline. In my opinion, predators have as much right to deer as hunters do. They certainly earn their kills. If human hunters were as skillful as predators at getting close to deer, there would be no need for this book.

Before leaving the subject of predators, I would like to add that their populations may, at times, reach higher levels than desirable. When they overpopulate they also have an adverse impact on their food supply. For this reason, predators must be managed, too, but they don't deserve the reputations and treatment they have gotten from many deer hunters who would like to eliminate them entirely.

One of the biggest barriers to blanket acceptance of deer-management decisions is getting hunters to accept the validity of population figures. They spend hours in the field and many of them see few whitetails or mule deer. This leads them to believe there are few animals around, unless they are able to see plenty of tracks, droppings, or other deer sign. Anyway, the next season when wildlife biologists say there is an over-abundance of deer and more does have to be harvested, the hunter becomes skeptical.

There are two primary reasons for opposing assessments of deer numbers. Some hunters spend each season, year after year, in the same area. They come to accept the territory they are familiar with as representative of their region, if not their state. Actually, there can be tremendous differences in deer densities in areas separated by fifty miles, or less. Most states are divided into management units to compensate for these differences, but it isn't always possible to separate accurately all units. Major roadways are often used as boundaries. These seldom coincide with differing deer-herd considerations.

The second major reason for differing opinions on deer abundance is that many hunters give themselves too much credit and deer too little. They expect that if there are a lot of deer in the area they will see a lot, if there are only a few they will see a few. It works this way sometimes, but not usually. Both whitetails and mulies are adept at avoiding hunters. And many hunters aren't as keen at sneaking through the woods or picking a stand as they think they are. I have been skunked while deer hunting enough times myself when there were plenty of deer around. I've learned to realize a hunter's limitations.

To illustrate my last point I will leave you with some facts and figures from a couple of closely monitored hunts in Michigan. One took place on a five-square-mile island in Lake Michigan — South Fox Island — during 1970. At that time the population of deer on the island was estimated to number approximately 600 animals. That meant there were about 120 deer per square mile!

The bag limit was three deer, two of which had to be antlerless. There were a total of 612 hunters who took part. They bagged 382 animals. Only 1 percent of the hunters collected three deer, 14 percent got two and 31 percent took one. A whopping 54 percent of the hunters were unsuccessful; some of them didn't even see a deer during their hunt!

The second closely monitored Michigan hunt was held inside a one-square-mile enclosure with a known population of deer. There were thirty-nine of them: seven bucks, fourteen does, and eighteen fawns. Seven experienced deer hunters hunted in the enclosure for four days. A total of eight deer were taken — three does, four fawns, and one buck. Only one of the seven bucks was sighted during the course of the hunt!

Hunts were held in the enclosure for seven years. The results each time proved that hunters are inefficient, only sighting a fraction of the population present in an area. This study was conducted in an area of limited size. On larger tracts of land hunters probably see an even smaller percentage of the actual number of deer present.

18

Bonus Seasons

All I could see was a group of bobbing antlers heading toward my brother and me. Six mule deer bucks were taking their time, feeding as they came. There were two bucks with big racks in the bunch. The one in the lead looked the best, so I riveted my attention on him.

When the lead animal was 150 yards out and still coming, I put the crosshairs on his shoulder, uncertain about waiting any longer to take him.

Bruce's reassuring words were what I needed: "Let him come. Take your time."

When the buck was between 100 and 125 yards away he turned to our right and was broadside. I figured that was the closest he would get. The buck jumped straight in the air when my 150-grain .30-06 slug connected; then he took off running. A second hit put him down for keeps. The mule deer's rack had five points on a side.

Another time when I was hunting whitetails with a muzzleloader there was a pair of young bucks working toward me across an opening that had been recently logged. One had spikes, and the second had a small rack with four points. When the bigger-antlered buck was still about eighty yards away it looked like he scented me, so I decided to try a shot.

I aimed for his shoulder and touched the trigger on my .50-caliber Hawken made by Thompson/Center Arms. The breeze whisked the smoke from the shot away quickly enough for me to see the buck bounding away with its tail wagging—a sure sign of a miss.

Something happened next that I probably will never experience again. Three magnificent bucks, each with racks carrying at least eight points, appeared one after the other from a lane to my left and trotted by me only thirty-five yards away! They continued by me into a swamp. I simply stood there and watched them disappear, almost not believing what I saw.

There wasn't enough time to reload the muzzleloader. Even if there would have been, I couldn't have shot anyway. I felt sure my round ball missed the buck I shot at because of his actions, but I couldn't be positive until I checked.

I recount these deer-hunting experiences because they both occurred during bonus seasons. They were special hunts designed to increase the harvest of an underutilized segment of the deer population or to increase recreational opportunities for deer hunters.

I collected the mule deer in Colorado during late August. The buck's antlers were still in velvet. The early-season rifle hunt was only held in certain high-country wilderness areas that were often inaccessible to hunters because of snow during the state's regular deer season. As a result, bucks that reside in these mountainous retreats were underharvested. An early season provided better harvesting of these deer and an excellent opportunity for hunters to collect trophy bucks.

Incidentally, this bonus season was suspended in Colorado for a number of years to allow the deer herd to increase. The early hunt may be reinstated in the future.

That unusual concentration of whitetail bucks crossed my path on a December hunt in Michigan after the close of the regular firearms season. The late season was established to give muzzleloading deer hunters a bonus opportunity to collect a buck if they were unsuccessful in filling their regular-season deer tag. The added time afield is a boon to hunters and does not adversely affect the deer herd. It is difficult to overharvest bucks during a primitive-weapons hunt.

The best time to hunt deer is whenever you can, but bonus hunts such as those I've described often provide a better opportunity to see whitetails or mule deer and bag one than regular seasons do. Sometimes pre- or post-season hunts simply offer deer hunters additional time to fill one license, as was the case with Michigan's black-powder hunt. It all depends on the circumstances. Other times deer taken during bonus seasons won't affect hunters' regular-season bag limits.

This is usually true in cases where an area has an overpopulation problem or an extra incentive is required to get hunters to participate. An example of such a situation is South Fox Island, which is part of Michigan and lies in Lake Michigan. Because it is remote (twenty-odd miles out in the lake), it is difficult to attract enough hunters there every year to harvest enough deer to prevent overbrowsing of the habitat. Deer tagged there

My best whitetail buck, an eleven-pointer, was taken on a late-season musket hunt.

with bow or rifle don't count on a hunter's regular license. Post-season hunts were held on the island for a couple of years, but now the season there coincides with deer hunts on the mainland.

A change in weapons may be all that is necessary to take advantage of bonus deer-hunting seasons in many cases. As I've already mentioned, switching from a modern rifle to a muzzleloader will give hunters added time afield in Michigan. The same is true in other states. Hunting with bow and arrow in addition to firearms often opens the door to additional deer-hunting opportunities. Most states have separate seasons for archers and firearms hunters. Archery hunts usually precede firearms seasons, but some are also held afterward. A few states restrict deer hunters to the use of only one weapon a year, so be sure to check local regulations.

My only regret about bowhunting for deer is that I didn't start sooner. The first years I hunted deer were with firearms exclusively. Then I started bowhunting. I wasn't as successful in bagging deer with a bow as I had been with a rifle, at least at the outset. More important though, I saw more deer than I had ever seen before, had plenty of opportunities to score, and

Hunting with bow and arrow as well as with firearms makes additional hunting time available to deer hunters.

learned a lot more about deer. The pleasant weather common during bow seasons added additional appeal to bowhunting for deer.

In the long run, I became a better firearms hunter because of what I learned while bowhunting and a better bowhunter because of my experience hunting whitetails and mule deer with rifles and shotguns.

Early fall bonus seasons are often rewarding because deer densities are at the highest levels possible. In addition, whitetails or mulies that haven't been hunted since the previous fall won't be extremely wary. It is not unusual to see bucks traveling together, especially mulies, at this time of year.

The only drawback to some early deer hunts is they are sometimes held in remote areas with rough terrain, which makes the territory hard to reach and the hunt a physical challenge. I was hunting between 10,000 and 12,000 feet above sea level in the Rocky Mountains when I downed the mule deer mentioned earlier. The going was tough, but the beauty of the surroundings at that time of year made the hunt worthwhile. The weather was pleasant for the most part on the mountain hunt, but temperatures commonly fell below freezing at night. Rain was almost an everyday occurrence, too, and snow fell occasionally.

The weather during late-season deer hunts can be downright miserable, but this is one factor that increases the vulnerability of whitetails and mule deer to hunters. Thermometer readings were below zero the day during muzzleloader season when I saw five bucks in a matter of seconds. Temperatures were the same throughout the hunt. All of those deer were feeding on the tops of trees that had been felled by loggers.

Cold weather had the deer moving and feeding. Bucks were feeding especially heavy during this period. The rut was over, and they were trying to regain some of the weight lost during their preoccupation with breeding activities.

Deer in larger numbers are sometimes more accessible to hunters during post-season hunts, too. Mule deer characteristically move to lower elevations with the approach of winter. Some whitetails also move to wintering areas, or "yards."

This movement concentrates large numbers of deer in smaller areas than they occupied earlier in the fall and makes animals easier to find.

Late hunts are a great time to collect big bucks. Deepening snow usually forces them out of inaccessible haunts to areas where hunters have more chance to see them. Despite the fact that deer may be concentrated and feeding more during late seasons, they can be difficult to bag. The animals are often extremely wary because of earlier hunts.

Bonus deer seasons that are held on a statewide basis are usually open to an unlimited number of hunters. The number of participants is normally regulated by a permit system when special deer hunts are held in limited areas. Permits are often allocated during a random drawing from the selection of applicants or on first-come-first-served basis.

An advantage of bonus deer seasons, whether early or late, is light hunting pressure, even in situations where participation is not limited. While the odds of seeing other hunters are low during special hunts, the opportunity to get a look at deer may be better than any other time of the year. At the very least, these seasons provide extra hunting time. For what more could a deer hunter ask?

19

Sportsmanship and Hunting Ethics

Ethics, sportsmanship, and safety have always been important in deer hunting, and will continue to be. In recent years and in the future, however, they have had and will have a new emphasis. They will not only be determining factors for the quality of each individual's hunting experience, but also who, if anyone, will hunt.

There are people who don't understand or approve of hunting. They not only don't hunt, but also many of them don't want anyone to do so. These individuals are organized in an effort to stop, or at the very least restrict, hunting. Examples of unethical, unsportsmanlike, unsafe behavior provide them with ammunition that can be used against hunters and hunting. Any and every incident that may portray hunting or hunters in a bad light is seized and amplified, sometimes distorted.

A television special on hunting labeled as a documentary and called "The Guns of Autumn" is a perfect example of this technique. It was aired in September 1975. Many, if not all, of the sequences in the show were atypical of hunting as most of us know it. Some of the scenes and sound effects were allegedly changed, according to hunters who took part in the filming. Anyone not familiar with hunting could have easily accepted "The Guns of Autumn" as a fair representation of hunting and formed opinions against it. Conservation and hunting organizations filed a number of lawsuits against CBS over the show. Some were won and others were lost.

A similar case arising from a television program entitled "Say Goodbye" developed in the early 1970s. Alaska sportsmen were involved in this lawsuit. Film of a polar-bear-tagging project was changed to make it appear that hunters illegally killed a sow with cubs from a helicopter. The case was settled out of court in favor of hunters, according to lawyer John Hendrickson of Anchorage, who represented sportsmen in the case.

If there weren't any instances of behavior or actions that are derogatory to hunting, antihunters wouldn't have gotten as much attention as they have. Unfortunately, unethical and unsportsmanlike hunters do exist. In a way, the antihunting movement has been beneficial in focusing attention on undesirable hunters and hunting practices. Once identified, something can be done about them. If we as hunters fail to correct any problems that exist, there may come a time when none of us will be able to hunt. To clean house, so to speak, it will be necessary to insist that unethical and unsportsmanlike hunters be kept out of the field.

There was a time when each hunter was held accountable for only his or her actions. That is no longer the case. Every action of any deer hunter reflects on all deer hunters. How I represent myself as a hunter in the field, and anywhere else for that matter, affects you as a deer hunter; and your conduct, likewise, will affect me. For this reason, each deer hunter has a responsibility to all other deer hunters to behave in an ethical, sportsmanlike, safe manner.

What qualities does it take to be an ethical hunter, a safe hunter, a sportsman? Are the qualifications tough to meet?

The guidelines are so simple, such common sense things, that every hunter should easily be able to meet them. Before discussing them I want to point out something that should be obvious: all three qualities are interrelated, although they are not necessarily the same. It is difficult to possess one without the others, but it can be done. Generally, an ethical hunter is a safe hunter and a safe hunter is usually a sportsman, and so on.

My dictionary defines ethics as the "basic principles of right action." A sportsman is described as "one who abides by a code of fair play." Some people label anyone who hunts a sportsman. To my way of thinking that is the way it should be, but at this time I would consider it a misuse of the word. Safety is "the state or condition of freedom from danger or risk."

The way I read the definitions, sportsmanship is determined by following the rules and regulations of hunting, which in most cases are laws. An ethical hunter does what is right in a hunting situation even though he or she may not be specifically bound by law to do so. It isn't always possible, however, to draw a line between the two.

Consider this example. On my first mule deer hunt I spotted a huge-bodied deer while still-hunting that was no more than fifty yards away, with its head hidden behind an evergreen tree. Only bucks were legal. The shoulder area of the animal was visible, so I could have shot the deer. In all probability, due to the animal's size, it was a buck.

I didn't shoot, though. In fact, I didn't even consider it. I waited until the deer, which indeed was a huge-racked buck, showed himself before attempting a shot. As it happened, the mulie finally detected my presence and came in the open on the bounce. I missed.

When I told my story to the other hunters in camp one of them said, "Why didn't you shoot him when you had an easy shot? If it had been a doe, no one would have known the difference." That man, whom I wouldn't have been sharing a camp with if there were a choice, was wrong. I would have known the difference if I shot a deer without identifying the sex and it turned out to be a doe.

I can thank my father as the first among many who instilled attitudes in me becoming of a sportsman and ethical hunter.

Anyway, if I had shot that buck when I first saw him, even though I didn't know it was a buck at the time, I wouldn't have broken the law. Shooting before I saw antlers would have been wrong, however, because the possibility of breaking the law existed. So was what the other hunter suggested unsportsmanlike or unethical? In my opinion it was both.

There are times when, according to the definitions, ethical and sportsmanlike behavior can be separated. Suppose a freshly wounded deer comes by your stand. You have a moral and ethical obligation to finish that animal if possible, although you may not be required by law to do so.

The same considerations apply if the hunter who wounded the buck or doe comes on its track. You killed the deer, you can tag it. At least offering the whitetail or mulie to the person who drew first blood would be the right thing to do, depending upon the severity of the wound.

Deer hunters have an ethical responsibility to their quarry to first, use an adequate weapon and projectile that can be handled efficiently; second, try for a clean, killing shot; third, expend every effort possible to trail and finish a wounded animal; and fourth, clean and care for the meat properly.

One year my brother and I helped another party of hunters track a whitetail one of its members wounded. It proved to be a two-day effort to kill the doe. I dropped the deer, but relinquished it to the other hunters, as we planned to do from the start.

Hunters also have an ethical obligation to each other and hunting to pick up litter left by others; to avoid unnecessary public display of dead deer; to understand deer management practices; to avoid unnecessary conversation about the kill, dwelling more on the many other aspects of deer hunting such as sights, sounds, and feelings that are seen, heard, and experienced during days in the field.

I think it is extremely important that hunters be more conscious of what they say about hunting. I have heard tales from well-intentioned hunters that almost turned my stomach. Imagine how a nonhunter (not necessarily an antihunter) would take such accounts. Stories from hunters themselves may easily convert a nonhunter to an antihunter.

Something I have done a lot of thinking about is the classification of hunting as a sport. In the truest sense of the word I don't think hunting is a sport, but rather a sporting endeavor or pursuit. A sport is usually thought of as a match or contest between two willing teams or players that provides recreation. There is no doubt that hunting provides plenty of recreation. Take the word willing out and hunting fits the rest of the definition, too.

"Willing" is the key word, though, at least from the antihunters' point of view. Deer certainly don't participate in a hunt willingly. Calling hunting a sport can be and has been criticized for that reason.

No one can argue that hunting as it is practiced today is not a sporting endeavor. Regulations are largely designed to give deer more of an advantage than they already have over hunters by restricting the time and manner in which a hunter can harvest them. Many hunters handicap themselves further by using bows and arrows, muzzleloaders, and handguns in their pursuit of deer.

My line of reasoning here may be classified as nit-picking by some people, but I think it has merit.

To be sportsmen, deer hunters should hunt only during prescribed hours, not take more whitetails or mule deer than specified by law or those of a protected sex, not shoot protected species of wildlife, ask permission before hunting private land, not litter (spent cartridges are litter), and make sure of their targets before shooting; which leads us to the subject of safety.

As I mentioned earlier, sportsmen are usually safe hunters. Most hunting accidents, then, are caused by gun- or bowhunters who are acting in an unsportsmanlike manner. Carelessness also enters the picture in many instances.

I remember reading an account several years ago in which carelessness and breaking a game law proved to be a deadly combination on a deer hunt. A pair of hunters were working through some heavy cover when one of them spotted a grouse in a tree. Grouse season was closed, high-powered rifles shouldn't be shot in the air, and the fellow didn't know where his partner was. He shot anyway. The bullet killed his companion.

This is only one example of many. Another illegal activity that often results in hunters' ending up on the wrong end of their guns is carrying them loaded either in a vehicle or in camp. Leaning a loaded firearm against a tree or a building, or on a car is asking for trouble, too. Poor gun handling also accounts for its share of woundings and deaths. Shooting down a road, resting the barrel of a gun on an occupied boot, and disregard for the direction the muzzle of a gun is pointing are a few examples.

A firearm should always be treated as if it is loaded. Whenever picking one up check to see that the chamber is empty; don't take someone's word for it. After a day in the field make sure all shells are removed from magazine and chamber. Work the action over and over again; then look or feel in the head of the chamber and magazine to insure no unejected shells remain. Don't remove only the cartridges you thought you put in. Sometimes, somehow, there happens to be one more than there was supposed to be.

I will never forget an experience that taught me a lesson in this respect. When returning to my car after hunting I used to remove the number of shells I *knew* I put in, then point the firearm at the ground, away from the vehicle or anyone with me, and pull the trigger so the gun wouldn't be stored in a cocked position. One evening when I did that, my gun discharged. There was no real harm done, except the unexpected shot scared me. That lesson taught me to check and double-check to make sure all ammunition is ejected.

To illustrate that my experience wasn't a freak, a similar incident that happened to a friend of mine is worth mentioning. On his way home from deer hunting, my friend was stopped by a conservation officer who asked to see his gun. He assured the officer the rifle was unloaded, which he was sure of, but when the warden worked the action a cartridge came out.

Never point a gun or an arrow in the direction of people or buildings. Always know where hunting partners are. If there is a chance they are in the line of fire of a deer, don't shoot. No whitetail or mule deer is worth the possible injury or death of a person.

Horseplay and guns don't mix. Neither do alcohol and hunting. Always try to make sure there are no obstructions in the barrel of a gun, only use the proper ammunition, always keep the safety on until ready to shoot, and never shoot at a flat, hard surface or water.

If crossing a fence or some other obstruction pass the rifle, shotgun, or bow over or under first; break the action or unload it if it is necessary to carry it. Use a rope to lift and lower unloaded firearms and bows to and from tree stands. An unloaded gun can also be carried into a tree stand safely with a sling. Also try to use safety belts when in a tree stand to prevent accidental falls.

Above all else, be sure of your target. Seeing a movement or a color, or hearing a sound is not enough to warrant a shot. Also as a point of safety, firearms hunters should not wear garments of brown, black, or white. Many states now require gun hunters to wear fluorescent-orange in

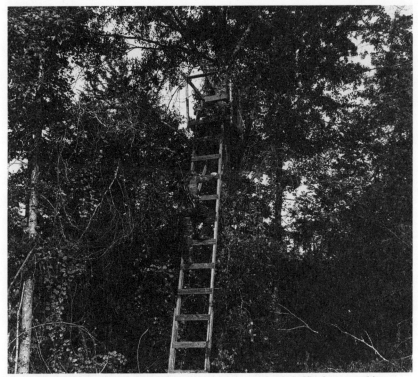

An early-season deerhunter climbs a tree stand with an unloaded rifle slung over his shoulder. Never do this with a loaded gun.

varying amounts, which has significantly reduced mistaken-identity accidents. It is a good idea to wear garments of this material even if it is not mandatory.

One other point: just because a deer hunter happens to be carrying a gun in the woods doesn't mean it must be fired. Shooting at tin cans and various other inanimate targets will only spook deer the other way. Target practice should be done on the range.

Bowhunters must be extremely careful with broadheads. If they are as sharp as they should be, they are capable of causing injury at any time, not just when released from a bow. Keep heads in covered quivers until ready for use. Never shoot a broadhead up in the air.

Many states now require young hunters to pass safety courses before they can obtain licenses. This is an excellent way to make sure future generations of hunters will be adequately versed in safe hunting practices. When young hunters are starting out is the best time to get them thinking of safety.

Tree-stand hunters should use a rope to lift their weapons to them once in position. A bow can be hung on a limb and retrieved when in position, as shown here.

Our father saw to it that my brother and I completed a hunter's safety course before we got our first hunting licenses. He also emphasized safety when in the field with us. From my experience I can appreciate the value of early introduction to gun and bow safety.

Each deer hunter should not only strive to be ethical, safe, and a sportsman, but he or she should also expect the same from hunting companions. This becomes especially important for safety. It is a proven fact that the vast majority of hunting accidents involve members of the same party.

One of the best ways to become acquainted with sportsmen in your area is to join a sportsmen's club. Another benefit of membership is that most clubs have facilities for target practice. Membership in sportsmen's clubs on the local, state, and national levels is also a great way to promote proper hunting practices and get the hunter's story to nonhunters.

National Hunting and Fishing Day, which is now an annual observance, is one of the best ways to do this. There are ways to tell your story on a continuing basis, too. One club in California, for instance, collects outdoor magazines from its members for distribution in school libraries, doctors' offices, and other key locations where they are sure to be read. Another way to reach people is through club-sponsored slide shows and lectures at schools or meetings of civic organizations. Deer and deer hunting are popular topics. Many groups are interested in learning more about both.

A sportsmen's club near where I live makes sure everyone entering and leaving the city gets a reminder about safety and sportsmanship in hunting. There is a sign along the highway that carries a message on each side. One side reads, "Stretch Your Story, Not Your Bag Limit," and the other, "Recognize Your Game First, Then Shoot." They are simple reminders, but passing motorists think about them. Drawing attention to these qualities is sure to help the image of the club as well as hunters in general.

Sportsmen's groups should also be constantly vigilant for newspaper articles or letters to the editor that make hunters look bad. Try to respond to them in a sensible manner in a letter to the editor. If facts have been twisted, do your best to straighten them out. Most people read their local newspaper, so this is an excellent way to reach nonhunters.

Clubs can display their disapproval of the shooting of protected animals or birds by offering rewards for information leading to the conviction of guilty parties. This helps the legitimate hunters' image.

One winter some poachers using bows and arrows got into a local deer pen that was part of a small zoo, killing three of the animals. Our archery club immediately reacted by offering a reward to help in locating the culprits. We let everyone know our disapproval through radio broadcasts and letters in the local paper.

The criminals were not apprehended, but at least the public was made aware serious bowhunters weren't going to take the blame for such actions.

Illegal hunting is probably one of deer hunting's biggest black eyes. Estimates in some states put the illegal deer-kill as high or higher than the annual legal kill. Always try to be on the watch for poaching or other infractions of game laws and report any incidents to local officials. Most

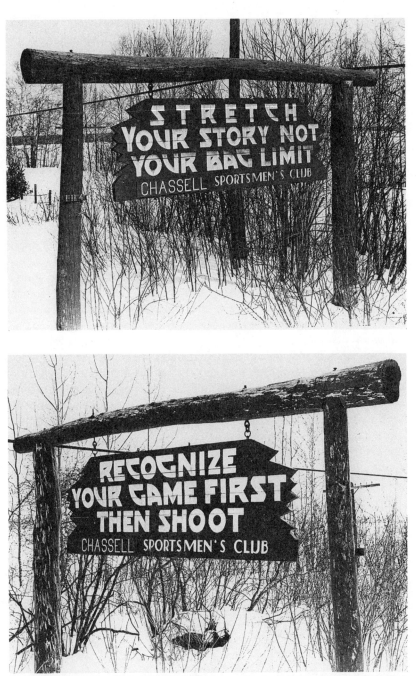

Reminders such as these help the hunter's image as well as make hunters more conscious of their responsibility.

states have toll-free numbers hunters can call to report violators. Under many programs of this type, tipsters turn in poachers anonymously and can claim a reward by using an identifying number.

Before concluding this chapter I would like to point out that a hunter's attitude toward hunting and the quarry probably has the most bearing on whether or not he will be ethical and exhibit sportsmanship.

Hunters who view hunting primarily as killing, for example, and feel they must get a deer at all costs, can't be ethical or sportsmanlike. They often must break game laws to attain their goal. These individuals miss out on the true benefits of hunting.

Hunting's primary benefit is recreational: simply to be in the outdoors; to relax in space unconfined by walls and buildings; to see, hear, experience, and learn about the many aspects of nature. Learning about and respecting deer is a major part of deer hunting; shooting a deer is of secondary importance. Nonetheless, all of us want to be successful in our attempts to bag a deer, even though the odds are against most of us. Realizing all of this is part of the attitude that breeds ethics and sportsmanship. You try your hardest against the odds, savor every moment afield, and hunger for every clue that will tell you something about a particular whitetail, mulie, or deer in general so that you *might* see one, *might* kill one.

Yet, when the season comes to a close and you haven't scored, you feel satisfied that you tried your best and can accept hunting for what it is: hours, days, months, and years of looking, learning, waiting, searching, and hoping — not killing. It is enough to whet a true deer hunter's appetite for the next season.

20

Success without Success

Features of my surroundings were losing their distinctness as the light faded at the end of a day of deer hunting. This time it was more than the end of a day, however; it was the end of a season, and I hadn't gotten a deer.

Actually, my attempts to bag a deer spanned three seasons: there had been a regular firearms hunt; the special muzzle-loading season; and a period for bow and arrow. These were the final minutes of that last season. My chances of getting a deer for the year faded with the light.

I climbed down from my tree stand and walked to a nearby road to wait for my partner to pick me up. I would be lying if I said I wasn't disappointed. I was. After all, anticipation of connecting with a deer was one of the primary motivating forces responsible for getting me in the woods in the first place. There was more behind my being in the outdoors day after day, though.

The disappointment wasn't solely because I didn't get a deer. The fact that I wouldn't get another opportunity to "hunt deer" until the next fall was as much, if not more, a part of the feeling. Reflecting on the past two months of deer hunting while waiting for my ride, I realized my lengthy season had been successful even though a deer wasn't tagged. A variety of experiences helped make it so.

One of the experiences happened when a white weasel came by my stand on the second day of the regular firearms hunt. Despite the fact the weasel was wearing its winter coat of white, it stood out in sharp contrast to its surroundings, since there wasn't any snow on the ground.

This white weasel added success to a day of deer hunting.

The streamlined predator thoroughly investigated a brush pile next to me, then started away after finding no prey. A squeak from my lips that imitated the sound a small mammal might make stopped the weasel in its tracks. After staring in bewilderment into the brush pile, it dove back in for another look around.

Then a red squirrel got into the act. It apparently saw the off-colored animal and came to investigate.

The squirrel made a couple of passes at the weasel as it came out of the brush pile for the second time. Oddly enough, the predator dodged the advances of the squirrel rather than attacking. Maybe it was still confused about the source of the squeak. At any rate, I let the weasel continue on its way that time, chuckling to myself as it went.

I have found that deer hunting is more than hours spent in the field with the sole intent of getting a shot at a whitetail or mulie. Deer hunting is a total immersion in the outdoors. From my point of view, any experience that makes the hunter feel more a part of the outdoors has to be considered a success. Seeing and shooting deer can be part of that success, but it doesn't have to be.

Success is the sum of all the experiences on a deer hunt that make the hunter's days afield worthwhile, the little and big things that make time in the outdoors richer. Hearing, seeing, and interacting with all forms of wildlife, such as the weasel I mentioned, are part of the success of a deer hunt, to me.

There are other things, too, such as witnessing a beautiful sunrise or being so enchanted with the stillness of the forest you hesitate to interrupt it by moving. Many of the experiences that add to the success of a hunt are difficult to share with others. They can't be brought home like a deer. Even fellow hunters may find it hard to appreciate the singular value of your particular moments in the field.

Experiences that add to the success of a hunt are not always individual things. Good companionship and sharing the good fortune of another member of the party who tagged a deer are also part of it. The afternoon I saw the white weasel, my brother dropped a buck. His success made my day more successful.

If downing a deer were necessary for every hunter to have a successful hunt, the number of those going afield after deer each year would be declining. Instead, their ranks are increasing. Only a small percentage of those who go afield score. The remainder find something compelling about deer hunting other than the kill that brings them back year after year. Most hunters enjoy a hunt without bagging a deer: success without success.

Success without success is one of the easiest things to achieve on a deer hunt. No one can tell hunters how to do it; it just happens. Consistently being successful in collecting a whitetail or mule deer, on the other hand, is one of the most difficult aspects of deer hunting. That is why this book and others like it devote most of their content to the know-how involved in getting close enough to deer to shoot them, rather than the peripheral joys of deer hunting.

I think such lopsided treatment tends to emphasize the kill rather than the hunt and its sidelights, no matter how unintentional this highlighting is. But the trees, plants, shrubs, insects, birds, reptiles, amphibians, and mammals other than deer are just as much a part of the deer hunter's world as whitetails and mulies.

As I mentioned in previous chapters, killing a deer should be considered a bonus of the hunt. If it is viewed as a necessary part, few will be truly successful.

Seeing that white weasel and sharing in my brother's kill were only a couple of highlights of that year I didn't get a deer. One extremely successful day during the muzzleloading season I saw no less than thirty-three deer. Every last one of them was bald — no antlers. Only antlered bucks were legal during the hunt, but it was nice to look over that many animals. The frequent sightings kept up my hopes of eventually seeing a buck.

A comical show put on by a ruffed grouse that day made it a little more successful. All the trees were coated with ice from freezing drizzle.

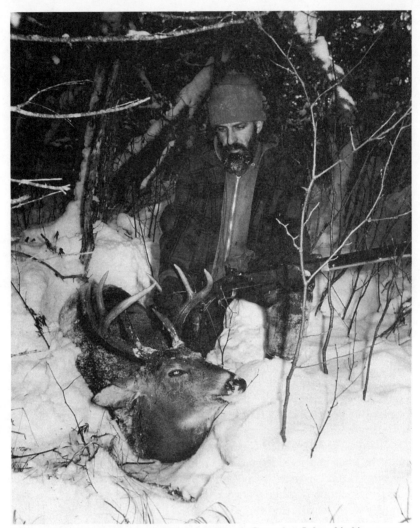

Bruce Smith with a black-powder buck in Michigan in December. I shared in his success.

The bird landed in a maple tree near me to pick at buds. It was slipping and sliding as it tried to maintain a grip on the icy branches. From its actions the grouse looked intoxicated.

The more I thought about the days I hunted deer as I waited for my ride on that last day of hunting, the more I realized how successful they had been. I smiled as I remembered an antler I found in December. I was hunting with bow and arrow then. There were three of us, and I was making a drive toward my friends Bill and Kirwin when I spotted an antler in the snow. It had four points. The beam had been shed recently; there was still blood on the base.

I tucked the shed antler in my pocket and when I reached my partners I tried to convince them I got a shot at a buck and my arrow knocked the antler off. I have a hard time keeping a straight face when trying to fool someone. They knew I was pulling their legs.

Two days later Kirwin arrowed a beautiful buck that had shed one antler. It wasn't the same animal that dropped the antler I found, though. The beam remaining on the deer's head was much more massive than the one I picked up. The deer was killed miles from where we had been before, too.

Kirwin's success and finding that shed antler contributed to my successful year of deer hunting.

My reminiscing was interrupted by approaching headlights that I knew would be my partner. "Maybe Bill got one," I thought. But I knew it didn't matter. The collective seasons had been successful even though I didn't get a deer. Bill would feel the same way if he hadn't scored.

Conclusion

Writing about deer hunting is great, but it doesn't get as high a rating from me as actual hunting. Since Michigan's firearms deer season arrived before I completed this book, I took time out to take part. After all, I reasoned, it would be an opportunity to do some last-minute research.

I got a deer, a buck, the day after Thanksgiving. He had three points. Antlerless deer weren't legal in the area I hunted. It took me six days of hunting to connect. I spent better than sixty hours in the field hunting, and the kill took all of five seconds. I'm not complaining; I'm just pointing out that there is a lot more to hunting than killing.

It was 11:30 in the morning when the yearling buck walked past my stand. My vigil began four hours earlier at first light. There was snow on the ground. The evergreen trees surrounded me. It was windy and cold.

There was a noise off to my right. When I looked, my buck was there, thirty-five to forty yards away, moving across a small opening at a brisk walking pace. The antlers were easy to see against the backdrop of snow. He was in the scope as soon as I brought the rifle up.

The crosshairs were on his shoulder as he passed through a small opening between two trees. I waited. If I would have shot then, I think my bullet would have hit farther back than I wanted because of the deer's speed.

He was in a bigger opening in a fraction of a second. The crosshairs were on the mark, and I squeezed the trigger. My 150-grain soft-point knocked the whitetail off his feet, dead instantly. The bullet hit where the neck joins the body.

An hour later I was relaxing at my post after dressing the deer and taking some photos. I took a bite out of a sandwich from my lunch and saw another deer just beyond where my buck had fallen. Seconds later, a huge eight- or ten-point buck walked quickly through an opening.

It may have been the same buck I saw two days earlier from the same stand. He was running then, so there was no time for a shot. Maybe that buck will be around next year.

I had seen still another buck earlier in the season. This one was in heavy brush. I didn't shoot at that one on the chance he would present a more open shot. He didn't.

The deer were moving more the day I got my buck than they had the entire season. My brother may have helped the situation. He was tracking during most of the morning and may have pushed my buck to me.

While dragging the whitetail I shot to my car, a strange thing happened. At one point a doe came bounding through the hardwoods, bleating as she went. She circled downwind of me and stopped no more than forty yards away. The deer stood there for some time looking at me and calling. I think she was in estrus (ready to breed) and smelled the buck. Eventually, she left.

The sound the doe made is hard to describe, but I'll bet if a commercial call could be manufactured to imitate it bucks would be attracted by the sound during the rut.

You may be wondering why it took me six days to collect a deer. It wasn't because I didn't scout my area ahead of the season. I did. The stand I picked for opening day looked good, but I didn't see anything there. That's right, not one deer! The weather may have contributed to my failure. It was foggy and drizzly all day.

There was success that day among the Smith party though. Uncle George got a spikehorn first thing in the morning. I spent several hours helping him get it out of the woods.

The third member of our party, my brother Bruce, missed a shot at a buck while still-hunting the second day of the season. Now, with two people to move deer for him, there is a good chance he will fill his tag before the season is over.

I have learned a lot about deer and deer hunting while writing this book. If you learn something, too, it will have been worth my time in the writing and yours in the reading. I wish I could say everything there is to know about deer and deer hunting is included in these pages, but it's not. There is a lot of information though, enough that I hope this book will be beneficial to a lot of people who, like me, are interested in deer — hunters and nonhunters alike.

There is one last point about hunting deer that I want to make before closing: luck plays as much a part, if not more, in the success of some hunters as skill or knowledge. You can apply every last bit of how-to information in this book and still not get a deer. Yet, another guy who heads into the field deer hunting for the first time in his life and doesn't know a thing about the pursuit can kill a trophy buck.

It is hard to understand, but it happens. Deer are simply not predictable all the time. Nonetheless, for consistent success it pays to be as conscientious and as knowledgeable as possible.

Deer hunting has its share of disappointments, but there are also rewards. Most of the time rewards overshadow disappointments. I know they have for me. The greatest benefit I derive from deer hunting is its contribution to my good health—both physical and mental. I hope deer hunting is at least as rewarding for you.

Bibliography

Brakefield, Tom. *The Sportsman's Complete Book of Trophy and Meat Care.* Harrisburg, Pa.: Stackpole Books, 1975.

———. *Hunting Big-Game Trophies: A North American Guide.* New York: E. P. Dutton Co., 1976.

Brister, Bob. "Rattle 'Em Up, But Safely." *Field & Stream,* vol. 130, no. 8, December 1975, pp. 42–48.

Carmichel, Jim. "Good Gun Care in Foul Weather." *Outdoor Life,* vol. 156, no. 5, pp. 90–94, November 1975.

———. "Sight In Now." *Outdoor Life,* vol. 158, no. 4, October 1976, pp. 94–102.

Cartier, John O. "Guide to Hunting Deer from a Stand." *Outdoor Life,* vol. 156, no. 4, October 1975, pp. 85–92.

Dalrymple, Byron W. *The Complete Book of Deer Hunting.* New York: Winchester Press, 1973.

East, Ben. "The Big Lie." *Outdoor Life,* vol. 149, no. 6, June 1972, pp. 65–67, 100–106.

Elman, Robert, ed. *All About Deer Hunting in America.* New York: Winchester Press, 1976.

Fawcett, Joel S. "Try This for Whitetails." *Sports Afield,* vol. 160, no. 3, September 1968, pp. 44–45, 120–121.

Geagan, Bill. "How Indians Hunt Deer." *Field & Stream,* vol. 125, no. 8, December 1970, pp. 36–37, 59–66.

Harbour, Dave. "21 Deer Taking Tips." *Sports Afield,* vol. 170, no. 3, September 1973, pp. 46–50, 139–141.

Helgeland, Glenn. "What the Compound Bow Will Do." *Field & Stream,* vol. 131, no. 6, October 1976, pp. 82–89.

Kal, Paula D. "A Cold Woman Never Got a Whitetail." *The American Rifleman,* vol. 125, no. 1, February 1977, pp. 28–29.

Koller, Lawrence R. *Shots at Whitetails.* New York: Knopf, 1970.

Meryl, Karl, and Boue, Ken. *The Deer of Nebraska.* Nebraska Game & Parks Commission Bulletin.

Miller, Peter. "Masters of the Tracker's Art." *Sports Afield,* vol. 172, no. 4, October 1974, pp. 60–63, 166–172.

O'Connor, Jack. "Sighting In Your Rifle." *Outdoor Life,* vol. 148, no. 4, October 1971, pp. 96–100, 104–106.

———. "Where to Place the Shot on Big Game." *Outdoor Life,* vol. 147, no. 1, January 1971, pp. 90–99.

Oertle, V. Lee. "Mule Deer Are Where You Find Them." *Outdoor Life,* Vol. 160, No. 1, July 1977, pp. 76–79, 144.

"Planning a Big Game Hunt." *The American Hunter,* vol. 5, no. 8, August 1977, pp. 69–123.

Richardson, Arthur H., and Petersen, Lyle E. *History and Management of South Dakota Deer.* South Dakota Department of Game, Fish & Parks, Bulletin No. 5, 1974.

Rue, Leonard Lee III. *The Deer of North America.* Danbury, Ct.: Grolier Books, 1989.

Schuyler, Keith. *Bowhunting for Big Game.* Harrisburg, Pa.: Stackpole Books, 1974.

Slade, Glenn. "How to Rattle Up a Buck." *Sports Afield,* vol. 172, no. 5, November 1974, pp. 47, 133–139.

Stone, Jim. "After Your Deer Is Hit." *Archery World,* vol. 22, no. 5, September 1973, pp. 24–28.

Taylor, Walter Penn. *The Deer of North America.* Harrisburg, Pa.: Stackpole Co., 1956.

Wootters, John. "Of Peeps & Posts." *Field & Stream,* vol. 131, no. 12, April 1977, pp. 142–145.

Index